Many Faces of Mulian

Many Faces of Mulian

THE PRECIOUS SCROLLS OF LATE
IMPERIAL CHINA

Rostislav Berezkin

UNIVERSITY OF WASHINGTON PRESS
Seattle and London

THIS BOOK IS MADE POSSIBLE BY A COLLABORATIVE GRANT FROM THE ANDREW W. MELLON FOUNDATION.

Additional support was provided by the James P. Geiss Foundation, a nonprofit foundation that sponsors research on China's Ming dynasty (1368–1644).

Copyright © 2017 by the University of Washington Press

Printed and bound in the United States of America

21 20 19 18 17   5 4 3 2 1

All rights reserved. No part of this publication may be reproduced or transmitted in any form or by any means, electronic or mechanical, including photocopy, recording, or any information storage or retrieval system, without permission in writing from the publisher.

University of Washington Press
www.washington.edu/uwpress

Cover design: Katherine Wong
Cover illustration: Mulian, his mother, and two demons in hell. Based on the frontispiece of the woodblock edition of *Dizang baojuan* (1679). Private collection of Li Shiyu. Drawing by Rostislav Berezkin.

Library of Congress Cataloging-in-Publication Data on file

ISBN (hardcover): 9780295742519
ISBN (paperback): 9780295742526
ISBN (ebook): 9780295742533

The paper used in this publication is acid-free and meets the minimum requirements of American National Standard for Information Sciences—Permanence of Paper for Printed Library Materials, ANSI Z39.48-1984. ∞

To my parents

CONTENTS

Foreword, by Victor H. Mair	ix
Acknowledgments	xiii
Prologue: Mulian *Baojuan* in Jingjiang	xv
Introduction	3
1. *Baojuan* about Mulian and Performance Literature	11
2. The Mulian Story in Chinese Literature	35
3. An Early Example in *Baojuan*	48
4. Sectarian Examples in *Dizang Baojuan* and *Baojuan of Benefiting Living Beings*	72
5. Beliefs and Practices in Sectarian *Baojuan*	98
6. Late Examples in *Baojuan of Three Rebirths* and *Precious Account of Mulian*	118
7. The Religious and Performative Context of Late *Baojuan* about Mulian	144
Conclusion	171
Appendix 1: Major Texts in Chinese Literature Dealing with the Mulian Story	177
Appendix 2: *Baojuan* Texts Dealing with the Mulian Story	181
Appendix 3: Translation of the First Passage of *Baojuan of Maudgalyāyana* (Manuscript of 1440)	187
Notes	189
Glossary of Chinese, Japanese, and Korean Terms	213
Bibliography	223
Index	243

FOREWORD
by Victor H. Mair

From relative obscurity half a century ago, *baojuan* ("precious scrolls") have emerged to become a major focus of interest and investigation among scholars of Chinese popular religious literature of the last millennium. This is the result primarily of five major scholars of this genre: Sawada Mizuho, Daniel Overmyer, Che Xilun, Wilt L. Idema, and Rostislav Berezkin. The first three scholars introduced *baojuan* as a subject deserving of serious study, described the basic corpus and its development through history, and presented newly discovered materials. Idema translated many texts of *baojuan* into English. The fifth scholar, Berezkin, takes up where the others have left off and brings *baojuan* studies to an exciting new pinnacle of sophistication and exactitude.

Among the previously inadequately explored territories that Berezkin is opening up or expanding are the religious dimensions of the texts, the social and literary implications of the genre, and, above all, the performative aspects of these prosimetric works.

The earlier researchers have investigated the religious associations of *baojuan*, but Berezkin goes deeper into the relationship between *baojuan* and specific scriptures and noncanonical sources. He also adroitly illuminates the function of *baojuan* in the religious life and thought of Buddhist believers.

Despite their wide circulation, especially in the middle and lower levels of society, the role of *baojuan* in the development of the literary tradition, both sectarian and secular, has not been delineated sufficiently clearly. In this volume and in his other, closely linked publications, Berezkin shows how *baojuan* fit into a lengthy process of evolution that comprises sūtras and sūtra-explanation texts (*jiangjingwen*), transformation texts (*bianwen*), tales of causation (*yinyuan*, *yuanqi*, Skt. *avadāna*, *nidāna*), and dramatic works.

Above all, what Berezkin does uniquely is document the performative features of *baojuan*, both historically and in contemporary settings. Most exciting, Berezkin goes into the field, down to the countryside, as it were, and records how *baojuan* are presented to the faithful today. This ethnographic dimension of Berezkin's investigations is completely unprecedented for *baojuan* and is scarcely to be encountered for any other type of Chinese popular religious literature that has deep roots in history.

This is the first research project on Chinese popular Buddhist literature that introduces the methods of folklore studies as an integral component of its overall design. This is a most welcome side effect of Berezkin's research on *baojuan*, for only in this way can studies of Chinese popular Buddhist genres be incorporated into the wider world of popular and folk literature outside of China.

On a quite different vector, Berezkin is unique in the detailed attention that he pays to formulaic, codicological, and linguistic characteristics of *baojuan*. Such empirical data are valuable for assessing the actual social and literary nature of *baojuan*.

Another signal contribution of Berezkin's book that sets it apart from previous studies is its sensitivity to women's issues. In a sense, Berezkin may be said to be in the vanguard of those scholars of popular religious literature who consider with utmost seriousness issues of gender.

Berezkin's research also has significance for literacy studies in that it reveals degrees of literacy and orality that cannot be accurately reflected in a simple binary of literate versus illiterate or oral versus written.

Particularly during the period of the Cultural Revolution (1966–1976), but even before then, *baojuan* performance was suppressed, the production of *baojuan* scrolls was prohibited, and existing manuscripts were confiscated and destroyed. Berezkin's investigations show unmistakably that somehow or other—though it may have lain dormant for decades—the tradition of *baojuan* production and recitation survived through countless political and ideological vicissitudes. I personally am much heartened by the perduring quality of folk and popular culture in the face of official opposition.

In the early 1980s, I traveled extensively in the Gansu/Hexi corridor, where many of the recently recovered *baojuan* were found. This was just after the slight relaxation of the anti-religious proscription of the preceding decades. The owners of *baojuan* in remote towns would approach me (the lone foreigner in the region in those days) and show me their collections of forbidden, hidden *baojuan* texts. I carefully noted the titles and other pertinent information about these scrolls in the possession of the country folk. How tremendously gratifying it has been that—during the last thirty or so years—most of the hitherto unknown scrolls whose existence I recorded have now been published, studied, and in some cases translated by Berezkin and his fellow researchers.

Another facet of Berezkin's scholarship, especially as it is embodied in this monograph, that is thrilling for me is the fact that—although his vision ranges far and wide—Berezkin keeps his eye on the story of Mulian (Skt. Maudgalyāyana) rescuing his mother from hell. Not only is this story among my own favorites in the whole of Chinese literature, it has been one of the most treasured narratives for countless generations of Chinese devotees of this ultra-filial Buddhist saint, even those who are not practicing religious Buddhists per se.

If we trace the story of Mulian back to its Indian roots, where he was known as Maudgalyāyana or Moggallāna (Pali), we learn that he is one of the best loved of the Buddha's disciples, revered for his firm devotion and supernatural powers. Furthermore, Mulian, the Buddhist saint is thoroughly domesticated and assimilated as a Chinese filial hero. Thus it is entirely fitting that the author has chosen the Mulian story as the quintessential representative of the entire genre.

The manuscript tradition for the Mulian *baojuan* and related genres in China is particularly rich. Berezkin masterfully tracks down dozens of different editions and variants that appeared during the six-century period of his purview. What he does with this abundant assemblage of data is not merely to catalogue or even to describe them (although he does that too). Rather, Berezkin analyzes and interprets the data in ways that help us better understand how *baojuan* served as a vehicle for the transmission of cultural verities and religious truths.

It is my great pleasure to write this foreword for Rostislav Berezkin's impressive opus. It affords an excellent vantage for viewing the superlative documentation and striking insights of a young Sinologist of the twenty-first century. At the same time, it will make all of us wiser about precisely what the Chinese popular religion tradition consists of and how it serves as a complement to the elite Chinese tradition that is so much better known. Moreover, beyond providing such an enormous amount of knowledge about the Chinese performative tradition of *baojuan*, Berezkin skillfully compares and contrasts it with relevant manifestations of folk and popular literature elsewhere in the world, thus enabling us to understand and appreciate both better. For all of these reasons, *Many Faces of Mulian* is a pathbreaking achievement that will irrevocably transform the field of Chinese popular Buddhist literature studies.

ACKNOWLEDGMENTS

I would like to acknowledge Victor H. Mair first and foremost for his model of thorough scholarship and his University of Pennsylvania colleagues Nancy S. Steinhardt, Paul R. Goldin, Nathan Sivin, and Linda H. Chance, who helped me with diverse sources relevant to my research for this book. In Russia, my research on *baojuan* texts owes much to the guidance of Lev N. Menshikov (1926–2005) (Institute of Oriental Manuscripts, Saint Petersburg) and Evgenii A. Serebriakov (1928–2013) (Saint Petersburg State University). Their help and advice contributed a lot to the present research, in terms of both materials and methodology used.

I am also grateful to the following individuals who shared with me materials pertaining to this study and provided criticism and comments during various stages of the project: Academician of the Russian Academy of Sciences Boris L. Riftin (1932–2012), Wilt L. Idema (Harvard University), Neil Schmid (North Carolina State University), Maria L. Menshikova and Kira F. Samosyuk (State Hermitage Museum, Saint Petersburg), Susan Naquin (Princeton University), Stephen F. Teiser (Princeton University), David Wang (University of Florida), Wang Qiugui (Tsinghua University), Che Xilun (Yangzhou University), Liu Zhen (Research Institute of Drama in Chinese Academy of Arts), Chen Ganglong (Beijing University), Dai Yun (Research Institute of Drama in Chinese Academy of Arts), Li Shiyu (1922–2010) (Chinese Academy of Social Sciences, Tianjin), Pu Wenqi (Chinese Academy of Social Sciences, Tianjin), and Martin Heijdra (Gest Library of Princeton University). Their comments and criticisms saved me from a variety of errors. Duan Baolin (Beijing University), Chen Qinjian (Huadong Normal University, Shanghai), Zhu Hengfu (Shanghai University), Yu Yongliang (Department of Culture of Zhangjiagang city), Yao Fupei (Department of Culture of Jingjiang city), Yu Dingjun, Zhang Mingwei, Dou Heng, and Hu Xiaochen helped me a lot with the organization and carrying out of the fieldwork on modern *baojuan* performances in China. Finally, I would like to thank all performers of precious scrolls I met in Zhangjiagang, Changshu, Jingjiang, Kunshan, Wuxi, and Suzhou, who were hospitable and kind in providing me with fascinating evidence on their ancient performative art.

The completion of this project was made possible by a research fellowship from Academia Sinica and a research grant from Fudan University.

PROLOGUE: MULIAN *BAOJUAN* IN JINGJIANG

My first experience with live *baojuan* (precious scrolls)[1] performance was also the most memorable. April 13, 2009, was a rainy and misty day in the village of Xinhua in Xieqiao township of Jingjiang city, Jiangsu, on the northern bank of the Yangzi River. Typical of late spring in the Yangzi delta, the weather was already warm and comfortable.

With the help of local cultural workers, whom I had contacted on the recommendation of Duan Baolin, a professor emeritus of the Chinese Language Department of Peking University and a friend of one of my teachers in Russia, I was able to witness a performance of a *baojuan* text about Mulian in a private house, a rare occasion nowadays and a fortunate opportunity for me. Being primarily trained as a student of texts of this performative tradition, I was fascinated to listen to their recitation by the folk performers. As I had learned in Russia, these recitations still took place in different areas of China. Now *baojuan* are designated as a part of the "intangible cultural heritage" of the country, so the value of these performative traditions is officially acknowledged by the state, and the events have become more and more open compared to the time of religious persecutions during 1950–1980s. They still represent archaic storytelling, mainly dealing with religious themes, the style of which can be traced to the Ming (1368–1644) and Qing (1644–1911) dynasties; and they are based on the stories taken from the written scripts. Nevertheless, few scholars, especially Westerners, have been able to witness these performances in their natural setting.

The tradition of Jingjiang, known locally as "telling scriptures" (*jiangjing*), is unusual in many respects. Originally it must have been part of the performance art of *baojuan* recitation that was widespread in the southern part of Jiangsu, or to use the poetic Chinese name for this region, "the lands to the south of the Yangzi River" (Jiangnan). The majority of old settlers of the Jingjiang area (originally an island in the Yangzi) came from the southern bank and apparently brought with them many old traditions of Jiangnan. Even the dialect used in telling scriptures, called "the old bank speech" (*lao'an hua*), belongs to the Wu group of dialects (or "topolects")[2] that are spread in the areas south of Yangzi and is different from language of neighboring areas of Jingjiang on the northern bank that belong to the city of Taizhou.

However, telling scriptures in Jingjiang today differs from the performance traditions of the areas to the south. The most important difference concerns the use of text in performance: while many other old traditions of *baojuan* recitation in Jiangsu as well as in northern China employ written texts (either printed copies or manuscripts) as performance scripts, storytellers of Jingjiang, known by the name of Buddhist disciples (*fotou*, lit., "the Buddha's head"), mainly present oral versions of traditional stories, which do not have the fixed texts and are re-created each time by the performers. The emergence of this form of performance is usually explained by the influence of other genres of storytelling art in neighboring areas, most prominently *tanci* (plucking lyrics; *chantefable*) and *pinghua* (expository tales) of the Suzhou and Yangzhou city areas.[3] Apparently many "secular" subjects of telling scriptures (*caojuan*, "grass scrolls") were borrowed from these other types of storytelling. Nevertheless, telling scriptures remains a ritualized art, taking place during religious assemblies, now organized mostly in private houses, at what are known as family assemblies (*jiahui*).

When we arrived at the house of the sponsors of the religious assembly, around 8:00 a.m., everything had already been prepared for the performance of telling scriptures. On that day a telling scriptures in the house of the Wang family took place on the occasion of the anniversary of the lady of the house, aged seventy-three, called the "assembly of prolonging life" (*yanshenghui*) after the purpose of the assembly, or "assembly of Guanyin" (*Guanyinhui*) after the main text performed during it. Both of her sons, who were workers in the nearby factory, her daughters-in-law, and her grandchildren, as well as other distant relatives, were present. Their participation, required by custom, served as an expression of their respect (filial piety) toward an old couple. Besides these, many neighbors and friends of the family participated, which contributed to the general joyous atmosphere of the event.

Figure P.01. Altar used for telling pictures in Jingjiang, 2009. Photo by the author.

Three performers—*fotou*—participated in the assembly. The leading performer, responsible for most of the rituals, was a relatively young *fotou*, Liu Zhengkun (b. 1962), who is a famous representative of Jingjiang tradition. Early in the morning they set up "the room for telling scriptures" (*jingtang*) with the altar for deities in the central hall (living room) of this modernized, three-story rural building. A permanent altar with the images of the whole local pantheon, called "sacred images" (*shengxiang*), painted on glass with a modern technique (located on the wall opposite to the entrance from the village street), was used for arranging small icons of deities, called "paper horses" (*zhima*), who were invited to assist the assembly. These icons, together with "the dipper [lamp]" (*xingdou*, also known as "the votive lamp"), four candles, three incense burners, statues of Bodhisattva Guanyin and the God of Wealth, the tablet representing ancestors of the host family, paper flowers, and numerous offerings to the deities (all vegetarian), were placed on the special narrow table standing in front of the altar. "The dipper [lamp]"—the wooden bucket filled with rice and decorated with several ritual implements, representing the stars of the Northern Dipper, which govern a person's destiny—is a common device in different ritual traditions of China, including Daoist services in its southeastern areas.[4]

While the altar represented the presence of deities, telling scriptures in honor of them took place around a big table, called the "scriptures stand" (*jingtai*), placed against the right wall of the hall, thus closer to the main entrance of the room. *Fotou* together with the chorus sat around that table. That table was decorated with the images of deities, painted on a small screen, known as the "dragon placard" (*longpai*), as well as with bunches of paper flowers (all prepared by the old women who participated in the assembly). Big red candles were lit, and smoke from incense burners, also placed on that table, was swirling in the air, thus creating the mystical and solemn atmosphere of the sacred assembly. The assembly started at 8:00 a.m. with the recitation of a text on "bowing with the vow" (*bai yuan*) and recitation of Buddhist prayers (*nian gongke*). Then the leading performer, standing in front of the altar, invited the deities with a special text, called *Gāthā on Invitation of Buddhas* (Qing fo ji). Only then did the performer start the narrative of the "sacred scrolls" (*shengjuan*), which in that case included *Baojuan of Guanyin* (Guanyin baojuan), *Baojuan of the Great Saint* (Dasheng baojuan), and *Baojuan of Zitong* (Zitong baojuan). All these texts narrate the stories of deities especially venerated in Jingjiang: Bodhisattva Guanyin, Great Saint (a Buddhist monk), and Lord Zitong (or Lord Wenchang [Wenchang dijun]).[5] At the beginning of the performance of the main narrative text, performers in Jingjiang sing four lines of "sacred words" (*shengyu*) and invoke "three friends" (Confucius, Laozi, and Buddha) and four mercies (Heaven and Earth, sun and moon, water and soil, and both parents), which constitute a ritual introduction to *baojuan* texts.[6]

Telling scriptures alternates the recitation of prose parts with the singing of verses typical of *baojuan* texts.[7] The prose part is narrated with different voice "registers" that create the lively descriptions and dramatic dialogues. As for the poetic parts of the text, the *fotou* sing them with different melodies, which are also related to different meters of the verse. The most common melodies are those of "plain tune" (*pingdiao*), used for the seven-syllable verse, "ten-syllable verse" (*han shizi*), and an aria of "Wearing the Golden Lock" (Gua jin suo), with their different modifications. These melodies are

Prologue   XIX

Figure P.02. "Scripture hall" during the "extending longevity" meeting in Jingjiang, 2009. Photo by the author.

traditional, originating from the music of *baojuan* of the sixteenth and seventeenth centuries. Only percussion instruments—wooden fish (*muyu*, a sort of small drum), clapper (*qipai*), and small bell (*lingyu*)—are used for accompaniment; this constitutes the archaic form of *baojuan* music in southern Jiangsu, called "recitation with the wooden [fish] accompaniment." A set refrain, known as "echoing the Buddha's name" (*hefo*), forms a peculiar feature of *baojuan* music. At the moment the performer finishes each second (rhymed) line of verse, the chorus sings the last syllable in the line together with the storyteller and chants the name of Buddha Amitābha: "Homage to Buddha Amitābha!" (Namo Amituo Fo); different forms of refrain are used. In Jingjiang, usually pious old women (six to eight during the "family assembly") who are familiar with the story and manner of performance form the chorus. Chorus members are also engaged in the preparation of ritual paraphernalia—ritual money (made of foil) and paper flowers—right at the time of performance. They also form the primary audience of performance, as they are constantly present during recitation.

During the assembly on April 13, recitation of major narrative texts, interspersed with the rituals of worshiping deities, took the whole day (with intermissions for lunch and late dinner). After dinner the worship of the deities of the underworld, who judge a person's soul in the afterlife and decide on its future rebirth, started. This ceremony took most of the night. It started with the recitation of *Baojuan of Li Qing* (Li Qing baojuan, alternatively called *Baojuan of Repaying Ancestors* [Bao zu baojuan]) dealing with the journey of an ordinary person in the underworld and introducing the Ten Kings of Hell and rituals of their worship. Then the performers recited *Baojuan of the Ten Kings* (Shi wang baojuan), which included rituals of asking pardon for the host's soul, called "sacrifices to the [Ten Halls]" (*jiao dian*). Ritual money and special "memorials [of pardon]" (*diewen*) were burned for every king of hell, while descendants together with the *fotou* were praying for the salvation of their elders. Only at 4:00 a.m., just before dawn, did the performance of *Baojuan of the Blood Pond* (Xuehu baojuan), the local variant of *Baojuan of Mulian* (Mulian Baojuan), start.

Performance of *Baojuan of the Blood Pond* is related to traditional Chinese beliefs about the physiological impurity of women: because they pollute water and soil with menstrual and childbirth blood, they are predestined to suffer in the underground Blood Pond after death. Special rituals conducted by pious descendants are required to rescue a mother of the family from afterlife torments. Recitation of *Baojuan of the Blood Pond* in Jingjiang is a local variant of the ritual of the "breaking of the Blood Pond" (*po xuehu*) in modern religious traditions of China. It enacts the salvation of a mother by descendants, who follow the example of pious monk Mulian rescuing his mother's soul from the underworld.

The performance of "breaking of the Blood Pond" takes place in front of a special altar called the "sacred stand" (*shentai*), constructed on the left side of the permanent altar with the deities' images. On the occasion I witnessed this sacred stand was represented by a small table under which the "treasury of the Blood Pond" (*Xuehu baoku*) was placed. The "treasury" was made of paper and represented the offerings for the officials of this compartment of hell. Three small icons ("paper horses") representing Dizang (Skt. Kṣitigarbha), Mulian, and the Dragon King (Longwang), and five kinds of offerings (noodles, sweets, rice cakes, and fruit, all decorated with pieces of red paper, as well as a plate with the paper flowers) were put in front of the "treasury."

The bowl with red water, representing the Blood Pond, and the bigger basin were placed on the table, while a stick with a pink towel on top of it, which symbolized the pewter staff presented to Mulian

Figure P.03. Performance of *Baojuan of the Blood Pond* in Jingjiang, 2009. Photo by the author.

by Bodhisattva Dizang, was stuck in the back of the chair, which was also placed in front of the table. The water in this bowl was dyed with the use of a plant called *lignum sappan* (*sumu*, commonly used in Chinese medicine). Brown sugar (*hongtang*), which is cheaper, is often substituted for it. While reciting the text of *Baojuan of the Blood Pond*, which he knew by heart, Liu Zhengkun knelt in front of this temporary altar most of the time. He wore a piece of red cloth, which symbolized Mulian's cassock (see figure P.03). Therefore, all magic objects that appear in *baojuan* about Mulian and his mother (pewter staff, cassock, and the Blood Pond) were materialized in this ritual performance. The woman's descendants (children, grandchildren, and daughters-in-law) knelt on the floor behind the *fotou* and performed the bows and prostrations required by the ritual. The recitation of *Baojuan of the Blood Pond* started with the invocation of the underworld deities, including Bodhisattva Dizang, the Ten Kings with their spouses and retinue, the guards of each hell, and demons (*yakshas*, Ch. *yecha*) serving there. While reciting the text of the *baojuan*, Liu Zhengkun at first narrated the story of Mulian and his mother. The text was recited in topolect, but it was possible to follow the main story line, especially as I had read the written version of it.

Figure P.04. "Breaking of the Blood Pond" in Jingjiang, 2009. Photo by the author.

The *fotou* personified different characters in the Mulian story with the use of different voice registers. In this narrative we hear the voices of Mulian, his parents, and souls of the deceased in hell.

Mulian, whose original name was Fu Luobo, was a son of rich landlord Fu Xiang in Fuxian village near the southern capital during the end of the Tang dynasty (ca. ninth century). In fact, however, Mulian was an incarnation of a star deity, who had been banished to earth to be born in the family of Fu Xiang and his wife, Liu Qingti. After his father died in an accident, a heavenly immortal descended to the world to teach Mulian how to rescue his father from underworld sufferings and attain salvation himself. Mulian and his mother were converted to Buddhism, which required worshiping the Buddha and observing a vegetarian diet. In addition, Mulian had to travel to Mount Jiuhua (in Anhui), where he became a Buddhist monk and a disciple of Bodhisattva Dizang (the savior of souls from the underworld in Chinese Buddhism). However, while he was on leave, Liu Qingti, who stayed at home, listened to the instigation of her evil brother Liu Jia and started to eat meat and drink wine. Furthermore, after Mulian had returned home, she lied to him and said she had not broken the vegetarian diet. This was a grave sin for which her life was immediately taken away, and her soul first confined to the Blood Pond in the underworld. After undergoing all the torments of the underworld, her soul was imprisoned in the City Enclosed in Iron (Tiewei Cheng; that is, Avīci, the deepest level of the underworld). With the use of magic objects that Dizang bestowed on Mulian, including a pewter staff, a cassock, and a pearl, Mulian was able to descend to the underworld to seek his mother's soul. While he traveled through the hells, he passed by the Blood Pond. Liu Qingti was not the only soul who was tormented there, as other women also found themselves there because of their sins of pollution.

At this point we learn the way of deliverance from sufferings of the Blood Pond: descendants, in place of their mother, need to drink blood from the pond. Meanwhile, Mulian traveled to the Buddha, who taught him how to rescue his mother's soul by organizing the Assembly of the Blood Pond. In addition, the Buddha bestowed on Mulian the "Penitence Text of the Blood Pond" (*Xuehu chanhuiwen*), which listed the seventy-two sins of a woman that should be recited during the Assembly of the Blood Pond. The *fotou* recites this text and bows each time a new sin is mentioned; kneeling descendants repeat his actions. After the penitence is recited, the *fotou* breaks chopsticks placed in the basin, which symbolize the railings of the Blood Pond. While Mulian's mother leaves hell, all other women in the pond also can escape their sufferings and be born in heaven: "The Blood Pond turns into white jade, eighteen layers of hell turn into heaven palace, all women in the Blood Pond escape from the sea of suffering and are born in the heavenly realm, they are happy and at ease."[8]

After this, the *fotou* calls the woman's descendants to drink red water from the bowl, following Mulian's example: "Pious daughters and sons in the sponsors' family come to the Buddha and drink three cups of crimson water; this means that they repay the mother's mercy of birth and nurture."[9] Before relatives are allowed to drink from this bowl, they should give tips to the *fotou*, which means the purchase of "the bloody water." Performers feel quite happy for this reason, and they should drink the rest of water in the bowl after the descendants.

After the Blood Pond is broken, the *fotou* takes the imitation pewter staff and knocks the ground thrice; this symbolizes the destruction of the City Enclosed in Iron and liberation of all souls imprisoned there. Then the narration continues: the *baojuan* tells that after Liu Qingti's soul had been rescued from hell, she was reborn as a dog, and Mulian took trouble to rescue her again until she was reborn in a human form. Mulian, in his turn, had to undergo another rebirth, because he had to collect souls of sinners, who had escaped when he destroyed the City Enclosed in Iron. In his next reincarnation he became the rebel leader Huang Chao (d. 884), an important historical figure of the Tang dynasty (618–907), who killed the required number of people and thus restored the world order. Thus a religious legend and historical events are intertwined in this oral narrative. According to *Baojuan of the Blood Pond* from Jingjiang, the title of dragon was eventually bestowed on Mulian,[10] which explains the use of the paper horse representing the Dragon King in the ritual setting of the recitation.

"Breaking of the Blood Pond" was the final part of the regular telling scriptures assembly to celebrate a woman's anniversary in Jingjiang. On April 14 it finished at 6:00 a.m., when it was already light outside, and was followed by a breakfast. Afterward, the *fotou* performed the concluding rituals, including "closing scroll" (*jie juan*), "presentation of tea" (*shang cha*) to the deities, "untying the karmic knots" (*jie jie*), "recitation of memorial" (*nian biao*), and "sending-off buddhas" (*song fo*). All paper ritual implements (treasuries with the offerings for the underworld deities, paper horses, and a paper "lotus boat") were burned by the performers.

Here the main focus is on the Mulian narrative, with many elements of rituals of the telling scriptures session omitted. On the whole, the assembly of "prolonging life" in Jingjiang differs from similar events involving *baojuan* performances in southern Jiangsu. First, it preserves the traditional scheme of overnight performance that is now rarely found in neighboring areas, especially in the case of an assembly organized for the welfare of living people. Thus it is very rich in content, with many texts and rituals included. Second, presentations of *Baojuan of Mulian* in neighboring areas are usually performed during funerals of old women, as in the case of telling scriptures traditions of Changshu and Zhangjiagang (located on the opposite bank of the Yangzi from the city of Jingjiang and belonging to the jurisdiction of Suzhou). Thus the joyous atmosphere of the Xieqiao assembly, which also served as the occasion of an extended family reunion, was quite special in comparison with other similar cases. Finally, rituals and an early meal became the start of the happy new day. The assembly in Xieqiao represents just one version of enactment of the multifaceted Mulian *baojuan*, a story whose history illuminates the development of the *baojuan* genre and its significance in Chinese religious culture.

Many Faces of Mulian

Introduction

Baojuan as a genre of Chinese popular prosimetric literature, written in language that mixes classical Chinese with vernacular elements, arose around the thirteenth through the fourteenth century and flourished in many areas of China until the beginning of the twentieth century. *Baojuan* texts were transmitted as manuscripts or in printed editions and were intended for a type of performance usually called "scroll recitation" (*xuanjuan* or *nianjuan*).[1] The history of *baojuan* encompasses three periods.[2] During the first period (thirteenth through the fifteenth century), *baojuan* propagated popularized Buddhist doctrines; in the second (sixteenth through the eighteenth century), most *baojuan* were the scriptures of sects;[3] and in the third (nineteenth through the twentieth century), *baojuan* mostly lost their connection with sectarian teachings and simply narrated popular stories. I call these periods early, middle, and late, respectively, breaking with the terminology of several classical studies of *baojuan* that designate the period of the sixteenth through the eighteenth century as "early" and that of the nineteenth through the early twentieth century as "late."[4]

Early on, scholars noted that some texts that traditionally are included in the corpus of *baojuan* use different generic names in their titles. These include "liturgy" (*keyi*), "scripture" (or sūtra, *jing*), "precious/miraculous scripture" (*baojing, miaojing*), "precious penitence text" (*baochan*), and "precious account" (*baozhuan*).[5] We can treat all of these as a single genre, however, on the basis of common features in their form and contents.

HISTORY OF BAOJUAN

External sources provide little information about the history of the *baojuan* genre, especially in the early and middle periods of its development. This paucity of historical data about *baojuan* of the thirteenth to the eighteenth century can be explained by their connection with popular sects and beliefs. During the Ming and Qing dynasties, sectarian groups were persecuted by the state, as their ideas of salvation were regarded as heterodox by the imperial government. Officials confiscated and destroyed sectarian *baojuan*. Nevertheless, many expensive woodcut editions of sectarian *baojuan* survived from the end of the Ming dynasty (sixteenth to early seventeenth century), indicating that persecutions were not as severe as those that followed under the Qing dynasty at the end of the seventeenth century.[6] The late Ming elites' lenient attitude toward sects and their scriptures implies that some aristocracy and courtiers supported the sectarian beliefs and sponsored the production of beautifully executed and decorated woodcut editions of *baojuan*. During the later Qing persecution of the sects, the confiscation of *baojuan* increased greatly, and the expensive printed editions of *baojuan* gradually disappeared, giving way to cheap editions and manuscripts.

A type of *baojuan* that became popular in the nineteenth century, however, was different from the sectarian scriptures. Texts of this type usually included moralistic stories about pious men and women who experienced many hardships in the course of their spiritual cultivation but in the end were rewarded with sainthood. During this period, many *baojuan* with secular subjects appeared; these materials often came from folk legends, novels, and drama. The *baojuan* genre developed from serving purely religious purposes into a combination of religious devotion and entertainment. Unlike the earlier sectarian *baojuan*, most of which came from northern China, the nineteenth-century *baojuan* became popular in the south, mainly in Jiangsu and Zhejiang provinces.

In the south, primarily professional storytellers, usually called "masters of scroll recitation" (*xuanjuan xiansheng*), performed *baojuan*. Although some were disguised as monks or Daoists, they were not ordained clergy. They earned their living from *baojuan* recitals and performed in public places (pilgrimage sites, temple fairs, teahouses, and entertainment quarters) and in private houses. The recitation of *baojuan* with more traditional religious subjects was connected closely with folk religious ceremonies; those with secular subjects were performed mainly for entertainment purposes. On the other hand, *baojuan* developed in an interchange with morality books (*shanshu*), didactic literature of the late imperial period, although, unlike *baojuan*, morality books usually were not used as scripts for oral performances, especially in the early period of their development.[7] At the end of the nineteenth and into the early twentieth century, publishers of morality books printed the texts of *baojuan* mostly in southern cities.

BAOJUAN IN THE MODERN PERIOD

After the 1950s, the practices of *baojuan* printing, copying, and recitation declined because of a new government policy that restricted popular religious activities; mass media took the place of the *baojuan* performances as a means of entertainment. In the 1980s, *baojuan* performances survived mainly in the rural areas of Jiangsu and Zhejiang in the south and in some areas of Gansu (mainly in the so-called Hexi corridor), Qinghai, Shanxi, and Hebei in the north. In Jiangsu and Zhejiang, the local traditions of performances experienced a revival in the 1980s and 1990s. In Gansu, Shanxi, and Hebei, however, they gradually declined and almost disappeared. Several *baojuan* still are recited by folk religious associations in remote areas of Gansu and Qinghai.[8] The centers of *baojuan* survival in Jiangsu and Zhejiang are the cities of Jingjiang, Zhangjiagang, Changshu, Suzhou, Wuxi, Changzhou, and Shaoxing. In those places, recitation of *baojuan* usually appears incorporated into religious assemblies on such occasions as anniversaries, house consecrations, and funerals or when there is a need for requests for the protection of children and healing.

In the 1980s, *baojuan* performances in several areas of China attracted the attention of local scholars.[9] In the 1990s–2010s, Chinese and foreign scholars continued fieldwork research on *baojuan* in various areas and published a number of reports that demonstrated the value of this literature in the context of traditional culture.[10] During the same time, the PRC government recognized the surviving traditions of *baojuan* performances as folk art, and several living traditions of *baojuan* performances were proclaimed an "intangible cultural heritage" (*fei wuzhi wenhua yichan*), with efforts to preserve them with government support.[11] In several places, scholars have collected *baojuan* texts and published them.[12]

Interestingly, while the southern traditions of *baojuan* are related to the third (late) period of the genre, several northern traditions still use texts that belong to the second (middle) period. For example, a folk music association in the South Gaoluo (Nan Gaoluo) village of Laishui county in Hebei (only 120 kilometers away from the national capital, Beijing) still recites several texts dating back to the sixteenth and seventeenth centuries, albeit out of their original sectarian context.[13] Several sectarian *baojuan* of the same period also are still used by folk associations in Gansu.[14] This situation reflects the historical development of *baojuan* texts and demonstrates that the performance of *baojuan* traditionally classified as second-period texts persisted into the third period and survived into the twenty-first century. Therefore, modern evidence of *baojuan* performance is an important source of information on the state of the *baojuan* genre during various periods of its development.

GOALS AND CONTRIBUTION OF THE PRESENT RESEARCH

In this book, I discuss the development of the story of Mulian in texts of the *baojuan* genre from the fourteenth through the nineteenth century, and its relationship with the religious and social background of these texts. This story of how a disciple of Buddha Śākyamuni, Mulian (Skt. [Mahā]Maudgalyāyana, Ch. [Mohe]Mujianlian or Muqianlian, usually abbreviated as Mulian),[15] rescued his sinful mother from rebirth in hell was widespread in the popular literature of China from the Tang dynasty onward (see appendix 1).[16] The tale of Mulian is also a unique example of a subject continuously used in *baojuan* since examples occur in the texts of all three periods. Furthermore, the earliest available specimen of the *baojuan* text—*Baojuan of Maudgalyāyana*, an incomplete manuscript dating to 1372—deals with this story.[17] *Baojuan* texts on Mulian are also important for understanding the popular religion of premodern and modern China, and they are still are performed in a number of storytelling traditions in China, mostly in conjunction with local ritual activities.

Nevertheless, *baojuan* texts concerning Mulian have not received sufficient attention from Chinese and foreign scholars. Among works dealing with the *baojuan* genre as a whole, studies of sectarian scripture-type *baojuan* in various languages still outnumber works devoted to texts of the narrative type.[18] Although Chinese and foreign scholars have long paid attention to the narrative texts of *baojuan*, they produced only a few general studies,[19] followed by analyses of several narrative *baojuan* texts.[20] Most of these studies demonstrate the transformation of a plot in different genres of Chinese literature or analyze types of stories in narrative *baojuan*, such as the stories of female salvation.[21] Narrative *baojuan* are of growing interest to scholars of Chinese literature and culture, especially as many such texts have been reprinted recently in mainland China and Taiwan and are available to the public.[22] Several of these have been translated into English.[23]

Current studies, nevertheless, have paid little attention to the succession of texts of *baojuan* that deal with the story of Mulian. Several important monographs have focused on the development of the Mulian story in China and neighboring countries but have devoted little space to the *baojuan* about Mulian.[24] Studies of texts about Mulian in several other genres have analyzed texts from the medieval period (fifth to eleventh century) and the history of the Mulian drama and its local varieties.[25] An important 1995 article discussed the performance context and religious meaning of a late text, *Precious Account of Mulian Rescuing His Mother in the Underworld* (Mulian jiu mu youming baozhuan; Che no. 690, hereafter *Precious Account of Mulian*),[26] although little was known at that time about the living traditions of *baojuan* performances in China, and this influenced the author's conclusions about the nature of the text. Another late variant of the Mulian story, *Baojuan of Mulian Rescuing His Mother in Three Rebirths* (Mulian san shi jiu mu baojuan; Che no. 694, hereafter *Baojuan of Three Rebirths*), was published in English translation but without an outline of the complete succession of *baojuan* texts on Mulian and detailed explanation of their ritual and cultural significance.[27]

This book thus fills a need in providing a comparative study of the major texts of the *baojuan* genre that relate the Mulian story. Studying this story as it is used in *baojuan* of different periods contributes to our knowledge of the evolution of the narrative texts of the *baojuan* genre. I analyze their contents against the background of the development of this subject in other genres of Chinese literature, focusing on the texts' performative and ritual aspects. Concentrating on this example of the Mulian story contributes toward a deeper understanding of the *baojuan* genre's nature, origin, historical background, and evolution.

MAJOR SOURCES

The five major texts analyzed here are the most representative examples of the use and transformation of the story of Mulian rescuing his mother in the *baojuan* genre. These are *Baojuan of Maudgalyāyana*, which dates to approximately the fourteenth century; *Baojuan of Bodhisattva-King Dizang Governing the Underworld* (Dizang wang pusa zhizhang youming baojuan; Che no. 160, first edition dated 1679, hereafter abbreviated as *Dizang baojuan*); *Baojuan Expounded by the Buddha of Benefiting Living Beings and Understanding of the [True] Meaning* (Fo shuo li sheng liao yi baojuan; Che no. 236, ca. seventeenth century, hereafter abbreviated as *Baojuan of Benefiting Living Beings*); *Precious Account of Mulian* (ca. early nineteenth century; I am using the reprint of the 1893 edition); and *Baojuan of Three Rebirths* (ca. second half of the nineteenth century; I am using the reprint of the 1898 edition).[28] These texts can be classified chronologically into three groups that correspond to the above-mentioned three periods in the development of the *baojuan* genre. There is one text from the early period (*Baojuan of Maudgalyāyana*), two texts from the middle period (*Dizang baojuan* and *Baojuan of Benefiting Living Beings*), and two texts from the late period (*Precious Account of Mulian* and *Baojuan of Three Rebirths*). In the corresponding chapters I outline special features of the form and contents of texts in each group; compare the texts in the second and third groups to detect characteristic features of contemporaneous *baojuan*; and compare these characteristic features with those of the text/texts in the preceding group, thus demonstrating the continuity and transformation of the form and content of *baojuan*.

I consulted other *baojuan* on Mulian for comparison in state and private libraries in China, Taiwan, Hong Kong, the United States, Russia, and the Czech Republic. In addition, I collected several related texts during my fieldwork in the Jingjiang, Changshu, Suzhou, and Wuxi areas in 2008–13.[29] Several local recensions of *baojuan* about Mulian that are modified from the editions of *Baojuan of Three Rebirths* have been performed in these areas up to the present. Many texts evaluated here were not published previously; nor have they been discussed by scholars. A list of different *baojuan* texts on Mulian (seventeen in total) supplements existing catalogues of *baojuan* (see appendix 2).

Introduction 9

Whereas studies of *baojuan* mostly rely on written sources, the present volume draws on both written materials and on live performances of *baojuan*. This method, substantiated by modern folklore theories, enriches our understanding of the functioning of the early texts and clarifies several issues concerning their history. I concentrate on traditions from the Changshu and Jingjiang areas, although I have also used materials from Suzhou, Gansu, Hebei, and other areas published by other Chinese and foreign researchers.

CHAPTER 1

Baojuan about Mulian and Performance Literature

What is the place of *baojuan* about Mulian in the discourse on folk and popular literature in China? The usual distinction between these two categories concerns the oral versus written form of their creation and transmission (if we omit some nuances of theories of folklore). Defining the status of extant *baojuan* texts from the point of view of literary theory remains an important problem. One fascinating feature of *baojuan* texts is their double role in the realms of both written and oral literature. Although the interplay of orality and textuality has attracted the attention of scholars of Chinese literature,[1] *baojuan* so far have not been analyzed from this point of view.

The texts of *baojuan* were intended for performance, and the very name "scroll recitation art" points to the fact that actual material texts were used in it. There is evidence that *baojuan* of the early and middle periods were recited during different kinds of religious assemblies. For example, the novel *Lyric Tale of Plum Flowers in the Golden Vase* (Jin ping mei cihua, later abbreviated as *Plum Flowers*, ca. 1594) by the Scoffer of Lanling (Lanling Xiaoxiaosheng) portrays a performance of *baojuan* by Buddhist nuns in the female quarters of the merchant Ximen Qing's house.[2] According to *Sequel to Plum Flowers in the Golden Vase* (Xu Jin ping mei, ca. 1660), ascribed to Ding Yaokang (1599–1669), Buddhist nuns also performed *baojuan* in the nunnery for a female audience.[3] *Plum Flowers* furthermore mentions texts of *baojuan* that were read aloud: "Then nun Xue opened *[Bao]juan of Lady Huang* [Huang shi nü juan][4] and recited in a loud voice."[5] Followers of the Vast Yang Teaching in the village of

11

Yixingbu near Tianjin, whom the Chinese scholar of sectarian teachings Li Shiyu discovered in 1957, recited texts in the same way.[6]

As for the modern *baojuan* performances, these are of two different types. The first type is called "recitation following the text" (*zhaoben xuanke*), which is practiced in the Changshu and Wuxi areas, Gansu (Hexi), and Hebei. For example, in Changshu the texts of *baojuan* are necessary attributes of the performance. Professionals who perform *baojuan* in this area, called "masters of telling scriptures" (*jiangjing xiansheng*), always carry texts with them.[7] During a performance, a master of telling scriptures puts the text on the table and constantly consults it. These usually are manuscripts copied by the performers themselves. However, they also keep some old editions of *baojuan* that were printed in the nineteenth and early twentieth centuries (including *Baojuan of Three Rebirths*). The second type of performance, as we have already seen, takes place in Jingjiang. There, professional performers (*fotou*) usually do not have records of the texts they perform as oral versions. In the earlier period (before the 1980s), most *fotou* were illiterate, and the art of *baojuan* performance was transmitted primarily orally.[8] Most texts recently published by local scholars were obtained by recording storytellers' oral versions on tape.[9] The content of the oral recitations delivered by performers in Jingjiang can differ from the texts with the same subjects as those of editions and manuscripts from the end of the nineteenth through the early twentieth century.

Although the special features of *baojuan* performance in Jingjiang have been used to classify it as a folklore genre,[10] it is clear that the case of Jingjiang is an exception among modern traditions of *baojuan* performance. There is also some evidence that *fotou* in Jingjiang in the past possessed written and even published texts. Judging primarily by the contents of the texts, it has been suggested that "sacred scrolls" (as opposed to the texts with "secular" subjects in these traditions) and "liturgies" (*keyi*) originally existed in written versions in Jingjiang.[11] *Fotou* and their assistants possess the texts of *keyi* that can be used in performance at the present time (see figure P.02). This situation is similar to that of modern *baojuan* performances (scroll recitation) in the suburbs of Suzhou, which usually address mostly entertaining secular subjects.[12] The transfer to the oral mode of performance in both places is due to the influence of the oral genres of *tanci* and *pinghua* that are popular in those areas or places close to them.[13]

Taking into consideration modern evidence of *baojuan* performance traditions in different areas of China, I agree with literary historian David Johnson that "texts seem to have always been part of hsüan chuan [*xuanjuan*] performances, either as props or as actual scripts" and that "the pao-chüan [*baojuan*] printed by the morality-book shops in the late nineteenth century probably were closely related to pao-chüan that were performed."[14] At the same time, one should remember that professional storytellers in the south, if they used *baojuan* editions, adapted these texts for performance. They used topolect pronunciation to recite them, embellished the story line, and added a ritual frame.

The usage of a promptbook during a performance constitutes a very specific feature of *baojuan* literature. Real folk storytellers usually do not use promptbooks for their performances, either in China or in other countries.[15] The use of promptbooks in *baojuan* performances can be explained by the origin of the genre from the recitation of scriptures by Buddhist and Daoist monks and nuns. At the same time, the usage of script facilitates the practice of amateur performances of *baojuan*.

In the Yangzi valley, scroll recitation has been performed by professionals or semiprofessionals who are paid for performances. In Hexi, on the contrary, professional performers of *baojuan* did not even exist before 1949. There, the recitation of text usually takes place within the family and is conducted by a literate man. The performer does not ask for any reward except for religious merit.[16] In the past, the situation in Jiexiu county, Shanxi was very similar to that in Gansu, though *baojuan* are rarely performed there now.[17] These performances may be regarded as amateur in nature.

Baojuan texts were most in demand for female audiences.[18] There is evidence that editors produced printed *baojuan* with this audience in mind. For example, the postface to the text of the 1919 edition of *Baojuan of Rectifying the Heart* (Zhen xin baojuan; Che no. 1550) by the Shanghai Hongda Morality Book Publishers (Hongda Shanshuju), called "Eight Methods for the Spread of Baojuan" (Baojuan liutong ba fa), mentions women as one of the targeted audiences and, more important, as performers: "Old men in the villages and ladies of inner chambers, when they have spare time, often enjoy telling stories, performances of *tanci*. If you encourage them to read this book aloud—either to perform [the script] themselves, or transmit it to other people, it will rectify the hearts of listeners as it enters their ears."[19] It appears that *baojuan* scripts were primarily used as promptbooks for professional storytellers and secondarily as materials for amateur performances and even individual reading.

PRODUCTION OF WRITTEN TEXTS OF *BAOJUAN*

Baojuan should thus not be treated like a typical folklore genre. Little is known about the history of the creation of the texts of early *baojuan* and their connection with oral literature, and almost all relevant information must be extracted from the texts themselves, with little external historical evidence on which to rely. For example, *baojuan* of the middle period sometimes boast connection with oral literature. One analyzed text is labeled as a recorded sermon of an illiterate sectarian teacher (see chapter 5, "Composition of Sectarian Texts and Their Buddhist Themes"). This is, however, highly suspicious, as was the case with other texts. Sectarians certainly employed subjects popular in folk storytelling; the story of Mulian rescuing his mother is a perfect example. They also tried to imitate the manner of the storyteller in terms of language, musical components of the text, and so on. Nevertheless, the term *oral-derived texts*, sometimes employed in regard to Chinese popular literature, is problematic in application to *baojuan*. In Western theories, these are texts that reveal features of the traditional oral literature but have reached us only in written form.[20] *Performance-style text*, as used to describe fifteenth-century *cihua* (stories with passages in verse) discovered in the Xuan family tomb in Jiading county near Shanghai in 1967,[21] is more appropriate. Such texts form a subcategory of popular (written) literature. On the other hand, some late *baojuan* possibly were oral-derived texts. Their production corresponded to the flourishing of the scroll recitation art in the nineteenth through the early twentieth century, and some texts were recorded from oral versions.

Not only storytellers but also members of the audience participated in the recording of texts. There were different reasons to edit and print *baojuan* texts. First, not only sectarians but also many Buddhist, Daoist, and popular cult believers considered *baojuan* sacred books. The motives of gaining religious merit, fulfilling a vow, and so on often underlay the donation of funds for printing *baojuan* at all periods of development. When in the 1950s the printing of *baojuan* was forbidden, pious people copied texts by hand.[22]

Second, the production of late *baojuan*, regarded as a category of morality books, undoubtedly was supported by the local elite. In the nineteenth through the early twentieth century, groups of well-to-do people regarded *baojuan* as books that maintained traditional values and were interested in their production and dissemination. It is likely that local elites primarily were interested in *baojuan* that contained moral instructions. The aforementioned "Eight Methods for the Spread of Baojuan" in *Baojuan of Rectifying the Heart* contains a direct call to donate funds for the publication and dissemination of *baojuan* texts.[23] It refers to the philanthropic societies in Chinese cities (in this case the Hall of Benevolent Support [Renjitang] in Yancheng in northern Jiangsu, later a part of Tongshanshe (Unity in Goodness) religious association) that collected and donated money for printing morality books, including *baojuan*. Around the second half of the nineteenth century, special publishing houses for morality books (*shanshuju*) appeared. *Baojuan* constituted an important part of these publishing houses' production.[24] Among the most famous of the morality book publishing houses was Yihuatang in Shanghai, which was active from ca. 1857 to ca. 1939, and produced Buddhist and Daoist scriptures, morality books, and *baojuan*.[25] Some editions of late *baojuan* discussed in this book also bear signs of a connection with this "philanthropic" publishing.

Third, *baojuan* texts of high narrative quality were in demand by fans of storytelling. They wished to own texts of performances so as to recall the experience of real-life storytelling through the process of reading. Commercial publishers edited and published such texts, especially of *baojuan* with entertaining subjects. For example, in the postface to one such edition by Shanghai Xiyin Publishers (Xiyin Shuju), its editor, Chen Runshen, said that he collected "folk manuscripts" of this text (presumably those used by storytellers), revised the text, and then published it in calligraphic script and embellished with illustrations.[26]

SOCIAL BACKGROUND OF *BAOJUAN* PERFORMANCES

Although printed texts of *baojuan* were edited by literate individuals, this does not negate the value of these texts as products of popular culture. During different periods of the development of this genre, these written texts often were formed as a result of cultural interchange between higher levels of society and commoners. "Popular culture," understood as shared by the people in general, across social boundaries, has been often discussed in works on Chinese religious beliefs and practices.²⁷ "Popular religion" (and culture) can also be seen as an arena of conflict, in which cultural categories are debated constantly and reconstructed in the process of interaction between representatives of different social strata.²⁸ These two approaches can be reconciled in the research of Chinese culture, as they do not really conflict with each other. We can easily imagine that there was room for debate and even conflict in the growth and development of cultural traditions in China, though they were shared by different categories of the population. For example, the evidence of *baojuan* texts shows that they were used by people of different social standing.

Originally these texts were recorded and edited by literate people and intended not only for commoners but also for well-to-do families. As for the early, presectarian period, the earliest manuscripts and editions of *baojuan* about Mulian (late fourteenth to early sixteenth century) were commissioned by a courtier, a concubine, and eunuchs (see chapter 3). Sectarian leaders, such as the nun Guiyuan (ca. 1559–after 1590) of the Western Mahāyāna Teaching and Piaogao (Han Taihu, 1570–1598), founder of the Vast Yang Teaching, who lived in the second half of the sixteenth to the beginning of the seventeenth century, also intended their writings for members of elite circles, including nobles and courtiers.²⁹ There is even a legend told in a sectarian *baojuan* text that the Ming emperor Zhengde (Wuzong, r. 1506–1521) read *baojuan* by Luo Qing (1442–1527), the founder of the Teaching of Non-Interference (Wuweijiao), called *Five Books in Six Volumes* (Wubu liuce), and ordered them to be printed and disseminated in 1518.³⁰ These texts, first published in 1509, are considered the earliest printed *baojuan* of popular religious movements.³¹

Though it cannot be proven that there was imperial support for the printing of *Five Books in Six Volumes* with the use of official records; nevertheless, "dragon placards" (dedicatory inscriptions in the form of a rectangular stele with wings and a top element covered with a pattern featuring dragons that often contained auspicious wishes for the ruling emperor) as a claim of court sanction for printing regularly appear in editions of sectarian *baojuan* in the sixteenth and seventeenth centuries. At that time, the powerful sponsors of the printing of sectarian *baojuan* usually were not scholar-officials but still were people of high social standing, including court functionaries (eunuchs), female members of the imperial court, and high-ranking military personnel.³² These categories of sponsors were the primary intended readership/audience for these texts. The evidence that women of well-to-do families enjoyed scroll recitation also comes from the novels of the sixteenth to early seventeenth century.

At the same time, we can see that the audience for *baojuan* performances was quite broad and varied. The atmosphere of these performances is evident in the novel *Pacification of the Demons' Revolt* (Ping yao zhuan; the complete title is *The Three Sui of the Northern Song Pacify the Demons' Revolt* [Bei Song San Sui Ping yao zhuan]), edited by the famous writer Feng Menglong (1574–1646) around 1620.[33] In the eleventh chapter there is a detailed description of a recitation of popular narratives by the Buddhist nun Sage Nun (Sheng Gugu), who is in fact a transformed fox, during the Great Assembly of No Obstacles (Wuzhe Dahui). This passage does not mention *baojuan* or "scroll recitation" but uses the terms "telling scriptures" and "talks on karmic causation" (*shuo yinguo*) instead.[34] Both terms often refer to *baojuan* performances: the first one is still in use in Jingjiang and Changshu; the second (also in the form of *jiang yinguo*) appears in the text of *Plum Flowers* as well.[35] Furthermore, the performer of texts in *Pacification of the Demons' Revolt* is called a *fotou*—the same term that denotes *baojuan* performers in Jingjiang today. Although *Pacification of the Demons' Revolt* does not mention *baojuan* scripts, we can guess that they were used in the performance. The performance mode—alternation of the prose narrative with the singing of verses (accompanied by the chanting of the Buddha's name) is typical of *baojuan*. The stories mentioned in this text—those of spiritual cultivation of Princess Miaoshan and Luobo (Mulian)—also were long associated with *baojuan*.[36] To my knowledge, this is the earliest external textual evidence of a performance of *baojuan* dealing with Mulian.

The Sage Nun in *Pacification of the Demons' Revolt* emphasizes the narrative nature of the texts recited and the broad audience for them:

> This assembly is called the Great Assembly of No Obstacles, or "telling scriptures," to clarify one's mind and realize the true nature. It is also called the recitation of the Buddha's [name], preparation for the rebirth in Western Land. Talking about the natural abilities of people in this world, there are many narrow-minded ones, but there are few smart. This time I would better talk about the karmic causation in order to teach people of the world to recite the Buddha's names. No matter whether they are male or female, lay or monastic, everyone who wishes can come to listen.[37]

Although the assembly was convened in a private space, the western garden of the house of a county official, Inspector Yang, and had the aim of expressing gratitude for the recovery of his wife, it was a public occasion. Many spectators came, some praying to the Buddha, some just taking the chance to eat vegetarian food for free.[38]

Three major observations can be made about this passage. First, this assembly was considered the popular type of Buddhist service that included preaching the doctrine for the laity. The main aim is rebirth in the Western Land, the stories are about Buddhist figures, and no messianic ideas and sectarian deities (such as the Unborn Venerable Mother) are mentioned. There is, however, a hint that it was not an authentic Buddhist occasion, if we take into account the deviant nature of the performer.[39] Second, the assembly was nevertheless organized by the county official, and Yang even reported it to his superior, the county magistrate. That means that local officials tolerated this type of religious performance at the beginning of the seventeenth century, a period of revived interest in Buddhist ideology and ritual practice during the late Ming dynasty, especially on the part of the wealthy gentry.[40] Third, it attracted people of different social standing, including women of rich households, commoners, and vagabonds. These characteristics of public performances are similar to those mentioned in the *baojuan* text of the seventeenth century—*Dizang baojuan*.

At the same time, there is abundant evidence that *baojuan* had been used by people at the lowest levels of society since the very beginning of this genre. For example, in his two arias the poet Chen Duo (active ca. end of the fifteenth to the beginning of the sixteenth century), who came from Shandong, mentioned the poor itinerant performers of *baojuan*, "men of the Way" (*daoren*), who traveled around in search of clients for their services—the recitation of sacred texts.[41] Both arias mention the text of the *Scroll of the Diamond Sūtra*, apparently the abbreviation for *Liturgy Based on the Diamond Sūtra with Full Explication* (Xiaoshi Jingang jing keyi; Che no. 1346), written ca. 1242 by the monk Zongjing,[42] which is a ritual explication of the popular scripture of Chinese Buddhism in prosimetric form and an important antecedent of *baojuan* texts.[43] The performers of this text are described as "promiscuous, ignorant and poor commoners from the military quarters," who, though they "pretend to be Buddhist followers, do not have any line of transmission from the teacher."[44] They wear the most common clothes and straw shoes. According to Chen

Duo, their clients also were poor commoners, who wanted to substitute proper Buddhist services with this "scroll recitation": "They take charge of the Buddhist feasts [*zhaishi*] and ask around [for clients]; families of humble origin just strive to save on this."[45] Apparently these "vegetarian feasts" had similar purposes as the big Buddhist assembly described in *Pacification of the Demons' Revolt*, though certainly on a smaller scale.

By the nineteenth century *baojuan* performances were firmly associated with people of lower status: there is plenty of evidence about these performances for peasants in both the north and south. By the end of the nineteenth century "scroll recitation" had also spread to the urban centers in the south where it gained popularity among common townsfolk.[46] Most notably, at the end of the nineteenth century *baojuan* enjoyed popularity among sing-song girls in Shanghai. Those performances are mentioned in the famous novel *Stories of Flowers on the Sea* (Haishang hua liezhuan, usually translated into English as *Sing-Song Girls of Shanghai*), written by the Shanghai journalist Han Bangqing (1856–1894) ca. 1892.[47] These performances in the brothels obviously were related to the cultural traditions of the neighboring areas.

This gradual narrowing of the social sphere is characteristic of popular genres in other countries as well. For example, in the fifteenth and sixteenth centuries (the period when it flourished), German *Volksbuch* (lit. "folk book," pl. *Volksbücher*), a European equivalent of such vernacular genres as *baojuan* and other lay vernacular narratives in China, found a readership among both the aristocracy and the bourgeoisie. In the seventeenth and eighteenth centuries, however, these reading materials moved from the upper classes of society to the lower ones, and folklorists of the nineteenth to the twentieth century found their printed copies among peasants and workers.[48] Western scholars often apply the term "folklore" to such materials, concluding that it is not possible to determine clear boundaries between folklore and written literature in the highly developed societies of the modern period.[49] Despite this fact, I prefer not to treat published *baojuan* texts (even those of the late period) as folklore; at the time of their circulation, they coexisted with pure oral storytelling.

Baojuan, like German *Volksbuch*, was a kind of literature with a long and complex history that eventually entered the mass-market book trade around the nineteenth century, but there were significant differences between late *baojuan* editions and the cheaply printed books for the masses of the eighteenth and nineteenth centuries in the West. Though *baojuan* were printed and sold for a general readership at the end of the nineteenth through the early twentieth century, the genre retained a measure of religious ideology. It did not become pure entertainment literature but rather preserved numerous traces of its development in the religious movements of the sixteenth to nineteenth century. Significantly, *baojuan* texts still retained the special status of books intended for recitation. This form of genre functioning was a product of the unique amalgamation of Buddhist rites and literature, sectarian beliefs, popular forms of religious devotion, and folk storytelling. This peculiarity of *baojuan* texts provides us with a new insight into the study of the interaction between written and oral forms of literature in China and elsewhere.

ORAL TRADITIONS AND ORIGINS OF *BAOJUAN*

The theory of oral-derivation texts also concerns the history of the *baojuan* genre on the whole. Scholars disagree on the question of its origins. Zheng Zhenduo (1898–1958), the first scholar to study *baojuan* texts in China, started the search for the antecedents of *baojuan*; he considered *bianwen* (transformation texts) to be their ancestors.[50] *Bianwen* are prosimetric texts in semivernacular language that were connected with a form of popular storytelling called *zhuanbian* (unrolling/reciting transformation [scrolls]) that existed in the Tang (618–907) and Five dynasties (907–960) periods. *Bianwen* seem to be the earliest extant texts of true prosimetric form in China. After their performances ended by the eleventh century, they were lost for many centuries until their rediscovery in Dunhuang in 1900.[51] Zheng Zhenduo argues, however, that this genre continued in the Song dynasty (960–1279) in the form of *tanjing* (talks on scriptures), also called *shuojing* (narratives on scriptures). This was a genre of storytelling about religious subjects that was performed in the entertainment quarters in the twelfth to thirteenth century.[52] Zheng Zhenduo claimed that *baojuan* were direct descendants of *bianwen*, and "talks on scriptures" was simply another name for the latter.[53] These conclusions fit into his general view that all later genres of Chinese storytelling developed out of the *bianwen* form.

Later Chinese and Japanese scholars, who mainly studied sectarian *baojuan*, did not agree with Zheng Zhenduo. First, they believed *baojuan* emerged too late (ca. fifteenth century) to have any links with *bianwen*.⁵⁴ Furthermore, they argued that the form and contents of the earliest known *baojuan* were much different from those of *bianwen*. *Baojuan* were closer to serious religious literature than to either *bianwen* or the Song dynasty *tanjing*, both of which were performed mainly for entertainment. In these views, *baojuan* developed out of real Buddhist preaching and were connected closely with the *keyi* (liturgies) and *chanfa* (texts of penitence rituals) that belonged to Buddhist religious literature.⁵⁵

Japanese scholar Sawada Mizuho pointed to the close antecedent of *baojuan*, *Liturgy Based on the Diamond Sūtra*, which also was called *baojuan* in a number of later editions.⁵⁶ It is the extended commentary in prosimetric form on the *Diamond Sūtra* (Skt. Vajracchedika-prajñāpāramitā-sūtra, Ch. Jingang bore boluomi jing) in Kumārajīva's (344–413) translation, a popular scripture of Chinese Buddhism.⁵⁷ *Liturgy Based on the Diamond Sūtra* is very different from typical *baojuan* in terms of form and content; it was recited, however, in a manner similar to other *baojuan*. Its ideas also had a significant influence on *Five Books in Six Volumes* by Luo Qing.⁵⁸ According to Sawada, the earliest *baojuan*, similar to *Liturgy Based on the Diamond Sūtra*, were composed by Buddhist monks, and later this form was employed by sectarians for their scriptures.⁵⁹ His view of a close connection between *baojuan* and penitence books also is well substantiated, and these texts are relevant to our study of Mulian (see chapter 2, "The Apocryphal Buddhist Scripture").

Further research on the popular literature of Dunhuang has brought new perspective to the search for antecedents of *baojuan*. Now it is accepted that there were several different genres in Dunhuang popular literature. Victor H. Mair divides them primarily into two groups: *jiangjingwen* (sūtra-explanation texts) with several groups of texts connected to them, such as *yuanqi* (tales of conditional origin) and *bianwen*. He has emphasized that *jiangjingwen* and *bianwen* had different forms and that their social and performance contexts were dissimilar.⁶⁰ *Jiangjingwen* were the texts of popular Buddhist sermons called *sujiang* (lectures for laity), which took the form of the recitation of a passage from sūtra with expanded commentary in the form of prose and verse.⁶¹ *Yuanqi* illustrated the working of karma through stories, also mainly borrowed from Buddhist literature.⁶² *Bianwen*, on the other hand, never expounded sūtras but rather narrated popular stories, in many cases not connected with Buddhism. *Jiangjingwen* presumably were recited by actual ordained monks while *bianwen* were performed by professional storytellers.⁶³

Taking into consideration this distinction, Che Xilun argues that *jiangjingwen*, and not *bianwen*, were the ancestors of *baojuan*.⁶⁴ The structure and performance qualities (accompanying rituals) of early *baojuan* are strikingly similar to those of *jiangjingwen*, as can be shown through analysis of the form of early *baojuan*. Significantly, a close antecedent of *baojuan*, *Liturgy Based on the Diamond Sūtra*, was similar to *jiangjingwen* as it was a text that explained quotations from the sūtra. Che Xilun, like Sawada, denies the supposed connection of *baojuan* with the Song dynasty *tanjing*.⁶⁵ He argues, however, that the tradition of expounding sūtras persisted during the Song in another literary form, called "talks on karmic causation" (*shuo yinyuan*), which were performed by monks invited to the homes of wealthy families. There are some references to this practice in sources of the twelfth to the fourteenth century.⁶⁶ This proselytizing apparently gave birth to *baojuan*, the earliest specimens of which expounded Buddhist stories. Apparently three *baojuan* texts survived from the early period (thirteenth to fourteenth century), although two of them exist only in later copies: *Liturgy Based on the Diamond Sūtra*, *Baojuan of Maudgalyāyana*, and *Baojuan of Merciful Rite of the Buddhist Disciple's Journey to the West* (Fomen Xiyou cibei daochang baojuan, hereafter abbreviated as *Baojuan of Journey to the West*).⁶⁷ Significantly, the two latter texts narrate popular stories: the Mulian story and the story of monk Xuanzang's (ca. 602–664) journey to India,⁶⁸ the latter of which had also been popular in religious storytelling since the early period.⁶⁹ Thus the subjects of earliest *baojuan* were derived from Buddhist storytelling.

Unfortunately, evidence about Buddhist popular lectures in the eleventh to fourteenth century is scarce. This led Daniel L. Overmyer, the most authoritative scholar of *baojuan* in the West, to conclude that there are no extant close antecedents of *baojuan* texts.⁷⁰ Nevertheless, as oral traditions of proselytizing are close sources of *baojuan* literature, *baojuan* texts dealing with the Mulian story, originally a Buddhist subject, are especially valuable because there is much evidence about their connections with the popular religious literature of the earlier period. The ways of transmission of *baojuan* texts in comparison with those of Buddhist scriptures (sūtra-explanation) are represented in table 1.01. It shows my view of the initial stages in the development of *baojuan* literature (thirteenth through the sixteenth

Table 1.01. Transmission of religious texts, thirteenth to sixteenth century

Type of texts	Authors	Performers (oral transmission)	Recipients (oral transmission)
Buddhist sūtras and texts of sūtra-explanations	Buddhist monks	Buddhist monks	Illiterate laity
Baojuan manuscripts	Buddhist and sectarian clergy	Baojuan performers	Illiterate audience
Baojuan printed copies	Buddhist and sectarian clergy	Baojuan performers	Illiterate audience

century), when it was greatly influenced by the Buddhist texts and related performance practices.

PERFORMANCE CHARACTERISTICS OF *BAOJUAN* TEXTS

The connection of the *baojuan* texts on Mulian with oral literature can be seen in several specific features of these texts: formulaic language, repeated narrative motifs, and multiple story lines. *Baojuan* texts should also be compared to performance-oriented texts in other world literatures and other genres of Chinese literature.

Scholars long ago noticed that the repetition of words, expressions, and similar narrative episodes was a particular feature of folklore and a necessary device for the creation and functioning of oral texts. American folklorists Milman Parry (1902–1935) and Albert B. Lord (1912–1991) proposed the theory that a frequent formulaic usage in a written text indicated that there was an underlying oral tradition (the so-called oral-formulaic theory). They studied the formulaic language of twentieth-century Yugoslavian storytellers (*guslary*) and discovered a proximity to the language of epics ascribed to Homer. Therefore, they argued that Homer's epics and similar texts from medieval times were oral derived.[71] Since the 1960s and 1970s, scholars of ancient and medieval literature have applied the oral-formulaic theory to a wide variety of traditions. Many scholars adopted it as a device to demonstrate the origin of a given text in oral literary tradition. A high degree of formulaic repetition at the levels of the language, theme, and story pattern was taken as a criterion for the classification of a text as oral derived.[72] Later, several scholars of texts with oral epic characteristics who did not agree with Lord's method of using formulaic usage as a sign of the oral origin of the text started to develop their own theories. An important change took place in the theoretical approach toward the texts—instead of seeking the orality presumably embedded in a written text, scholars turned to the exploration of the specific reading practices and social context of texts exhibiting characteristics of oral literature.[73]

A more recent theory of oral literature, that of "word-power," was suggested in the 1990s by John M. Foley. It is based on the close study of several traditions of oral literature and its derivatives (ancient Greek, Yugoslavian, Old English, Native American, etc.) and combines several approaches to folklore and oral-derived texts: the Parry-Lord Formulaic Theory, Foley's own Immanent Art, the Ethnopoetics (Dennis Tedlock and Dell Hymes), and Performance Theory (Richard Bauman).[74] These four theories share the conception of the folklore performance as the enabling event and tradition as its enabling referent.[75] According to Foley, the folklore performance constitutes communication that is received in a particular way in reference to tradition. The oral literature possesses the characteristics of performance arena, register, and communicative economy.[76] Performance arena is the locus where the event of performance takes place; register is the idiomatic version of the language used in the traditional oral performance; and communicative economy signifies the interactive work of the performer and the audience in which signals are decoded and gaps are bridged with extraordinary fluency.[77] With the use of these devices (together constituting the so-called word-power), oral performance introduces metonymic extratextual meaning, peculiar to oral traditional literature. For example, formulaic language, standard themes, and story patterns discussed in the oral-formulaic theory constitute an important aspect of register. In addition to the meaningful signs, the gaps of indeterminacy that result in "blank spots" or logical cruces in the recorded text of a performance also contribute to the style of communication (communicative economy).[78] The performance arena notion implies the existence of an audience familiar with the conventions of tradition; they must be competent enough to detect and interpret the signals and blanks in the text. Only then can the communication in the performance be carried out.

An important aspect of Foley's theory is its application to the analysis of oral-derived and oral-oriented ancient and medieval texts. It is probable that writing was employed at any or all levels of their composition, transmission, or both. *Baojuan* certainly fall into this category. Dealing with this kind of text, with authorship that nevertheless assumed an oral traditional mode of expression, the emphasis was shifted from the detection of their oral origin to the study of their functioning: "This emphasis [on social function] entails the reversal of the usual heuristic perspective: instead of trying to gauge how much has been preserved or lost, we need rather to ask what the documents can tell us about how they should be read."[79] Though we probably never shall reconstruct the actual performance on the basis of the texts, the performative tradition of which is dead, there is still a lot to learn about their functioning. Oral-derived texts and their imitations can be regarded as an active remembrance of oral tradition. The characteristics of traditional oral literature—performance arena, register, and communicative economy—survive in the written text in modified forms: "As long as the communicative medium remains the dedicated register forged for and in performance to convey meanings that institutionally impinge upon the individual event, and with the proviso that there also remains an audience alive to the encoded signals for interpretation, then we must continue to respect that register's significant force, in short, its word-power."[80]

However, oral-derived texts retain only a measure of traditional oral register, performance arena, and communicative economy. The register in these texts is reduced to the idiom, which is still able "to make institutionalized reference . . . to performance and tradition, and thereby to engage fields of meaning that are otherwise beyond the reach of any performer or audience."[81] The paralinguistic features, which constitute an important part of register in the real performance, are, in most cases, inevitably lost. The performance arena transforms the real event of performance into a rhetorical frame. Nevertheless, "in both cases the experience of performance, real or projected, energizes the relationship between performer, now rhetoricized as well, and the reader/audience."[82] The influence of communicative economy remains in the blank spots (omissions) in the text. The approach Foley used to analyze written texts of Homeric hymns and the Old English poem *Andreas* in terms of textually transformed performance arena, register, and communicative economy is useful in the case of *baojuan* texts as well.[83] Because these texts were produced for storytellers as well as for the readership/audience that was familiar with real-life storytelling performances, the audience for these texts was fluent in their register.

Western scholars already have used concepts similar to Foley's theory in studies of Chinese popular literature. An example is the concept of "simulated context" developed by Patrick Hanan, who focused on the Chinese fiction of the Song-Qing dynasties, which is "the context or situation in which a piece of fiction claims to be transmitted." In Chinese vernacular fiction "the simulacrum is that of the oral storyteller addressing his audience, a pretense in which the author and reader happily acquiesce in order that the fiction can be communicated."[84] Victor H. Mair, following Hanan, applied the concept of simulated context to the study of *bianwen* texts from Dunhuang, where the simulated context appears as the phrases, devices, and techniques employed by an author or editor of a written vernacular text to create the atmosphere of live storytelling.[85] This notion of simulated context is close to Foley's concept of the rhetorical performance arena.

At the same time, Western scholars have different opinions about the use of formulaic or stock phrases and their connection with orality in vernacular literature. For example, Mair noted that the extensive use of a storyteller's formulaic expressions (especially those introducing verses) in a text signifies that the work was intended for a reader and not for a performer (the professional folk storyteller).[86] The real storyteller knew the technique of punctuating his performance without written notes. On the other hand, Vibeke Bordahl, a scholar of Chinese folklore, has recently shown by thorough comparison of oral and written versions of the same popular story that similar formulas appear in real-life storytelling and its written derivatives.[87] In this regard *baojuan* texts constitute a rare example in which the written elements of narrative frame are actively used in a real-life performance.

The rhetoricized storyteller's voice in *baojuan*, introductory formulas and interruptions, and notes prescribing the transmission of accompanying rituals all are signs of the establishment of the performance arena. The formulaic language, recurring story patterns, and musical pieces constitute peculiarities of a text's register. As we shall see, there also are several instances suggesting the relevance of the application of the communicative economy to these texts. This approach not only helps explain the special features of *baojuan* texts but also makes possible a measure of reconstruction of their characteristics of the performance and usage about which little is known from the historical records. The comparison with the information about modern performances of *baojuan* in China contributes to my analysis of the texts.

In speaking about the tradition as an enabling referent against which *baojuan* texts were set, we should note their connections with the traditions of Buddhist preaching and lectures on scriptures. Scholars of Chinese performance-oriented texts have noted their inseparability from the broader cultural tradition. For example, Anne E. McLaren regards constantly repeated elements in *cihua* texts, such as formulaic verse, stereotypical themes, and motifs, as "stock material" or "cultural lore."[88] This sort of material is used extensively in other genres of Chinese vernacular literature, such as the traditional novel. Stock material also played an important role in the composition and perception of *baojuan*. All the texts analyzed in this book contain stock material that was transmitted for centuries—certain expressions and scenes that can be traced to Buddhist scripture and *bianwen*. At different periods of history, additional stories were associated with the Mulian story in *baojuan* literature, such as the story of Huang Chao that we encounter in Mulian *baojuan* of the late period. They were derived from other sectarian scriptures, folklore, drama, and novels, and also can be considered stock material.

STUDYING THE FORMAL CHARACTERISTICS OF *BAOJUAN*

In connection with new theoretical approaches to performance-oriented texts, especially Foley's theory of "word-power," it is important to study in detail the form, verse types, and language of *baojuan* texts. These features of texts have not been analyzed in depth so far. An exception is the Japanese study of a part of *Baojuan of Maudgalyāyana* (manuscript of 1372).[89] Only brief studies have been devoted to the form of *Precious Account of Mulian* and *Baojuan of Three Rebirths*.[90] There has been no work published in regard to *Dizang baojuan* and *Baojuan of Benefiting Living Beings*. Therefore, in the following chapters, I pay close attention to the following features of the form of each major *baojuan* about Mulian:

1) material aspect of extant editions and manuscripts

2) division into volumes and sections; structure of each section (if a text is divided into sections)

3) introductory and concluding parts of the text (especially their verse passages)

4) peculiarities of use of different forms of verses in the text (repetition or new narration)

5) peculiarities of the forms of verse used in the text (meter and rhyme)

6) arias and other sung passages used in the text and their peculiarities

7) visual aids (in case of the illustrated manuscripts and woodblocks of *baojuan*)

8) characteristics of the language of a text

9) formulas in the text (especially introductory formulas of prose and verse passages)

Categories 3–9 in particular are connected with the performative context of the text (rituals, impersonation of characters, visual representations, and musical pieces). Using the terms of "word-power" theory, they provide information on the performance arena and register of *baojuan* texts' performances.

A thorough analysis of the form of *baojuan* texts also leads to redefining the development of the *baojuan* genre. Because of the differences in contents of *baojuan* of the middle and late periods (traditionally termed as the early and late periods), several scholars have treated late *baojuan* almost as an independent genre. For example, Overmyer insists on the necessity of differentiating between two types—scriptural (or sectarian) and narrative (or literary) *baojuan*—which, in his view, represent different phases in the development of the genre, early and late, respectively.[91] Later scholars of *baojuan* literature have made attempts to redefine this traditional view of the genre's development. For example, in her dissertation devoted to the role of *baojuan* in popular religious culture, Janet Kerr has demonstrated the continuity of characteristic features in the early and late *baojuan*. However, following Overmyer's conclusions, she also distinguishes them mainly into scriptural and narrative categories. In order to study the evolution of the genre, she analyzed three texts on different subjects from three periods: one scriptural and two narrative. In her view *baojuan* texts can be regarded as a unified genre as "the narrative and scriptural *baojuan* shared a common function as ritual and salvational literature."[92]

Kerr's conclusion about the common religious nature of *baojuan* texts of different periods appears to be even more applicable to narrative *baojuan* texts on Mulian, which possess a similar ritual function. The evidence of these texts that date to different time periods also confirms that the same subject matter was used throughout the entire history of the genre. At the same time, continuity in the formal characteristics of the texts is also important for understanding the integrity of the genre. A detailed analysis of the form of *baojuan* texts about Mulian and comparison of them reveals the evolution of the form of *baojuan* texts and their constant connection with the changing performative context.

Though Japanese and Chinese scholars who study *baojuan* have sketched the major outlines of the formal characteristics of the genre and their transformation during different periods of its development, there is still no consensus on some aspects of the origins and state of their musical forms.[93] Deeper analysis of the formal aspect of the texts, especially the peculiarities of individual examples, is necessary.

The only thorough study of all the types of verse and their combination in the sections of a specific *baojuan* was completed by Elvira S. Stulova (1934–1993), who worked in the Leningrad Branch of the Institute of Oriental Studies, Russian Academy of Sciences (now the Institute of Oriental Manuscripts, Saint Petersburg) and studied *baojuan* texts that were preserved there, including several rare and even unique printed copies from the sixteenth through the eighteenth century. Her representative work is the study on *Baojuan of Tathāgata Puming Who Understood the Meaning of Non-interference* (Puming rulai wuwei liaoyi baojuan; Che no. 794, hereafter abbreviated as *Puming baojuan*), a sixteenth-century text that at that time was considered to be unique one to that Russian collection (later it was also rediscovered in China).[94] Stulova's research, however, was limited because of the lack of materials on the performance of *baojuan*. An example is her interpretation of seven-character verse. The most common forms used in *baojuan* of all three periods are verses with seven-, five-, and ten-character lines. Seven- and ten-character verse also has been standard in other genres of Chinese popular storytelling and drama. This arrangement forms the "system of verse-recitation" (*shizanxi*), or "clapper-mode system" (*banqiangxi*). The opposite is the "system of arias" (*qupaixi*), or "system of lyrics and arias" (*ciquxi*).[95]

Baojuan was a mixed genre that employed both verse recitation and singing of arias.

Stulova treated verses with seven- and five-character meter in *Puming baojuan* as ordinary verses of the *shi* genre, the classical form of Chinese poetry.⁹⁶ *Shi* had five- or seven-character meters. Of the two forms of *shi* that developed in the course of evolution of Chinese poetry, the one with the most rigid rules, which spread during the Tang dynasty, is called "modern style verse" (*jintishi*). It requires following the special rules of tonal combination within a line (*gelü*), rhymes in level tone, parallelism of the phrases in certain lines, and so on.⁹⁷ The rules of tonal combination for the modern style verse were based on the pronunciation of medieval Chinese (ca. seventh century). There the even tone (*ping*) was juxtaposed with three other tones (rising: *shang*, falling: *qu*, and entering: *ru*), collectively designated as slanted (*ze*). At the same time, there was also the "ancient style verse" (*gutishi* or *gufeng*) that developed before the establishment of these rules but remained in use during the Tang and later. Nevertheless, during and after the Tang, poems written in this form were influenced by modern style verse to a certain degree. The rules were applied not so rigidly, however, in the ancient style poetry as in the modern. For example, syllables in both level and slanted tones could rhyme, parallelism was not obligatory, and so forth.⁹⁸ Stulova analyzed seven- and five-character verses in *Puming baojuan* as the ancient style verse, using the schemes of the combinations of tones in each line introduced by Wang Li (1900–1986) in his analysis of the ancient style poetry.⁹⁹ As a result, many schemes of combinations of tones in *Puming baojuan* were recognized as corresponding to variants of ancient style poems that Wang Li labeled as "not seen" or "used extremely rarely."¹⁰⁰

In modern performances of *baojuan* in Hexi and Hebei, seven- and ten-character verses are recited to special kinds of folk melodies known as the "Buddhist [chant] in seven-characters" (*qizi fo*) and "Buddhist [chant] in ten-characters" (*shizi fo*).¹⁰¹ A similar distinction of two basic melodies is also apparent in Jingjiang performances of *baojuan*. In Changshu "telling scriptures," there are more than a dozen melodies commonly used for seven-character meter verses in *baojuan*.¹⁰² While *baojuan* performances in the Jingjiang and Changshu areas (as well as in Hexi) usually have only percussion instrumental accompaniment, in the Suzhou and Shaoxing areas string accompaniment is mainly used.¹⁰³ In modern traditions of performances in the north as well as in the south, every other line of seven-character verse in *baojuan* has the refrain called "echoing the Buddha's name," usually containing "hail to Amitābha Buddha." This refrain appeared in the earliest specimens of *baojuan* genre. It thus turns out that since the early period, seven-character verses in *baojuan* were a kind of folk poetry that was far removed from the literary examples of ancient style verse. The authors of *baojuan* more likely would have tried to match folk melodies rather than follow the classical rules for the combination of tones as in classical verse, so analysis of seven- and five-character verses in *baojuan* according to the schemes of the *shi* poetry appears to be irrelevant.

Since the beginning of the sixteenth century at the latest, ten-character verses were used in *baojuan* texts. Che Xilun argues that ten-character verses probably first appeared in drama of the thirteenth century; however, in *baojuan* they came from the other genres of storytelling art.[104] For the analysis of rhymes in seven- and ten-character verses, most scholars of *baojuan* adopted the system of "thirteen tracks" (*shisan zhe*), which also has been used commonly in northern genres of Chinese storytelling since the Ming dynasty.[105] This rhyme system corresponds to the northern variants of Chinese and is used in poetry in modern Mandarin.[106] The rhyme in the verses of analyzed *baojuan* texts has several special features, and rhymes in their arias also were influenced by the older rhyme systems for arias of the thirteenth to fourteenth century.

Remaining problems in the definition of the forms of verses used in *baojuan* include a special meter of verse in *baojuan* of the early period that has different numbers of characters per line, with the usual structure of four-four-five or four-four characters in a line. Stulova considered this form a lyric (*ci*) without any indication of the name of the melody that it would have accompanied.[107] Che Xilun regards it as a particular form of eulogy or hymn (*gezan*).[108] This hypothesis is well proved by modern evidence of *baojuan* performances in Laishui (Hebei) where a similar kind of chant is sung at the opening of *baojuan*.[109] Therefore, it is logical to treat it as a hymn of unknown name.

There are also arias in *baojuan* that are especially numerous and varied in texts of the middle period. Che Xilun refers to these arias as "small arias" (*xiaoqu*) or "popular arias" (*suqu*).[110] They designate verses written to fit a certain melody. Huang Yupian, the Qing dynasty official in charge of persecutions of sectarians in what is now Hebei at the beginning of the nineteenth century, who also paid attention to their scriptures in his book, *Detailed Refutation of Heresies* (Po xie xiang bian, hereafter *Refutation of Heresies*; written between 1834 and 1843), supposed that these melodies could have appeared in the early *baojuan* under the influence of *kunqu* theater.[111] Che argues that arias in *baojuan* are not related to *kunqu*. They could be different from arias used in traditional theater because, though their melodies might have the same names, the ones used in *baojuan* were folk modifications.[112] Modern Chinese scholars of drama argue, however, that popular variants of commonly used arias often were modified very slightly compared to the classical schemes used in drama.[113] A musicological study of the arias in some early *baojuan* preserved in Laishui reveals that they were close to classical forms.[114]

A comparison of arias used in *baojuan* and classical arias (mostly specimens of the Yuan and Ming dynasties) demonstrates the difference in their meters. The most appropriate source of such classical aria schemes is *The Imperially Approved Register of Arias* (Qinding qupu; later referred to by its popular name, *Register of Arias of Kangxi [Reign]*) compiled by Wang Yiqing et al. around 1715. As a book written on imperial order, it was clearly an attempt to standardize the form of aria verses.[115] It provides the schemes of tonal combinations in the selected examples of arias mostly taken from the plays of the Yuan and Ming dynasties (fourteenth to sixteenth century).

In the prosody of arias, rules of tonal combination also existed. They were not the same as in the *shi* and *ci* genre verses owing to changes in pronunciation of Mandarin by the thirteenth century when arias started to be composed. The main division into even and slanted tones nevertheless was preserved. In the majority of aria schemes, there were prescribed positions for the even (by that time divided into upper and lower even), rising, and falling tones.[116] Comparison of the tonal combination in the arias from the *baojuan* under discussion with that prescribed by the schemes is impractical, mainly because of the phenomenon of "padding words" (*chenzi*), common in arias. Extra words, and even sentences, could be added to the main scheme in the actual verses of arias; in some cases the omission of words was allowed.[117] Extra words were sung quickly, to fit to the melody. Thus it is very difficult to distinguish between main and padding words in the arias, and analyzing tonal combinations in them is problematic. Still, the focus on comparison of the overall structure of the pieces (number of sentences) and the position and tones of rhymes is sufficient to show that the general schemes of arias in *baojuan* about

Mulian of the early and middle periods of development, namely *Baojuan of Maudgalyāyana*, *Dizang baojuan*, and *Baojuan of Benefiting Living Beings*, were quite close to the classical ones in the registers of arias of the imperial times. However, in the case of the late texts, *Baojuan of Three Rebirths* and *Precious Account of Mulian*, we do not have such direct correspondence, which indicates the even more popular nature of these texts, which borrowed melodies from folk music.

CONCLUSION

Baojuan often have been regarded as folklore or oral-derived texts. Although the *baojuan* analyzed in this book are not necessarily oral-derived literature, they were deeply rooted in the popular performance tradition. Numerous vernacular elements in the language of these texts made them comprehensible for an audience not very sophisticated about classical Chinese books, including illiterate people. Detailed analysis of poetic parts of *baojuan* texts from different periods of their development shows their close connections with the musical culture of the late imperial period. The musical aspect of their performances was quite complex and varied, as it included melodies of different quality and origins, from the arias related to the theatrical genres to folk songs. These performance qualities of *baojuan* texts—use of colloquial language and musical accompaniment—developed in the traditions of *baojuan* recitation that survive in different areas of China. *Baojuan* are performance-oriented texts that still can be used in performances today, though they essentially are cultural relics.

The double role of *baojuan* as books that can be used for recitation and for individual reading has analogues in traditional Chinese as well as in old European literature. These internal and international parallels help explain the circulation of *baojuan* texts in the broad social strata as well as its present survival in rural society.

Baojuan texts dealing with the story of Mulian were created for a different audience, and the aims and mode of their production, as well as the social background and manner of performance, changed over the centuries. At the same time, the texts contain common themes, ideas, and formal characteristics. An analysis of texts from different periods reveals both changes and continuities in their contents and form. Among the research methods used in this volume are detailed analysis of the characteristics of content and form of the *baojuan* texts that were closely related to the changing context of their performance and reception and investigation of features of interaction of oral and written literature in these texts with reference to the performance theory concerning oral-oriented literature. The result is a more complete picture of the history of the *baojuan* genre and its place in Chinese popular literature. At a certain level, it illuminates the origin and antecedents of the genre, its integrity, and the classification and evolution of its texts.

CHAPTER 2

The Mulian Story in Chinese Literature

In spite of extensive research by international scholars, the origin of the story of Mulian rescuing his mother is still unclear. There is almost universal agreement that the earliest known account of the story is the *Sūtra of Ullambana, Expounded by the Buddha* (Fo shuo Yulanpen jing; *TSD*, no. 685, hereafter *Sūtra of Ullambana*).[1] Traditionally, it is assumed that a monk of Tocharian origin, Dharmarakṣha (Ch. Zhu Fahu), translated it into Chinese at the beginning of the fourth century.[2] Another Chinese recension of this scripture, *Sūtra of Offering Bowls to Repay Kindness* (Bao en feng pen jing; *TSD*, no. 686), dates to the period between 317 and 420.[3] If an original sūtra ever existed in an Indian or Central Asian language, it has not been found.

The term *Ullambana* (*Avalambana*, Ch. *Yulanpen*) stands for the basin in which offerings for Buddhist monks are presented. The sūtra claims that such an offering is the best way to obtain the salvation of ancestors; Mulian did this to rescue his mother from rebirth in the form of a hungry ghost. The Ullambana offering was performed during the Zhongyuan (Middle Primordial) Festival on the fifteenth day of the seventh moon, also known as the Ghost Festival, which flourished in China in the medieval period. Traditionally, the word *Ullambana* was interpreted as "hanging upside down" (*daoxuan*), a description of the sufferings of sinners.[4] This etymology is doubtful, especially as this kind of offering is not known in the traditions of Indian Buddhism. Modern scholars have suggested different hypotheses to explain the etymology of the word *Ullambana*.[5] On the basis of thorough philological analysis, it has been proposed recently that this word is the transliteration of the Sanskrit colloquial form *olana* (from "odana"), meaning "rice."⁶ Thus *Ullambana* should be interpreted as the "rice bowl," which is logical in the context of the Chinese ritual.

The story of rescuing his mother's soul is a part of the literature concerning the activities of Maudgalyāyana/Mulian, one of the first disciples of Buddha, who is an important figure in the canonic literature of Buddhism in both Indian and Chinese traditions.⁷ The story of Mulian rescuing his mother with the use of Ullambana, however, does not appear in the Indian Buddhist texts. Several scholars who have studied the origins of the story have concluded that it is apocryphal and was created in China.⁸ Others, with the use of the materials of Indian Buddhist literature (mainly its Chinese translations), have demonstrated that the Mulian story fit into a significant, broad topic of parents' deliverance in Buddhist literature. Similar stories deal with the problem of filial duty among Buddhist believers.⁹ Therefore, this story appeared in a textual background that indicates its foreign (Indian or Central Asian) origin.

From the time of its appearance in Chinese literature, the story of Mulian rescuing his mother constituted an important point of reconciliation and unification for major religious traditions in China: Confucianism, Daoism, and Buddhism. This story clarified the attitude of Buddhists toward filial piety, one of the major values in Confucian literature. Buddhists often were accused of violating the principles of filial piety because they adopted the value of celibate monasticism. According to the *Sūtra of Ullambana*, however, the salvation of ancestors' souls with the use of the Buddhist ritual and the monks' prayers is the best expression of filial duty. In this respect, the ideas expressed in this scripture are in accord with the argument of many eminent early Chinese apologists of Buddhism, including Mouzi (ca. third century ce), Sun Chuo (ca. 300–380), and the monk Huiyuan (334–416).¹⁰ The important place of the *Sūtra of Ullambana* (and hence the Mulian story) in Chinese Buddhism is attested by the fact that the eminent Tang monk Zongmi (780–841) composed a commentary on this scripture (ca. 830) that emphasizes this new Buddhist concept of filial piety and draws on the popular narratives describing Mulian's journey to the underworld that had formed by that time.¹¹

The Mulian story quickly entered and influenced the culture of the general populace of the medieval period. It has been argued that stories of filial piety related to the mother and son bond such as the

Mulian story, constituted the basis for the social program of Chinese Buddhism that was aimed at family values. Apparently these stories supplemented the basic value of Confucianism that primarily concerned filial duty toward male ancestors.[12] Whether or not this conclusion is correct, the link with filial piety became an important factor in explaining the broad transmission of the Mulian story in China and in other countries of East Asia.[13]

Scholars also have noted indigenous Chinese, specifically Daoist, connotations of the Zhongyuan Festival in China.[14] In the sixth to the eighth century the Zhongyuan Festival and the Mulian literature connected with it already had a highly syncretic nature and were fully incorporated into popular Chinese culture.[15] Numerous studies have demonstrated that by the twelfth to thirteenth century, the Zhongyuan Festival had synthesized sacrifices to the monastic community and ancestors with offerings to the lonely spirits (*guhun*). In the traditional worldview, these lonely spirits (the souls of people who do not receive proper offerings) are very dangerous for the living and should be propitiated. The Ullambana ritual took the new extended meaning of "universal salvation" (*pudu*) of all living beings, and souls of the dead in particular, as it incorporated the emerging Buddhist rituals of feeding hungry ghosts (*shishi* or *yankou*).[16]

By the fourteenth century, when the Mulian story appeared in the texts of *baojuan* form, there was a long tradition of its development in Chinese literature, including its storytelling and dramatic genres.

THE EARLY VERNACULAR VERSIONS OF THE STORY

Because of its ideological significance, the story of Mulian rescuing his mother was featured in numerous pieces of Chinese Buddhist exegetical literature.[17] For the present study, the most important are the versions of the story presented in texts preserved in the library of the Buddhist cave-temple of Dunhuang, along the Silk Road, from the eighth to the tenth century, and presumably connected with Buddhist sermons for laity (*sujiang*) and storytelling traditions (*zhuanbian*). Among the Dunhuang manuscripts, there are four distinct texts connected with the Mulian story. These are fragments of *Jiangjingwen of the Ullambana Sūtra* (Yulanpen jing jiangjingwen), *Yuanqi of Mulian* (Mulian yuanqi), *Bianwen of Mahāmaudgalyāyana Rescuing His Mother from the Underworld* (Da Muqianlian minjian jiu mu bianwen, hereafter *Bianwen of Mahāmaudgalyāyana*), and a fragment of *Bianwen of Mulian* (Mulian Bianwen, more probably another version of *Yuanqi of Mulian*).[18] Two manuscripts of *Bianwen of Mahāmaudgalyāyana* are dated to the tenth century.[19] *Bianwen of Mulian* is mentioned in historical sources, however, in connection with two poets who lived at the beginning of the ninth century.[20] On this basis, the text of *Bianwen of Mahāmaudgalyāyana* has been dated to around 800.[21]

Yuanqi and *bianwen* represent close contemporary versions of the Mulian story that are very different from the original version in the *Sūtra of Ullambana*.[22] At the same time, scholars agree that in the vernacular narratives from Dunhuang this story took the basic form in which it appeared in later texts in Chinese literature, notably drama and *baojuan*.[23] The contents of *bianwen* (and most later versions of the story) and *Sūtra of Ullambana* differ in five major ways: (1) the punishment of Mulian's mother was transferred from the realm of hungry ghosts to Avīci (Ch. Abi) hell; (2) the journey of Mulian through all divisions of hell occupies a large space; (3) an account of the previous life of Mulian and his parents is included; (4) Mulian's mother is reborn as a dog after she is released from hell and the realm of hungry ghosts; (5) at the end, Mulian's mother is reborn in the Heaven of the Thirty-three Celestials.[24] This last detail apparently specifies the heavens where rebirth of ancestors is promised in the *Sūtra of Ullambana*.

In *bianwen*, Mulian also receives a secular name, Luobo (Turnip), that is different from the name used for him in Buddhist scriptures. This change is considered to be the result of the misinterpretation of a Chinese abbreviated transcription "Mulian" as the Sanskrit word for "turnip."[25] Furthermore, Mulian's parents also received personal names: Fuxiang (spelled as 輔相) and Qingti. All of these names were preserved in virtually all later dramatic and *baojuan* versions.[26] The appearance of these new details in the story in *bianwen* and *yuanqi* texts can be interpreted as the influence of expanded oral versions. Some of these new details already exist in the earlier Chinese Buddhist apocryphal and exegetic texts, the most important of which is the *Pure Land Ullambana Sūtra* (Jingtu Yulanpen jing, ca. 600–650), the apocryphal scripture, also preserved only among Dunhuang manuscripts.[27] Significantly, this early text relates the Mulian legend to the concept of the Pure Land, so important in later Chinese Buddhism, which is often juxtaposed with the torments of hell in the later works as well.

The detailed description of divisions of hell that we find in popular narratives about Mulian from Dunhuang (in particular *Bianwen of Mahāmaudgalyāyana*) was an important aspect of the development of the Chinese concept of afterlife punishment in hells, which occurred in the medieval period (third to the eighth century). This new understanding of the underworld was related to the Buddhist concepts that were transmitted to China from abroad (including karma), but it also had Chinese specifics, expressed for example in the aspect of the bureaucratic underworld administration, headed by the great king Yanluo (Skt. Yama), who judges the sinners and metes out justice. Merciful Bodhisattva Dizang, who rescues souls from the underworld, also appears in *Bianwen of Mahāmaudgalyāyana*. All of this is an important part of the traditional Chinese cosmology that also influenced the religious landscape of neighboring countries. Narratives of Mulian's journey certainly were part of the tradition of literary and artistic representations of hell, which became popular by the Tang period.[28]

Visual representations of hell, known as "the hell tableaux" (*diyu bian*), must have been closely related to the Buddhist preaching on retributions and popular narratives that developed out of it, including *bianwen* texts. The use of visual aids during performances appears to have been one of the characteristics of the *bianwen* genre. It is now generally accepted that picture scrolls, showing the events of the narrative, regularly were displayed during the oral performances of *bianwen*, based on the usual verse-introductory formula: "Please look at the place, where X occurs, how should I present it?"[29] There is also evidence that manuscripts of *bianwen* dealing with the Mulian story were illustrated. One of the manuscripts of *Bianwen of Mahāmaudgalyāyana* (S 2614) has the words "With Pictures, One Scroll, With Preface" in its title. However, the two characters for "with pictures" were crossed out, and the illustrations are missing from this manuscript.[30] Another manuscript of this text, PK 876, has blank spaces alternating with portions of the text, perhaps to accommodate illustrations.[31] These illustrations may have been replicas of picture scrolls that were unrolled by the performers of *bianwen* in front of their audience.

To my knowledge there are no murals illustrating the Mulian story in the Mogao caves in Dunhuang where the vernacular texts of the tenth century were discovered. We can only speculate about the reason for their absence, as many other well-known Buddhist stories from canonical literature were depicted in these caves. A pictorial version of the Mulian story, however, dating to approximately the tenth century was discovered in the Yulin caves near Dunhuang. The details of these images suggest a connection with the *bianwen* or *yuanqi* versions of the story. Several scenes reproduce the contents found in *Bianwen of Mahāmaudgalyāyana*.[32] Images from Yulin support the hypothesis of the connection of Buddhist preaching and the nascent *bianwen* genre with murals in temples. The precise nature of this connection is still not clear, but there also is evidence of correspondence of other subjects in *bianwen* and murals.[33]

Representations of the underworld torments in *bianwen* of the Tang period, in both their textual and visual aspects, continue in the later popular narratives on Mulian and his mother, including early *baojuan*, especially *Baojuan of Maudgalyāyana*. They influenced the development of this story in the literary traditions of neighboring countries, where the story also has a setting of hells, and where numerous pictorial versions of related narratives were created.[34]

THE APOCRYPHAL BUDDHIST SCRIPTURE OF THE TWELFTH TO THE THIRTEENTH CENTURY

A version of the story close to that in *bianwen* appears in the later apocryphal scripture *Sūtra of Mulian Rescuing His Mother Expounded by the Buddha* (Fo shuo Mulian jiu mu jing, later abbreviated as *Sūtra of Mulian*). This text, like *bianwen*, was lost in China but was discovered in the twentieth century in later editions in Japan and Korea. The Japanese illustrated edition was reprinted in 1346 from the Chinese original printed in Yin county of Zhedong (in the modern city of Ningbo in Zhejiang), dating to 1251.[35] The Japanese reprint survived in a unique copy in the Kinkōji monastery in Kyoto. It is illustrated in the "picture above text" manner, in which illustrations appear in the running lane taking about one-third of the scroll height; they also have explanatory labels.[36] The colophon of the Japanese edition does not indicate the name of the translator (compiler) of the text.

The text reprinted in Korea is titled *Sūtra of Great Mulian, Expounded by the Buddha* (Fo shuo Da Mulian jing, hereafter abbreviated as *Sūtra of Great Mulian*). Its text is almost identical to that of the Japanese reprint; however, the form of its editions is different. *Sūtra of Great Mulian* survived in several woodblock editions, the oldest of which (dated 1537) comes from the monastery Yonngisa.[37]

Several Korean editions are illustrated, but the pictures greatly differ from those in the Japanese reprint: they are much cruder and appear inside the text and not on the top of it. Though the Korean editions date to a period later than the Japanese reprint, this text apparently was transmitted to Korea quite early, around the end of the eleventh to the early twelfth century. Sermons on *Sūtra of Mulian* that should refer to this scripture are mentioned in the Korean historical chronicle under the year 1106.[38] Furthermore, the Korean editions indicate that *Sūtra of Great Mulian* was translated into Chinese by the monk Dharmadeva (Ch. Fatian, fl. 973–1001); however, his connection with this text is very doubtful and not substantiated by other sources.[39]

Nevertheless, it is clear that *Sūtra of Mulian* dates to the eleventh to the early twelfth century. It might have been connected with another apocryphal *Glorious Sūtra of Reverend Mulian* (Mulian zun sheng jing), mentioned in the book *Records of Bright Dreams about the Eastern Capital* (Dongjing menghua lu) by Meng Yuanlao (ca. 1147). Meng Yuanlao says that this sūtra was sold in the markets of the Song dynasty capital Bianliang (modern Kaifeng) during the Zhongyuan Festival before 1125.[40] Unfortunately, we do not know more about its contents. It is clear, however, that Meng Yuanlao was talking about a certain popular variant of the Mulian story that should have been very similar to the extant text of *Sūtra of Mulian*.

Sūtra of Mulian received considerable influence from vernacular narratives such as *bianwen* and *yuanqi*. This is illustrated in the following features of the text: (1) proximity of its content to *bianwen*, (2) usage of some elements of colloquial language, and (3) presence of visual aids—illustrations that closely follow the story line. Unlike *bianwen* and *yuanqi*, however, *Sūtra of Mulian* is not a prosimetric text. It is written completely in prose. It is certainly not the record of an oral sermon; and based on the special features of this text (its earliest available edition), it seems to have been intended for individual reading.[41] If Meng Yuanlao and the Korean chronicle indeed refer to the currently available *Sūtra of Mulian*, it and *Bianwen of Mahāmaudgalyāyana* appear to be not very far apart in time: the first dates to beginning of the twelfth and the second to the middle of the tenth century. Unfortunately, it is hard to establish direct connections between them, as no other relevant materials have been discovered.

One should especially note the third point of proximity between *Sūtra of Mulian* and *bianwen*, as it is important for the interpretation of performances and texts of *baojuan* dealing with the Mulian story. In spite of the fact that both *bianwen* and *Sūtra of Mulian* were illustrated, there was a considerable difference in the quality of the illustrations: while in the first case picture scrolls were used in picture storytelling, in the second case they apparently were designed to attract and assist readers. Illustrated editions of *Sūtra of Mulian* (as far as we can judge by the Japanese reprint of 1346) most probably did not serve as genuine picture storytelling. Their illustrations were too small for convenient demonstration during live performance of the text, although they were well suited for individual reading.

The format of the Japanese reprint edition is especially close to that of illustrated editions of *pinghua* ("Five completely illustrated pinghua" [*Quanxiang pinghua wu zhong*]) that were printed by Yu publishers of Jian'an (modern Jian'ou in Fujian) around 1321–23 and preserved in Japan in the Library of the Cabinet of Ministers (Naikaku bunko). They also have the "picture above the text" form and bear indicative labels. These *pinghua* editions usually are regarded by modern scholars as reading materials rather than storytelling promptbooks.[42] Pictures accompanying the text of *Sūtra of Mulian*, however, testify that it must have been used by a specific reading audience. Semiliterate readers, especially women and children, could use pictures to supplement their understanding of a text and probably were the target audience. As it discusses the ritual of female salvation and filial piety, its contents were appropriate for such audiences. Furthermore, illustrations contribute to the entertaining side of the reading. Pictures that continuously illustrate narration also appear in two early manuscripts of *baojuan* about Mulian, and the contents of that *baojuan* text are very close to *Sūtra of Mulian*. Therefore, illustrated editions of *Sūtra of Mulian* should be considered as an intermediate stage between the *bianwen* and *baojuan* genres.

Although *Sūtra of Mulian* was lost and forgotten in China, it had an important influence on the development of religious literature dealing with the Mulian story. The contents of the apocryphal scripture were included in the "penitence book" with the title of *Cibei lanpen Mulian daochang chanfa* (Penitence at the Ritual Place of Merciful Ullambana of Mulian), a text accompanying the ritual of penitence to be performed at the ritual area (*daochang*, lit. "place of the Way/Path"; Skt. *maṇḍa, maṇḍala-māḍa*), which is quite close to the performance of *baojuan* with the special purpose of penitence of sins by the means of invocation of Buddha's names.[43] Although the earliest edition available to me (kept in the library of Saint Petersburg State University) is dated 1617, its preface is dated 1351.⁴⁴ Therefore, it predates the earliest available text of *baojuan* dealing with the Mulian story and constitutes its close antecedent.

DRAMATIC VERSIONS

During the Song dynasty, the ritual drama of the Mulian story appeared in China. Along with storytelling and vernacular religious literature, it was an important factor in the development of story in the *baojuan* genre. The earliest evidence of the Mulian drama, which was performed during the Zhongyuan Festival in Bianliang, comes from the book by Meng Yuanlao, *Records of Bright Dreams about the Eastern Capital*. *Zaju* (variety play) with the title *Mulian Rescues His Mother* (Mulian jiu mu) was staged in the entertainment quarters (*gousi*) of the capital during the seven days before the fifteenth day of the seventh moon before 1125.⁴⁵ There was much discussion of the contents of this drama, but there is no other evidence about this performance other than Meng Yuanlao's record.⁴⁶ There is also information on the existence of Mulian dramas of other genres in the thirteenth to fifteenth century; however, none of these scripts mentioned in historical sources survives today.⁴⁷

The earliest extant script of a Mulian drama was compiled by Zheng Zhizhen (1518–1595), an author from the area of modern Anhui. It is titled *Newly Compiled Drama Exhorting Goodness of Mulian Rescuing His Mother* (Xinbian Mulian jiu mu quan shan xiwen, hereafter abbreviated as *Drama Exhorting Goodness*).⁴⁸ Zheng Zhizhen's preface in the earliest edition is dated 1583.⁴⁹ In the preface and remarks on the drama, Zheng Zhizhen said that he used the preceding text that he had arranged in three volumes (one hundred acts) intended for a three-night performance.⁵⁰ In the postface to the earliest edition of this drama, Hu Guanglu gives the name of the source used by Zheng Zhizhen—*Story of Mulian* (Mulian zhuan).⁵¹ In the aria opening the third volume of the drama, Zheng Zhizhen provides the name of the author of this source—a certain Chen.⁵² Chinese scholars concluded that Zheng Zhizhen abridged and edited the full-fledged script that was connected with popular drama or storytelling performance.⁵³ Zheng Zhizhen's drama is an important monument in the history of Chinese popular literature and its interaction with literati culture. There are numerous studies of the special features of the contents and form (music) of this script, so there is no need to provide much detail about it here.⁵⁴

Another early script of the Mulian drama is *Golden Rules Exhorting Goodness* (Quan shan jin ke, later abbreviated as *Golden Rules*). It exists in several versions, compiled at the end of the seventeenth to the eighteenth century, and was used for performances in the palace theater of the Qing dynasty emperors.[55] The most well-known version is the script edited by the court functionary Zhang Zhao and published in the middle of the eighteenth century. Zhang Zhao's script was intended for performance over the course of ten days. Many additional episodes were inserted in the main story line, so that Zhang Zhao's version consists of 240 acts. *Golden Rules* apparently represents an adaptation of a popular story for court performances with the emphasis on propagation of traditional ethical virtues of filial piety, chastity, and loyalty (substantiated by additional scenes). This text exercised considerable influence on later storytelling and dramatic versions; especially famous are some scenes from it staged as a modern musical drama of Beijing (*jingju*, popularly known as Peking opera).[56] Today the story of Mulian rescuing his mother is still performed in this genre of Beijing drama; in April 2002, I saw this performance by young actors of the Beijing theater academy in Lao She Tea House (Laoshe Chaguan), a famous tourist attraction in Beijing.

Besides Beijing drama, the Mulian story has been a popular subject in most local genres of Chinese traditional drama, which are almost innumerable. The Mulian story also has been used in pieces of different genres of storytelling.[57] Historical sources testify that Mulian dramas flourished in different provinces of China during the Ming and Qing dynasties.[58] Today many Mulian dramas in local genres still are staged in China. Some versions of the Mulian drama were transmitted orally, but many troupes relied on written scripts.

Many local versions of the Mulian drama became available recently, as they were published in the project *Studies in Chinese Ritual, Theater, and Folklore Series* (Minsu quyi congshu). This collection includes Mulian drama scripts from several provinces (some are transcriptions of orally delivered versions),[59] as well as collections of materials and fieldwork reports pertaining to Mulian dramas.[60] Much research also has been done in mainland China that resulted in the publication of drama scripts and collections of articles and materials on Mulian dramas in different regions of the country.[61] Several important studies based on extensive fieldwork have been published by Japanese and Western scholars.[62] This research even formed the trend in Chinese literary studies called "Mulian-ology" (Mulian xue).

The current literature on Mulian dramas is immense. For example, in the bibliography of works of Chinese literature related to the story of Mulian, Mao Gengru listed 98 different drama pieces (including separate acts) and 47 pieces related to storytelling.[63] A more recent bibliography by Dai Yun includes 185 drama scripts and 52 storytelling pieces (altogether 254 and 101 different editions/manuscripts, respectively).[64] They originated from approximately eighteen modern provinces in China. One should note, however, that these bibliographies are far from complete, even in documenting extant texts.[65] Only a few versions of local Mulian dramas, mainly scripts with an unusual treatment of the story line that pertain to the contents of *baojuan*, are relevant here.

In spite of the fact that much research has been conducted on the Mulian drama, many questions concerning the formation and spread of the local variants remain unanswered. For example, many local variants of full-fledged Mulian dramas have only slight differences. Most of them closely follow *Drama Exhorting Goodness* by Zheng Zhizhen, apparently because the latter was widespread due to its printed form.[66] At the same time, several represent greatly expanded versions of the Mulian story, as they contain the "prehistory of Mulian" (*qian Mulian*) and/or the "sequel of Mulian" (*hou Mulian*), or are accompanied by the performance of drama with other subjects, and in this last feature they are similar to *Golden Rules*. Therefore, many Chinese scholars argue that some local versions of the Mulian drama (the drama of Putian county, Fujian, in particular) had formed prior to the time when Zheng Zhizhen produced his recension. These scholars claim that the dramas from Putian and other areas in southern China preserve characteristics of the Song and Yuan southern drama (*nanxi*) genre on the basis of contents, scenic organization, and music.[67] Especially interesting are the conclusions of the musicologists who treated the local Mulian dramas in the south as the remnants of old *nanxi* music that spread in several provinces of China.[68]

There are several points concerning the functioning of Mulian plays in Chinese society that are important in connection with *baojuan* literature. The first is an obvious moralizing tendency (as declared in the title of Zheng Zhizhen's version of the drama) that makes them similar to *baojuan*. For example, the moralizing context of Mulian dramas (in modern Anhui in particular) can be seen as representing the values of the mercantile class that supported their performances.[69] Another important feature is the ritual context of Mulian dramas.

In this, one should note that there are two quite distinct types of Mulian dramas in China. The first includes full-fledged multiple-act dramas (*liantaixi*). The second is represented by short scenes inserted in funerary rituals. These two types also have differences concerning the status of performers. While long dramas are performed by folk actors, funerary dramas often are performed by folk Buddhist or Daoist priests (religious specialists whose main role is the performance of funerary rituals).[70] Today both types of dramas survive mainly in southern China. Multiple-act dramas have been performed in Hunan, Fujian, Anhui, Jiangsu, Jiangxi, and other provinces.[71] The Mulian dramas also are staged by Chinese people living in Southeast Asia. Especially famous are dramas staged by the descendants of Fujian people in Singapore.[72] Funerary Mulian dramas still are staged in Fujian, Taiwan, Guangdong, Zhejiang, and Sichuan.[73]

The first type of drama also is accompanied by various rituals aimed at warding off baleful spirits and bringing good fortune.[74] Results of such rituals are connected mainly with the prosperity of the whole community. For example, the Mulian drama has been staged regularly (once in ten years) by Chinese emigrants from Putian county in Singapore in order to pacify all the potentially malevolent spirits of the deceased in the community. Rituals and drama are staged in turn by Daoist priests and actors.[75] Some local versions of the Mulian drama preserve a connection with the Ullambana ritual and the Zhongyuan Festival. Although the latter is no longer celebrated in many areas of China, it was still popular in the recent past. Mentions of the festival in connection with Mulian drama in historical sources indicate that until recently performances often took place on the day of the festival.[76] This is often not the same, however, in modern performances.

In funerary performances, the main focus is personal (familial) welfare. Performers enact the process of rescuing the soul of the dead from hell and leading it to a better rebirth. In funerary performances, Mulian's deed of rescuing his mother serves as the model for activities of pious descendants who commission the funerary ritual for their deceased. Still, the two types of dramas are closely related. It has been suggested that full-fledged Mulian drama also developed out of the funerary ritual of a soul's salvation (*chaodu*), around the end of the Song dynasty.[77] The ritual function of the different kinds of Mulian drama has parallels in the religious context of *baojuan* dealing with the Mulian story. Most *baojuan* discussed in this book are connected with funerary or salvational rituals. In several cases, it is clear from the texts themselves, and sometimes fieldwork substantiates it.

CONCLUSION

The earliest *baojuan* of Mulian appeared around the fourteenth century; by then, the story of Mulian rescuing his mother had already undergone a very long process of evolution in Chinese literature. From the fourth to the fourteenth century, this story appeared in multiple forms including apocryphal Buddhist scriptures, oral storytelling accompanied by visual aids, folk drama, and ritual pieces. All of these forms were connected with the various representations of the core story that also had an impact on *baojuan* texts.

The earliest available manuscript of *Baojuan of Maudgalyāyana* is considered the earliest surviving specimen of the *baojuan* genre and probably dates to 1372, although scholars differ in their conclusions about its date and authenticity. Several of them accept the suggested date and regard the text as a popularized Buddhist narrative,[78] and some think the given date is forged and that this text dates to a later period.[79] The 1372 date is supported by the fact that another more complete manuscript copy of the same work, dated 1440, became available recently.

Thus *Baojuan of Maudgalyāyana* postdates many pieces related to the story of Mulian rescuing his mother (storytelling pieces, apocryphal sūtra, and the earliest dramatic versions already existed before it) but predates the earliest available recension of the Mulian drama and sectarian *baojuan* of the sixteenth through the seventeenth century. The earliest known *baojuan* text continued the old tradition of oral literature and its derivate that dealt with the same subject, and it also represented the intermediate stage in the development of this story in Chinese literature. The early origins of *Baojuan of Maudgalyāyana* are also evident in special features of the form and content of this text discussed in the next chapter and in its relationship to later recensions of the same story, such as *Drama Exhorting Goodness*.

CHAPTER 3

An Early Example in *Baojuan*

Baojuan of Maudgalyāyana is represented by two manuscripts, both of which are incomplete. The first, dated 1372, belonged to Zheng Zhenduo and was later donated to the National Library of China.[1] The second, dated 1440, originally belonged to Vladimir A. Desnitskiy (1878–1958) and now is kept at the State Hermitage Museum in Saint Petersburg, Russia. Until recently, it was relatively unknown.[2] Because the contents of both manuscripts (including text and illustrations) are identical, they may be considered as two copies, created at different periods of time. Even the size of the pages and the number of characters on each page in both manuscripts are quite similar.

There are two titles in these manuscripts: the title *Baojuan of Mulian Rescuing His Mother [and Helping Her] to Escape from Hell and Be Born in Heaven* appears at the end of both manuscripts.[3] The Hermitage manuscript, however, also includes the title *Baojuan of Reverend Maudgalyāyana Rescuing His Mother [and Helping Her] to Escape from Hell and Be Born in Heaven* at the beginning of it, which I use as the complete title of this work. Both manuscripts also refer to the text as *Baojuan of Mulian* (Mulian Baojuan 目連寶卷), but I use *Baojuan of Maudgalyāyana* here in order to distinguish this early text from the later recensions, also called *Baojuan of Mulian*.

The National Library manuscript of *Baojuan of Maudgalyāyana* is now mounted as an album although originally it was a large accordion-style book (Ch. *jingzheben*) with the pages pasted together to make one long sheet, written on one side only. This format was typical of Chinese manuscripts and editions of the Buddhist scriptures and *baojuan* of the sixteenth and seventeenth centuries. Significantly, the surviving three volumes of the Hermitage manuscript also have the form of an accordion-style book. All volumes of this manuscript have binding, apparently of later origin, that consists of a blue fabric glued on cardboard. The second volume is currently missing. Comparison of the two manuscripts reveals that the Hermitage manuscript is much more complete than the National Library one. The extant portion of the latter starts with the episode of Mulian's arrival at the gates of Avīci hell, which appears in the middle of the third volume of the Hermitage manuscript. The National Library manuscript also includes the episodes of the meeting of the mother and son, the liberation of the mother's soul from hell, the realm of hungry ghosts, and her rebirth as a dog, as contained in the third and fourth volumes of the Hermitage copy. In the Hermitage manuscript, this first episode follows the long description of all the departments of hell that Mulian traversed while searching for his mother (apparently starting in the missing second volume).

The text of *Baojuan of Maudgalyāyana* is divided into multiple sections with a set structure. There are twenty-five such sections in the National Library manuscript and fifty-two sections in the Hermitage manuscript. They basically correspond to the division into sections called *pin* or *fen* in *baojuan* of the sixteenth through the eighteenth century (see chapter 4, "The Formal Characteristics"). In *Baojuan of Maudgalyāyana*, however, unlike later *baojuan*, these sections are not titled. Every section of the text consists of a prose part followed by a seven-character antithetical couplet (*duilian*), eight lines of seven-character verse, a "hymn" (*gezan*) with an irregular number of characters per line, and four lines of five-character meter verse.[4] Several times arias also are inserted in the sections, and sometimes they substitute for several other verse forms, thus somewhat destroying the regular structure of the text. Arias appear four times in the extant part of the National Library manuscript and eight times in the extant volumes of the Hermitage manuscript, but only two aria melodies are used: "Sūtra in Golden Characters" (Jin zi jing) and "Wearing the Golden Lock" (Gua jin suo). Each such section of this *baojuan* text may be considered a scene, as the details of the narrative it tells usually also are depicted in the illustrations placed in front of it. In the more complete Hermitage manuscript, most (thirty-three) of the sections begin with illustrations, which are thus fairly evenly distributed throughout the whole manuscript. The illustrations tend to spread over multiple pages, in most cases occupying three pages, but some only occupy double pages.

ON THE HISTORY OF *BAOJUAN OF MAUDGALYĀYANA*

Both manuscripts seem to have been connected with the religious activities at the imperial court of the Yuan and Ming dynasties, respectively. This is indicated by their beautiful decoration. The National Library manuscript has a dedicatory "dragon placard" with the inscription written in gold against a dark purple background. The characters are partially faded, however, and very unclear. As far as we can determine the contents of this inscription, it says that the manuscript was made on imperial order with funds donated by a certain Tuotuo (Toghtō?) in the third year of Xuanguang reign (1372). The Xuanguang reign was the reign title proclaimed by the Mongolian prince Ayushiridara (Zhaozong emperor) in 1370.[5] It belonged to the Northern Yuan regime (1369–1404), which was established after Ming dynasty troops captured Dadu (modern Beijing), a capital of the Yuan dynasty, and the Yuan emperor fled to the steppes of modern Inner Mongolia (1368).[6]

The poor quality of the script in the colophon raises the possibility of an alternative dating of this manuscript. It has been argued that the faded characters in the colophon of the manuscript stand not for the Xuanguang but for the Zhiyuan reign title (1335–1340).[7] The date of production of this manuscript would then be 1337. This argument connects the name of the donor indicated in the manuscript with the famous statesman of Zhiyuan reign, prime minister Toghtō (Ch. Tuotuo, 1314–1355).[8] In *History of the Yuan [Dynasty]* (Yuan shi), his name is indeed transcribed in the same way as that of the donor in this manuscript. Toghtō was known for his sympathy toward Han culture and Buddhism; he also maintained close relations with the ruling emperor.[9] Therefore, it was proposed that he could have commissioned this manuscript of *Baojuan of Maudgalyāyana*. The association of this manuscript with the prime minister, Toghtō, however, is dubious. As I examined the manuscript in the National Library of China, I can attest that its colophon contains the characters of Xuanguang and not Zhiyuan; and Toghtō had died before the beginning of the Xuanguang reign. In addition, Toghtō (Tuotuo) was a common name of Mongolian nobility during the Yuan; this makes identification of the sponsor with the use of the single name we have virtually impossible.

Judging by the inscription in its colophon (also in the form of the "dragon placard" at the end of the manuscript), the Hermitage manuscript of *Baojuan of Maudgalyāyana* was commissioned by the imperial concubine and then donated presumably to an unnamed Buddhist monastery or chapel: "donated by the imperial concubine Jiang in the fifth year of Zhengtong reign of the Great Ming (1440)." I did not find her name in historical sources; apparently imperial concubines were too numerous to all be recorded.

Unfortunately, we do not know more about the origins and later history of either manuscript. The illustrations in both are of high quality. The names of the calligrapher and painter (or painters) who executed the text and illustrations, however, are unknown; it is not clear whether we can attribute either of manuscripts to the court artisans. Nevertheless, the existence of early texts of *Baojuan of Mulian* (or *Baojuan of Maudgalyāyana*) by the fifteenth century at the latest is proved by the mention of this text in other sources that date to the early sixteenth century. The first one is a work by Luo Qing, who mentions *Baojuan of Mulian* in the twenty-fourth chapter of *Baojuan of Deeply Rooted Karmic Fruits, Majestic and Unmoved Like Mount Tai* (Weiwei budong Taishan shengen jieguo baojuan; Che no. 1224). This text belongs to *Five Books in Six Volumes*, first printed in 1509. It mentions several *baojuan*, most of which Luo Qing considered deviant. *Baojuan of Mulian* is characterized there as "having seven parts of outer Path and deviant teaching."[10] It was obviously a scripture that propagated views other than Luo Qing's teaching, most probably another popular form of Buddhism, which is quite in accord with the contents of the extant *Baojuan of Maudgalyāyana*.

Evidence from another almost contemporary source—the colophon of the edition of *Liturgy Based on the Diamond Sūtra* made in 1528 with sources donated by the court eunuchs Zhang Jun and Wang Yin (in the collection of Zhou Shaoliang [1917–2005] and reprinted recently by Taiwanese scholars in the collection of scriptures of folk religions)—may prove this conclusion. There, *Baojuan of Mulian* is mentioned along with the other sixteen *baojuan* commissioned by those persons.[11] It has been argued that these early mentions of *Baojuan of Mulian* in other *baojuan* texts refer to *Baojuan of Maudgalyāyana*.[12] It is quite tempting to adopt this view. At the same time, we cannot confirm the connection between these manuscripts dating to the fourteenth and fifteenth centuries and the later references, as it is probable that several recensions of *Baojuan of Mulian* existed by the sixteenth century; another recension of *Baojuan of Maudgalyāyana* is also known (see "Baojuan of Maudgalyāyana and Later Sectarian Texts" in this chapter).

THE FORMAL CHARACTERISTICS OF *BAOJUAN OF MAUDGALYĀYANA*

Because *Baojuan of Maudgalyāyana* is the earliest *baojuan* text of a narrative nature that survived in the form of authentic early manuscripts, it occupies a central place in the early history of this genre and can provide valuable information about the initial stage of its development and transmission. Many elements in the two manuscripts refer to the performance mode of this text.

Decoration of Manuscripts

The decoration of the two manuscripts of *Baojuan of Maudgalyāyana* with detailed illustrations of narrative quality is extremely rare for *baojuan* manuscripts and editions. Usually, editions of *baojuan* of the middle period, such as those of *Dizang baojuan* and *Baojuan of Benefiting Living Beings*, have several printed illustrations at the beginning and end of the woodblock. There are usually no illustrations inside *baojuan* texts; if there are, they are black and white. There are analogies of several elements of decoration in *Baojuan of Maudgalyāyana*, however, that can be found in printed *baojuan* of the later period.

For example, the first volume of the Hermitage manuscript opens with illustrations, showing the assembly of monks and celestial beings presided over by the Buddha, seated on the throne. It occupies three folios. At the end of this group of images, there is the "dragon placard" with the inscription wishing longevity for the currently reigning emperor. "Dragon placards," which were usual in the imperial editions of Buddhist and Daoist scriptures, according to the sectarian legend, were bestowed by the emperor for the editions of Luo Qing's scriptures. Since then, they had regularly appeared in the sectarian *baojuan*. For example, the similar "dragon placards" with the auspicious words and wishes of longevity for the reigning emperor are placed at the beginning of woodblock editions of *Baojuan of Benefiting Living Beings* and *Dizang baojuan*.[13]

The images of deities' assemblies also appear on the opening illustrations of sectarian *baojuan* of the sixteenth to seventeenth century.

An Early Example in *Baojuan*

Figure 3.01. Buddhist assembly. Frontispiece illustration of *Baojuan of Maudgalyāyana* manuscript (1440), Hermitage Museum, Saint Petersburg, Russia.

At the same time, there is a significant difference in the contents of these images in *Baojuan of Maudgalyāyana* and in *Baojuan of Benefiting Living Beings*, for example. While in the first, the assembly is presided over by the Buddha only, in the latter, there are images of the seated founders of the Three Teachings.[14] This difference has to do with the syncretic nature of the religion that *Baojuan of Benefiting Living Beings* represents—the Teaching of Yellow Heaven. These Buddhist characteristics of the opening images of *Baojuan of Maudgalyāyana* are in accord with the orthodox Buddhist contents of this text.

At the end of both the National Library and Hermitage manuscripts, near the colophons in the form of the "dragon placards," are images of Skanda (Ch. Weituo), a guardian of Buddhist teaching, which is also typical of the editions of the Buddhist sūtras dating to the fourteenth to sixteenth century. Images of Skanda and colophons in the form of rectangular votive steles also appear at the end of the editions of *baojuan* of the sixteenth to seventeenth century.[15] Therefore, these decorative elements of manuscripts of *Baojuan of Maudgalyāyana* are quite typical of the manuscripts and editions of *baojuan* of the middle period, with the exception that the frontispiece illustrations of the first are in color. The evidence of *Baojuan of Maudgalyāyana* also demonstrates that "dragon placards," which signify the court sponsorship of the manuscript production, began to be used for the decoration of *baojuan* much earlier than when Luo Qing's works were written and printed.

Ritual Framework

The introductory and concluding parts of *Baojuan of Maudgalyāyana* merit discussion in detail, as they reflect the performance mode and the ritual use of this text. The introductions and conclusions are very complex. In the Hermitage manuscript, the introduction is still extant; it opens with ritual instructions for the performer and the audience of this text: "The believers at the ritual area should put palms together in prayer in front of the chest, sit upright according to the rules and recite the Heart Sūtra at the end of this scroll in vernacular language. The participants of the assembly should reverently chant the Buddha's name [following the performer], and this will create merits."[16] This passage clearly refers to the oral performances of *baojuan* at the religious assembly called the "ritual area" (*daochang*).

This passage is followed by a mantra written in Sanskrit: "Om a hom."[17] Then the sacred formula of paying obeisance to the three treasures of Buddhism—Buddha, Dharma, and Sangha—in all ten directions follows.[18] Next is a prosaic passage that briefly summarizes the contents of the text—the story of Mulian rescuing his mother.[19] This text can be classified as "the text of conditioned origin" (*yuanqi*),[20] which is a standard element in Chinese Buddhist literature, including *baojuan* of the thirteenth to fifteenth century.[21] Then there is a lengthy verse in twenty-two lines with seven characters per line, starting with the words "*Baojuan of Mulian* has been transmitted since antiquity until now" that praises Mulian's filial piety and puts it in the context of "twenty-four paragons of filial piety," common figures in traditional Chinese literature. The verse is followed by a prosaic passage starting with the words "thus have I heard" (*rushi wo wen*), typical of the Buddhist sūtras, which tells how the Buddha pronounced the sermon on the Mulian story. Then follows a verse in twenty lines with seven characters per line, starting with the words "Here we open *Baojuan of Mulian*,"[22] which we can label as the *gāthā* on opening sūtra (*kaijingji*), also an element standard in the *baojuan* texts of the thirteenth to fifteenth century.[23] All these elements of introduction are important to note, as they demonstrate how *Baojuan of Maudgalyāyana* imitates the form and contents of the Buddhist sūtras.

Similar ritual elements appear in the concluding part of *Baojuan of Maudgalyāyana*, which includes several special verse forms. After the last section of the usual structure, the "text of taking vows" (*fayuanwen*) follows. This is the expression of the wishes of the performer and audience of the text that all living beings would escape disasters and suffering. Then the "Hymn of Old Man Chuan" (Chuan lao song) appears. It is followed by the "text of transfer of merit" (*huixiangwen*, Skt. *pariṇāma*). These texts also express the wishes of salvation for all living beings. The text of transfer of merit claims that all sentient beings will realize the true nature (*zhenru*),[24] and all living creatures will ascend to the opposite shore (of salvation).[25] The text ends with two stanzas of aria, "Sūtra in golden characters," which emphasize the miraculous qualities of this text, its copying, and its recitation.[26]

The concluding part of *Baojuan of Maudgalyāyana* is nearly identical to that of *Liturgy Based on the Diamond Sūtra*. In both cases, the text of taking vows and "Hymn of Old Man Chuan" are basically the same; only the name of the religious meeting is changed in the latter into the "Ritual area of Ullambana" (Yulan da daochang), compared with *Liturgy Based on the Diamond Sūtra*.[27] Regarding the introductory part, which survives only in the Hermitage manuscript of *Baojuan of Maudgalyāyana*, there is also similarity between the two texts. *Liturgy Based on the Diamond Sūtra* opens with sacred formulas, invocations, prosaic "text of conditioned origin," a hymn on burning incense (*juxiangzan*), and a *gāthā* on opening sūtra,[28] but these elements differ in the two texts. The introduction of *Baojuan of Maudgalyāyana* is much shorter and simpler if compared with *Liturgy Based on the Diamond Sūtra*, though. Textual elements with the similar forms and contents also appear in the texts of *baojuan* of the sixteenth to seventeenth century; therefore, they can be characterized as standard in *baojuan* of both the early and middle periods. At the same time, they certainly testify to the connection of *baojuan* with earlier genres of Buddhist literature.

The terms used in the introductory and concluding parts of *baojuan*, such as *gāthā* (*ji*, an acronym for *jituo*), hymn (*zan*, Skt. *stava, stotra, stuti,* etc.), transfer of merit, Three Treasures, Prajňāpāramita, and four mercies, are of Buddhist origin. *Gāthā* is the form of verse commonly used in Buddhist scriptures. Hymns are also poetic forms sung with particular melodies. In the tradition of monastic Buddhism in China, special kinds of hymns and *gāthās* are sung as the introduction and conclusion of a sūtra-recitation ritual. Some of them have names close to those used in *baojuan*. For example, *kaijingji* is the usual term for an introductory verse in the recitation of sūtras in Buddhist monasteries in the modern period.[29] There are also hymns with names close to that of the "hymn on burning incense," such as *xingxiangzan*.[30] The text of vows is also an integral part of the Buddhist services: usually a patron writes it on the occasion of a religious meeting.[31] This text is a dedication, addressed to a Buddha or bodhisattva, that often also includes a prayer for the departed but also can include repentance for past crimes. This form of verse often is attached to Buddhist scriptures. The transfer of the merit is also a key notion in the Buddhist services: the related verse is recited at the end of Buddhist rituals in order to transfer the merit obtained through performing the ritual to all living beings or often specifically to benefit a deceased person.[32] Several textual fragments in *Baojuan of Maudgalyāyana* were directly borrowed from mainstream Buddhist tradition. For example, "Hymn of Old Man Chuan" in its concluding part of *Baojuan of Maudgalyāyana* is the orthodox work of the Chan school; it was composed by Shi Daochuan in the twelfth century and later included in the collections of Buddhist texts.[33]

The same terms (verses on opening sūtra, Sanskrit hymns, invocation of deities, and hymns) that apparently signified similar rituals were used in the sūtra-explanation texts of the Tang and Five dynasties periods. They are mentioned in the texts concerning their performance, including manuscripts from Dunhuang.[34] For example, the prose parts in the introduction of *Baojuan of Maudgalyāyana* roughly correspond to the explanation of the meaning of the religious meeting and the sūtra title (*kaiti*) in both prose and verse at the beginning of *jiangjingwen*.[35] Sūtra-explanation texts also ended with eulogies on the Buddha, making vows, and transfer of merit. The similarity of the introductory and concluding parts of *baojuan*, sūtra recitation, and sūtra-explanation proves that *baojuan* originally were connected to Buddhist sermons, and the manner of *baojuan* performance closely imitated the rituals accompanying recitation and explication of Buddhist scriptures.

The main aim of the introductory and concluding parts in *Baojuan of Maudgalyāyana* can be seen as the establishment of a performance arena, which in the text of *baojuan* is called the "ritual area." The last lines of "Hymn of Old Man Chuan" mention the ritual place of Ullambana, where all living beings receive salvation. Originally, "ritual area" meant the location where enlightenment is achieved. In Buddhist texts, it also means the place where religious practice is carried out or where the Buddha is worshiped. We can conclude that the text of *Baojuan of Maudgalyāyana* was intended to be performed during a special religious assembly. This assembly preserved the memory of the Ullambana ritual, which was so popular in Chinese Buddhism and was certainly related to the salvation of the souls of the dead.

The concluding verses of *Baojuan of Maudgalyāyana* emphasize its ritual function. First, special emphasis is put on the release from the afterlife punishment in hell:

> At first we wish that the mountains of knives would lose their blades.
> Secondly, we wish that the spikes of the trees of swords would break.
> Thirdly, we wish the flames of coals in the oven of [hell] would be extinguished.
> Fourthly, we wish the waves of rivers would become calm!

Later the text says:

> Furthermore, we wish that seven generations of ancestors, who died before,
> Would leave bitter suffering and attain rebirth in heaven;
> And all of them would escape
> The tortures for sins in hell.[36]

The desire to release seven generations of ancestors from hell is the stock phrase, related to the ritual of Ullambana and the earliest texts of the Mulian story in China. It appears in both the *Ullambana Sūtra* and *Sūtra of Mulian*.[37] This stock element also is used in later *baojuan* texts analyzed in this book.[38]

Structure and Verses

As to the form of the text, the structure of sections of *Baojuan of Maudgalyāyana* is similar to that of other *baojuan* that date to the thirteenth to fifteenth century. Significantly, every section in *Liturgy Based on the Diamond Sūtra* and *Baojuan of Journey to the West* has basically the same structure as this *baojuan*, except that the first two do not use arias.³⁹ In *Baojuan of Maudgalyāyana*, as with the first two, there are no ten-character verses, which are typical of *baojuan* starting from the sixteenth century onward. This peculiarity testifies to the early origin of *Baojuan of Maudgalyāyana*. On the other hand, the forms of five- and seven-character verse used in *Baojuan of Maudgalyāyana* are quite similar to those in *baojuan* of the sixteenth to seventeenth century, including the special features of their rhyme.⁴⁰ The same can be said of the hymns with four or five syllables per line, characteristic of *baojuan* texts in the early and middle periods. The infrequent use of arias in *Baojuan of Maudgalyāyana* makes it different from the typical *baojuan* of the sixteenth to seventeenth century, which use a great number of aria motifs. Thus *Baojuan of Maudgalyāyana* apparently represents the beginning of the practice of using arias in the nascent *baojuan* genre. It demonstrates that singing passages of different forms, including hymns and arias, already had become an important part of the performance register of these texts as early as the mid-fourteenth century.

At the same time, it is not surprising that *Baojuan of Maudgalyāyana* uses arias at such an early date. Arias appeared in popular religious works in the fourteenth to early fifteenth century. In this respect, an important antecedent of *baojuan* is the book of Buddhist chants: *Tunes with the Names of All Buddhas, World-Honored Rulai, and Reverend Bodhisattvas* (Zhu fo shizun rulai pusa zunzhe mingcheng gequ; hereafter *Tunes with the Names of all Buddhas*) that was compiled on imperial order at the beginning of the fifteenth century.⁴¹ It represents the adaptation of many popular tunes for religious purposes. *Tunes with the Names of All Buddhas* contains examples of both motifs, "Sūtra in golden characters" and "Wearing the golden lock," which are used in *Baojuan of Maudgalyāyana*.⁴² However, there are some differences in the schemes (and thus music) of these arias in both works. For example, while the scheme of "Wearing the golden lock" is almost the same in *Tunes with the Names of All Buddhas* and in *Baojuan of Maudgalyāyana*, the schemes of the "Sūtra in golden characters" are different in these two works. On the other hand, general schemes of arias used in *Baojuan of Maudgalyāyana* (including "Sūtra in golden characters") are similar to those of the same motifs in *baojuan* of the middle period. Furthermore, these arias are similar to those performed by Buddhist nuns in *Plum Flowers*, apparently derived from the *baojuan* texts of that period.⁴³ Therefore, *Baojuan of Maudgalyāyana* contains a special variant of the two popular arias that continued to be used in later *baojuan* texts (sixteenth to seventeenth century).

Verses in *Baojuan of Maudgalyāyana* usually serve to amplify and embellish the events introduced in the preceding prose parts (or anticipate the events narrated in prose later, as in the first section of this text). The hymns and arias at the end of the sections usually also have didactic contents that develop religious ideas appearing in the preceding prose. This particular style of prose and verse alternation was a special feature of the *baojuan* genre; however, verses also can have a different function in the later recensions of *baojuan* about Mulian. Therefore, this repetition of the contents in the verses of different forms constitutes a special feature of the performance register of *Baojuan of Maudgalyāyana*.

Language

The language of *Baojuan of Maudgalyāyana* also offers some keys to understanding the performance register of this text. At the very beginning, it refers to itself as "the scroll in vernacular language" (*baiwen juan*).[44] Direct speech is frequently included in both the prose and verse passages of this text, also common in several genres of living storytelling traditions in China.[45] The contents of direct speech passages in *Baojuan of Maudgalyāyana*, *Sūtra of Mulian*, and *Bianwen of Mahāmaudgalyāyana* have similarities, suggesting that these texts could be connected with the lost early dramatic tradition of Mulian.[46] However, though dramatic influence is possible, we cannot be certain of this, as the scripts of early Mulian dramas have been lost. The use of direct speech in *Baojuan of Maudgalyāyana* is intensified by colloquial words, characteristic of the literature in vernacular language during the Yuan dynasty and later.[47] We can assume that the performer could enact the characters of the text while reciting this direct speech—a feature observed in the modern performances of *baojuan*. This frequent inclusion and enactment of direct speech is an important characteristic of the performance register of *Baojuan of Maudgalyāyana* that continued in the later history of the genre.

The musical parts, use of direct speech, colloquial language, references to images, formulaic expressions, and stock elements thus constitute characteristics of the performance register of *Baojuan of Maudgalyāyana*. Though the form of the two manuscripts is extremely rare if compared with other surviving early specimens of the *baojuan* genre, many elements in both manuscripts have much in common with the later editions of *baojuan* (sixteenth to seventeenth century). We can observe the same peculiarities in the contents of *Baojuan of Maudgalyāyana*.

SPECIAL FEATURES OF CONTENTS OF *BAOJUAN* OF *MAUDGALYĀYANA*

The special features of the contents of *Baojuan of Maudgalyāyana* testify that it belongs to the Buddhist or presectarian period of the *baojuan* genre development, while one can find continuation of its ideas and beliefs in the later sectarian *baojuan* of the sixteenth to seventeenth centuries.

On the Source of Baojuan

How can we tell that *Baojuan of Maudgalyāyana* represents the early stage of the development of the story in Chinese literature? First of all, the details of the Mulian story in the extant part of the text are quite archaic. In terms of the story development and archaic language, *Baojuan of Maudgalyāyana* stands closer to *Bianwen of Mahāmaudgalyāyana* than to the later versions of the story in dramas and *baojuan*, *Drama Exhorting Goodness* (late sixteenth century) and *Baojuan of Three Rebirths* in particular.[48] It seems, however, that *Sūtra of Mulian* constitutes a closer antecedent to this text, as is evident through textual study. A sufficient example of the connection of *Baojuan of Maudgalyāyana* and *Sūtra of Mulian* are the episodes that appear in both texts but are absent from *Bianwen of Mahāmaudgalyāyana*.[49] At the same time, *Sūtra of Mulian* follows the tradition of *bianwen*. Thus this *baojuan*, composed approximately during the Yuan dynasty closely following *Sūtra of Mulian*, also is related indirectly to *Bianwen of Mahāmaudgalyāyana* through the means of this apocryphal scripture.

Buddhist Topics in Baojuan

Second, in *Baojuan of Maudgalyāyana*, there is no explicit expression of typical sectarian ideas, common for *baojuan* of the sixteenth to seventeenth century. Instead, quite a few Buddhist ideas and values appear. There are many terms and symbols of Buddhist origin, such as "sentient beings" (*hanshi*, Skt. *bhautika, sattva*), "living beings" (*zhongsheng*, Skt. *sattva, jana*), "true nature," "opposite shore" (*bi'an*), and "[numerous, as grains of] sand in the Ganges" (*Heng sha*, Skt. *gaṅgā-nadī-vālikā*). *Baojuan of Maudgalyāyana* also refers to the practices of meditation and recitation of the Buddha Amitābha's name. It consistently encourages its audience to recite the name of Amitābha in order to be born in "the Lotus Pond of the Ninth Grade" (*jiupin liantai*), the highest place in the Pure Land according to the Buddhist scriptures, and says that "one phrase of [A]mitābha originally is the ancient ritual area."[50] At the same time, there are also references to the teaching of the Chan school: Chan meditation (*Chanding*) and "instant enlightenment" (*dunwu*).[51] As a result, there is a mixture of the ideas and images of the Pure Land and Chan schools, namely the hope of rebirth in the western Pure Land through invocation of the name of Amitābha and the search for instantaneous enlightenment. The syncretism of the ideas of these two schools is quite obvious, as both schools were the most influential in China from the second half of the ninth century onward. These ideas were widespread even among prominent monks by the Ming period,[52] not to mention among lay Buddhist believers, who often drew little or no distinction between the teachings of different Buddhist schools. This syncretism of Chan and Pure Land ideas is also found in other *baojuan* of the early period, as well as in the writings of the Teaching of Non-Interference.[53]

In addition, the original Buddhist story as retold in this text was completely incorporated into the indigenous Chinese culture, a fact revealed in the contents as well as illustrations in the manuscript. For example, the introductory verses of *Baojuan of Maudgalyāyana* portray Mulian as one of the twenty-four paragons of filial piety (traditional Chinese concept), a tendency that can be traced to the popular literature from Dunhuang.[54] In addition, the illustrations depict the characters of the story in Chinese-style dress and in Chinese surroundings. These features make *Baojuan of Maudgalyāyana* a product of the indigenous form of Chinese Buddhism, oriented to lay believers.

The description of afterlife punishment in *Baojuan of Maudgalyāyana* is also traditional and even archaic. The most notable figures in the underworld are judges of souls, called Yan Lords of the Ten Lands (Shidi Yanjun) in this text, who appear in *baojuan* several times and are depicted in the figures in two manuscripts.[55] These certainly represent the conception of the "Ten Courts [of the underworld]," standard in Chinese popular religion since around the tenth century. According to popular belief, Yanwang governs the fifth of these courts, issues the order to bring a person's soul to the underworld, and judges the dead, as is described in *Baojuan of Maudgalyāyana*.⁵⁶ There is no clear division of hell into Ten Courts in this *baojuan*, however, the same as in the much earlier *bianwen* and *yuanqi* on Mulian. *Bianwen* and *yuanqi* have been seen as representing the transitional period of the formation of the cosmology of hell in Chinese popular religion, and therefore they do not deal with Yanwang in detail.⁵⁷ This is conspicuously different from the late literature about Mulian, for example, *Drama Exhorting Goodness*, where the Ten Courts of hell are portrayed. As the influence of this particular cosmology in *Baojuan of Maudgalyāyana* is limited, this also demonstrates a considerable difference between *Baojuan of Maudgalyāyana* and several late *baojuan* texts on Mulian, such as *Precious Account of Mulian*, on the conceptual level.

Baojuan of Maudgalyāyana and Later Sectarian Texts

At the same time there is conspicuous continuity between *Baojuan of Maudgalyāyana* and the later *baojuan* texts of the sectarian teachings. First, many ideas and terms in this text, though they have Buddhist origins, have equivalents in the sectarian teachings and appear in the *baojuan* of the sixteenth to seventeenth century. Many so-called sectarian movements during the Ming and Qing periods grew out of or were inspired by the popular or "folk" forms of Buddhism (lay Buddhist movements).⁵⁸ One particular religion, that of Non-Interference, recently has been defined as a lay form of Buddhism that did not rely on messianic prophecies (characteristic of such religions of the sixteenth to seventeenth century as the Yellow Heaven).⁵⁹ However, one should use such definitions with caution and acknowledge the syncretic form of teachings of most sects, which also included Daoist elements.⁶⁰ Terms and ideas that certainly were not derived from mainstream Buddhism appear in the cosmology of Luo Qing's and his followers' writings. In addition, such syncretism of ideas and practices of different origins was common in many religious traditions of China (obvious even for religious professionals, not to mention popular following) since the medieval period.⁶¹ In this light, though the self-definitions of groups are important, we do not need to completely accept them, especially as they do not appear very relevant in the complex religious landscape of late imperial China. "Sect" here refers to self-defined syncretic religions (with their own cosmology, scriptures, and rituals) that developed during the Ming and Qing dynasties and produced *baojuan* texts.

An Early Example in *Baojuan* 63

Figure 3.02. Ten Kings of Hell meeting Buddha. Illustration of *Baojuan of Maudgalyāyana* manuscript (1440), Hermitage Museum, Saint Petersburg, Russia.

Several scholars have noted that specific terms and ideas in *Baojuan of Maudgalyāyana* indicate probable sectarian influence. For example, the term "Unborn [Mother?]" appears in part of its text published by Zheng Zhenduo.[62] One of the concluding verses of *Baojuan of Maudgalyāyana* has the following lines:

Pay attention to the words of the Unborn [One],
Think about early return to the native land!"[63]

Although these lines can be seen as a reference to the sectarian deity, Unborn Venerable Mother, and as an indication that the text of *Baojuan of Maudgalyāyana* appeared sometime during or after the sixteenth century,[64] this wording does not necessarily mean Unborn Mother. In *Baojuan of Maudgalyāyana*, there is no extended explication of the myth about Unborn Mother, her children, exiled to the mundane world, and her emissaries descending to rescue humankind, as in *baojuan* texts of the sixteenth century.⁶⁵ In addition, the term Unborn occasionally appeared in mainstream Buddhist works where it was usually an abbreviation of "[that] without birth and death" (*wu sheng wu mie*), one of the Buddha's titles, as was even noted by the officials-persecutors of sectarian teachings in the early nineteenth century.⁶⁶

Other expressions that appear in *Baojuan of Maudgalyāyana*, such as "true emptiness" (*zhenkong*), "native place" (*jiaxiang*), "to return to the original land" (*huan benxiang*), and "boat of Dharma" (*fachuan*), also can have sectarian connotations in the later period. All of them have the meaning of salvation, which is represented as a return to the native (or original) land of the Unborn Mother.⁶⁷ There is also the notion of the elects, "predestined [people]" (*youyuan*), who attain salvation by receiving the "ideas from the West" (*xilai yi*) from an enlightened teacher and ascend the boat of Dharma.⁶⁸ All these terms often appear in *baojuan* of the sixteenth to seventeenth century. They do not necessarily challenge the authenticity, however, of the early dates in the manuscripts of *Baojuan of Maudgalyāyana*. These terms might have been borrowed by the later sectarian teachings from popular Buddhist works, including *Baojuan of Maudgalyāyana*, and reinterpreted by them. One case of such reinterpretation is the use of the images included in "Hymn of Old Man Chuan," which, as already mentioned, was composed by the Chan master in the twelfth century:

> Poor man will receive the treasure,
> The child will meet his mother,
> The floating boat will reach the shore,
> And lonely traveler will return to the native land.⁶⁹

The symbol of the child's reunification with his mother meaning salvation (way to the heavenly realm) fits with the main story line in *Baojuan of Maudgalyāyana*—the separation, travel through the hardships of the underworld, and ultimate reunification of mother and son. This metaphor also was employed in the meaning of salvation in the sectarian *baojuan* dealing with the story of Mulian. Significantly, other images from "Hymn of Old Man Chuan"—a poor man obtaining treasure, a boat reaching the shore, and travelers returning home—appear as metaphors of salvation in a sectarian context in *Dizang baojuan*.

Nevertheless, there are several episodes in the story line of *Baojuan of Maudgalyāyana* that significantly differ from the preceding versions of this story in Chinese literature, including *Sūtra of Mulian*. For example, Mulian is represented as a rebirth of the ancient Buddha Amitābha who "transformed [and manifested] in the Eastern land (i.e., China) in order to rescue his mother." Amitābha manifested as Mulian also in order to convert the people in delusion, who, with his help, will realize the true emptiness and return to their native land.[70] This interpretation of Mulian as a manifestation of the higher deity does not exist in the earlier texts, such as *bianwen* and *Sūtra of Mulian*; but, on the other hand, Luo Qing used this concept of rebirth in application to the Mulian story in his scripture. His *Baojuan of Self-determination [Needing] neither Cultivation nor Verification, which Rectifies Belief and Dispels Doubt* (Zhengxin chuyi wu xiu zheng zizai baojuan, hereafter abbreviated as *Baojuan of Self-determination*), included in *Five Books in Six Volumes*, says that Mulian and his mother, Qingti (written as 清提), were both miraculous transformations of the Limitless (or Limitless Sacred Ancestor), the highest deity in the system of Luo Qing's Teaching of Non-Interference, the creator and savior of all through self-manifestation in different forms.[71] The image of Qingti demonstrated the existence of the sufferings of hell and necessity of religious perfection, "studying the Path," to people in this world.[72] This interpretation of Mulian in *Baojuan of Maudgalyāyana* is also typical of the later sectarian *baojuan*. Furthermore, in *baojuan* of the sixteenth to seventeenth century, Amitābha, with the same epithet, Ancient, often acts as the highest deity and progenitor of mankind, comparable only to the Unborn Mother.[73] Thus this episode in *Baojuan of Maudgalyāyana* serves as a precedent for the new interpretations of the story in a sectarian context.

Another conspicuous detail that is similar in the later sectarian scriptures is the presence of a female deity who occupies an important place in the textual and visual levels of *Baojuan of Maudgalyāyana*. It is Celestial Mother (Tianmu) who welcomes Ms. Liu into heaven after the redemption of the latter's sins. This scene is represented in the last illustrations of both manuscripts.[74] Celestial Mother also appears in *Sūtra of Mulian*.[75] This deity is very hard to identify in the Buddhist, Daoist, or popular pantheon. In the Buddhist context Celestial Mother is one of the titles of the tantric deity Molizhi (Marīcī) or Zhunti (Cundī), also venerated as one of the forms of Bodhisattva Guanyin (Avalokiteśvara). Later on, this cult appears to have influenced the development of female deities in late imperial

China.⁷⁶ The usual iconography of Molizhi (three eyes and eighteen hands), however, is very different from the image we find in *Baojuan of Maudgalyāyana* (as well as in the Japanese reprint of *Sūtra of Mulian*); therefore, it is very hard to make any conclusion about the connection of these two deities.

Still, in *Baojuan of Maudgalyāyana*, Celestial Mother and her female suite certainly represent the importance of the female entity in the cosmology of this text. It fits superbly with the symbol of motherhood invoked there. The connection of Celestial Mother and the Unborn deity in *Baojuan of Maudgalyāyana* is not clear. Their confluence, which is very probable in the context of this text, however, will produce the Unborn Mother, similar to the sectarian deity portrayed in *baojuan* since the first quarter of the sixteenth century.

Despite these continuities between *Baojuan of Maudgalyāyana* and sectarian works, we can understand the strong difference between them after the comparison of this early *baojuan* with its sectarian adaptation. The latter is represented by an undated manuscript that has the same title as the manuscript dated 1440—*Baojuan of Reverend Maudgalyāyana Rescuing His Mother [and Helping Her] to Escape from Hell and Be Born in Heaven* (Che no. 693)—but contains an amplified recension of the early *baojuan* (hereafter abbreviated as *Baojuan of Maudgalyāyana-2*). This manuscript originally belonged to Zheng Qian (1906–1991) but now is kept in the Library of the Research Institute of Drama in the Chinese Academy of Arts (Beijing) where I was kindly allowed to consult it. This manuscript is also incomplete; only the last two volumes out of three (sections 31–86) survive, and a part of the conclusion is missing.

Baojuan of Maudgalyāyana-2 possesses an important difference in terms of contents: the explicit propagation of the Teaching of Non-Interference, which, in this text, is represented as having been propagated by the Buddha, and Maudgalyāyana becomes its adept in order to rescue his mother from the torments of hell.⁷⁷ Other peculiarities of its form and contents, such as the division into sections, use of numerous arias, references to inner alchemy practices, and elaboration of the story line, suggest that this *Baojuan of Maudgalyāyana-2* was composed in the sixteenth or seventeenth century.⁷⁸ The affiliation of *Baojuan of Maudgalyāyana-2* with the Teaching of Non-Interference is quite natural if one considers Luo Qing's usage of the Mulian story in his texts. Thus it is an early sectarian adaptation of the Mulian story.

An Early Example in *Baojuan*

Therefore, in terms of contents as well, *Baojuan of Maudgalyāyana* is a classical specimen of *baojuan* of the early (Buddhist) period. Although many details of it are different from those of the sectarian *baojuan* of the sixteenth to seventeenth century, there are also a number of similarities between them; furthermore, it must have served as a source for the later adaptation of this story in the context of the Teaching of Non-Interference—*Baojuan of Maudgalyāyana-2*.

ON THE USE OF *BAOJUAN OF MAUDGALYĀYANA*

It is obvious that *Baojuan of Maudgalyāyana* was designed to be read aloud. As stated in the guidelines for the performance, provided in the introductory passage of this text, the audience is encouraged to participate actively in the performance, and rewards are promised for the participants of the religious assembly at which *Baojuan of Maudgalyāyana* was recited. One of the introductory verses says:

> Now as we open *Baojuan of Mulian*,
> All buddhas and bodhisattvas descend [on the altar].
> If all the participants of the assembly chime in with the Buddha's name,
> They will be able to avoid eight difficulties and escape three disasters.[79]

Thus audience participation was embodied in the chanting of the refrain in verses (also mentioned in the prosaic introductory passage), as was common in later *baojuan* performances. Therefore, this special feature of the performance manner appears already in the earliest surviving example of *baojuan*. The special characteristics of form and language of *Baojuan of Maudgalyāyana*, analyzed earlier, also make it a convenient piece for oral performance.

At the same time, it also was transmitted in the written form: "If somebody copies this manuscript, and leaves it to the future generations, who will continue to recite it, one's ancestors in nine generations will be [saved the same as those] of Mulian."[80] Therefore, this text could also be used as a material for individual reading. In this respect, the beautiful decoration of the two extant manuscripts is of primary importance. As was already noted, the position of illustrations in the manuscript of *Baojuan of Maudgalyāyana* and their quality are outstanding.

In its visual aspect, *Baojuan of Maudgalyāyana* is similar not to the editions of *baojuan* of the sixteenth to seventeenth century but to *Bianwen of Mahāmaudgalyāyana* and *Sūtra of Mulian*, where illustrations also closely followed textual narrative. Both manuscripts of *Baojuan of Maudgalyāyana* reflect the practice of simultaneous perception of written text and illustrations. Thus *Baojuan of Maudgalyāyana* continues the form of an illustrated narrative that apparently originated from picture storytelling. But how exactly were these illustrations used? The first option is that storytellers displayed and referred to the illustrations during performance. This is improbable because neither of the illustrated manuscripts can be used effectively in this way. Their format is quite different from picture scrolls accompanying performances of *bianwen* that either contained only pictures or contained pictures of transformations on one side and text passages of *bianwen* on the other.[81] That format was much more convenient for displaying pictures during performances.

The second option concerns not oral performance but the individual reading of this *baojuan*. Significantly, illustrations in the manuscript of *Baojuan of Maudgalyāyana* usually precede written descriptions: they depict events discussed in the following section of the text. Thus the reader could look at the pictures first and then proceed with reading a relevant passage. This layout of figures also shows that these manuscripts were used by a specific reading audience. Semiliterate readers, such as women and children, could use pictures to supplement their understanding of a text.

Furthermore, illustrations in *Baojuan of Maudgalyāyana* are very elaborate; they contain many subsidiary figures and details of scenery that make them objects of a reader's scrutiny. In this way they certainly contributed to the entertaining side of reading by attracting the audience to the colorful and captivating images. The proposed association with the female audience is collaborated further by other two facts: the meaning of the religious assembly with which the text was associated and the female sponsorship of the Hermitage manuscript.

BAOJUAN OF MAUDGALYĀYANA AND FEMALE AUDIENCE

Baojuan of Maudgalyāyana mentions the Opulent Gathering of the Blood Bowl of Ullambana (Xuepen Yulan Shenghui), which helped Mulian rescue his mother from rebirth as a dog. This meeting was organized by Mulian on the day of the Zhongyuan festival (15th day of the 7th month), following the Buddha's advice.[82] Because the concluding passage of this *baojuan* in addition says that it was performed during the Ullambana Assembly,[83] we can assume that this text was also associated with the Blood Bowl beliefs and rituals.

The Blood Bowl was an important symbol in the literature about Mulian since around the twelfth to thirteenth century. As we have already observed in the case of telling scriptures in Jingjiang, there was a widespread belief in China that after death women are imprisoned in the Blood Pond. The earliest mention of these beliefs is in a ritual text dated 1194.[84] Sometimes the confinement in the Blood Pond is presented as a punishment for violation of postpartum taboos; however, more often it is presented as the inevitable consequence of female physiological impurity (for details, see chapter 7, "The Blood Pond in Texts and Ritual"). In any case it is the duty of pious descendants to perform the ritual of the salvation of their mother's soul.

These beliefs are founded in the Buddhist notions of the physiological impurity of a woman's body as well as in the principle of filial duty toward one's mother.[85] They are presented clearly for the first time in the *Blood Bowl Sūtra of the True Teaching in the Great Canon Pronounced by the Buddha* (Fo shuo Dazang zhengjiao Xuepen jing, hereafter *Blood Bowl Sūtra*), a short Chinese scripture of unknown date (ca. twelfth century). An important aspect of this text is its explicit reference to the story of Mulian rescuing his mother from Blood Pond.[86] Therefore, filial children perform rituals of their mother's salvation from the Blood Pond, following the example of Mulian.

This variant of the Mulian story that included the Blood Pond mythology became the core of the Buddhist ritual practice of salvation of women. Since the early period, the rituals of the Blood Pond also were used in the Daoist tradition.[87] The practice of the recitation of *Sūtra of the Blood Bowl* (and similar texts) during special rituals for the redemption of a woman's sins is mentioned in the literature of the sixteenth to seventeenth century (fiction and drama).[88] The Blood Pond as one of the compartments of hell also appears in *Drama Exhorting Goodness*.[89] Expanded versions of the *Blood Bowl Sūtra* from the later period usually have the form of "penitence books" and are used to cleanse all women's sins. Several texts of penitence books that deal with the salvation from the Blood Pond (one of them dated to the end of the Ming dynasty) and very close in terms of contents to *baojuan* texts have survived.[90] The image of the Blood Pond also was incorporated into the ritual systems of the sectarian teachings of the sixteenth to seventeenth century and thus often appears in *baojuan* of the middle period.[91] For example, *Baojuan of Maudgalyāyana-2* has an entire section devoted to the description of the Blood Pond where sinful women are suffering. The ritual of the salvation of deceased women from suffering in the Blood Pond still forms an important part of the ritual practice of folk believers in several parts of China today.

Therefore, the mention of the Blood Bowl in *Baojuan of Maudgalyāyana* is extremely important. It testifies to the connection of its ritual aspect with popular mythology and may even be the performance of a specific ritual. It represents the development of the ritual meaning of the Mulian story in popular Buddhist literature, as the Blood Pond is not mentioned in *Sūtra of Mulian*. The abundance of hell and salvation symbols in *Baojuan of Maudgalyāyana* suggests that this text was connected with funerary rituals,[92] but this cannot be confirmed since we simply do not have this information either in the text or in the external sources.

The topic of female salvation and its reference to the Blood Pond suggest that the text of *Baojuan of Maudgalyāyana* was created primarily for a female audience. In addition, the sponsor whose name appears in the colophon of the Hermitage manuscript of this *baojuan* is female. Therefore, it is likely that women of high social standing (the inner court in particular) were the target audience of this text. Furthermore, the fact that the manuscript was commissioned by an imperial concubine is quite in accord with the information about *baojuan* printing in the middle of the sixteenth century.[93] Thus, the evidence of *Baojuan of Maudgalyāyana* suggests that the connection of *baojuan* with female sponsors and audiences was established very early in the history of this genre.

CONCLUSION

There are two extant *baojuan* manuscripts dealing with the Mulian story, dated 1372 and 1440, that belong to the early stage of *baojuan* development. They are two copies of the same work—*Baojuan of Maudgalyāyana*—done in different periods. They were commissioned by representatives of the imperial court of the Northern Yuan and Ming dynasties; therefore, this work circulated among people of high social standing. The existence of such *baojuan* texts dealing with the Mulian story in the late fifteenth to early sixteenth century is also attested to by the contemporary sources. This early *baojuan* about Mulian is considerably different from the adaptations of this subject in the later sectarian works, such as *Baojuan of Maudgalyāyana-2*, and certainly represents a popular interpretation of mainstream Buddhist ideas and values. The similarity of the story line as well as of the mode of illustration in the 1346 edition of *Sūtra of Mulian* and manuscripts of *Baojuan of Maudgalyāyana* demonstrates the connection of *baojuan* and vernacular Buddhist scriptures. The link with *Sūtra of Mulian* also reveals the indirect connection of *baojuan* with *bianwen*, providing a new perspective on the study of the association of these two genres.

When we juxtapose the performative context (arena), register, and stock material of this early text with the later *baojuan* dealing with the Mulian story, we find many similarities between *Baojuan of Maudgalyāyana* and later texts. The decoration of its manuscripts and the inclusion of the formulas, mantras, and the poetic passages that represent the stock material of the Buddhist literature intensify the connection of the text with Buddhist preaching. At the same time, the style, verse forms, and performance mode of *Baojuan of Maudgalyāyana* have much in common with *baojuan* of the middle period.

However, both early manuscripts have a special illustration mode not typical of the later *baojuan* texts. It is reminiscent of the practice of picture storytelling, in which the Mulian story appeared since around the eighth to ninth century. On the other hand, these illustrated manuscripts were likely designed for individual reading, with the fine illustrations meant for the instruction and entertainment of readers (most probably mainly women and children). The narrative motif of Mulian being the transformation-rebirth of another deity and the special religious ideas that can be associated with the cults and practices of the sects as observed in this text also continue in *baojuan* of the sixteenth to seventeenth century.

CHAPTER 4

Sectarian Examples in *Dizang Baojuan* and *Baojuan of Benefiting Living Beings*

Of the several copies of the woodblock edition of *Dizang baojuan* that exist, I use the one reprinted in the *Folk Baojuan* (*MJBJ*) series, which apparently comes from the Library of the Research Institute of Drama in the Chinese Academy of Arts (Beijing). The text says the first edition was printed in Beijing in 1679, but the woodblock edition that I use gives the date 1710 in the colophon of its first volume (*juan*).[1] This may be the reprint date or consecration of this particular copy. Another copy of this text was found in 1957 in the Puyin temple of the Vast Yang Teaching in the vicinity of Tianjin, which demonstrates that the text continued to circulate in the sectarian milieus until the twentieth century.[2] Recently, another printed copy (also dated 1710) was discovered among the materials of the folk musicians' association of South Gaoluo village in Laishui county, Hebei.[3] Unlike another old text, *Baojuan of the Origin and Development of Merciful and Miraculous Earth Goddess* (Houtu niangniang lingying cibei yuanliu baojuan), however, folk musicians in Gaoluo do not recite this text at the present time.

Li Shiyu considered *Dizang baojuan* to have been composed in the Ming dynasty, presumably basing his judgment on the similarity of the contents of its text with other *baojuan* from the end of the sixteenth to the early seventeenth century.[4] The early date for this *baojuan* is doubtful primarily because there is not enough evidence; however, *Dizang baojuan* certainly existed by the end of the seventeenth century. The probable place of its composition is Beijing, and it circulated quite broadly in north China at the later period. In the nineteenth century Huang Yupian mentioned this text in the supplementary volume of his *Refutation of Heresies* where he discussed *baojuan* confiscated from sectarians.⁵ Based on his evidence, we can suppose that this text was used by sectarians in Hebei at that time.

Baojuan of Benefiting Living Beings is now represented by the only woodcut printed copy, reprinted in the collection of *Scriptures of Folk Religions of Ming and Qing Periods* (*MMZJW*), which is undated. Yu Songqing, who studied the original edition in the Library of the Chinese Buddhist Association in Beijing, concluded that it was printed, at the earliest, in the second half of the sixteenth century.⁶ This *baojuan* belongs to the Teaching of Yellow Heaven that emerged in this century.⁷ It deals with the early history of this religion, but still has not been used by scholars as a source on this history.

Baojuan of Benefiting Living Beings was not mentioned in scholarly works before the 1990s. There are some references in earlier sources, however, that probably indicate this text. For example, in 1947, Li Shiyu discovered a copy of the manuscript when he carried out fieldwork in Wanquan county of Chahar (northwestern Hebei), where some peasants still followed the Teaching of Yellow Heaven. There he obtained a manuscript without a title and date and reconstructed its title as the "xxxx *Mulian Baojuan*."⁸ The content of the text summarized in Li Shiyu's work is the same as *Baojuan of Benefiting Living Beings*, available in a modern reprint. The first part is about the spiritual cultivation of Mulian in the form of a shellfish and the salvation of the elect by buddhas and bodhisattvas. The second part deals with the propagation of the sectarian teaching by buddhas Puming and Puxian (apparently Puming's granddaughter and a female leader of the Yellow Heaven), who were still worshiped by locals in Wanquan in the middle of the twentieth century. On the basis of the contents and structure of this *baojuan*, Li Shiyu concluded that the text he had obtained was compiled in the early period of the development of the Teaching of Yellow Heaven around the sixteenth to seventeenth century.⁹

AFFILIATION AND DATES OF THE TWO TEXTS

Dizang baojuan was associated with the Western Mahāyāna Teaching. It mentions several nuns, abbesses of the Baoming nunnery (Baomingsi, Nunnery Protecting the Ming) at different times, who were venerated as the leaders of the Western Mahāyāna sect. These are the semi-legendary nun Lü, the founder of Baoming nunnery;[10] her successor nun Jinxi (secular surname Yang, ca. 1450–1530); and nun Guiyuan (secular surname Zhang, ca. 1559–after 1590), apparently the true founder of Western Mahāyāna.[11] Their surnames appear in *Dizang baojuan* in a disguised way—by splitting their family name characters—which is characteristic of sectarian materials of the late imperial period.[12] Furthermore, *Dizang baojuan* names the nun Lü as the founder of the teaching (*kaishan zu*); she is also proclaimed to be a reincarnation of Bodhisattva Guanshiyin. According to this text, she lived in Huang (Yellow) village (Huang cun) and "broadly rescued all the living beings."[13] This information corresponds to versions in other sectarian sources (mostly *baojuan*). Baoming nunnery, which originally was the court-sponsored Buddhist temple and later became the center of the Western Mahāyāna, was located in this village near Beijing.[14] *Dizang baojuan* also says that Patriarch Lü transmitted the "words of the Six Maxims" (*Liu Ju yanyu*), a moral injunction, which in *Dizang baojuan* is also called the Sacred Edict.[15]

Besides these three patriarchs, other followers of the sect are mentioned in *Dizang baojuan*: Fushan, Fubao, Fukun, Fuming, and Fuhai. Since they all have the same first characters in their names, it is possible that they belonged to the same generation in the sectarian hierarchy, as was typical of the sects in that period.[16] The text itself points to the participation of Fushan and Fubao in the production of *Dizang baojuan* (see chapter 5). Furthermore, Fubao and Fukun are said to have been seated in the "boat of Dharma" (*fachuan*), an allegory of salvation from the sufferings of the earthly world, in Beijing. The boat with Fubao and Fukun onboard brought the protagonists of the text to the realm of the Unborn Mother.[17] Presumably they constituted the immediate religious community that produced and venerated *Dizang baojuan*.

The affiliation with the Western Mahāyāna Teaching explains the fact that *Dizang baojuan* was published in Beijing and until the twentieth century circulated near the capital area. The Western Mahāyāna Teaching was active mainly in the Beijing area, and several *baojuan* affiliated with it were printed there at the end of the sixteenth century.[18] In the seventeenth century the Western Mahāyāna Teaching was able to escape the severe persecution of sects carried out by the Qing government. Presumably, the reason for this was that its followers were successful in presenting themselves as true Buddhists. Their religion was indeed quite similar to Buddhism and was not engaged in militant activities, though millenarian beliefs in the Unborn Mother were central to it. The imperial patronage of the Baoming monastery continued during the reign of Shengzu (Kangxi), while the cult of the nun Guiyuan (and thus Western Mahāyāna) also continued there.[19] *Dizang baojuan* was published at roughly the same time. The connection of *Dizang baojuan* with Baoming monastery may not be certain, but it definitely is a product of one of the groups of the Western Mahāyāna.

Baojuan of Benefiting Living Beings describes the establishment and propagation of the Teaching of Yellow Heaven by Li Bin (Buddha Puming, ?–1562/1563), dated 1554 and 1558, respectively (sections 12 and 13). Some details of these events correspond to the information in other scriptures of this teaching.[20] For example, section 12 of *Baojuan of Benefiting Living Beings* says that in 1554 Buddha Rulai (Tathāgata) Puming, who was the reincarnation of the Ancient Buddha of Medicine (Yaoshi gufo, Skt. Bhaiṣajyaguru), settled on Mount Tai (Taishan), the sacred peak of China, and became the Lord of Eastern Prosperity (Donghua Zhu, China?) with the alternative title of the Green True Bodhisattva (Qingzhen Pusa).[21] This is the same year in which Puming is said to have accomplished the refinement of an inner elixir in other scriptures.[22] Section 13 says that in 1558, Puming returned to the celestial palace (i.e., he died). Before that, he had been imprisoned in a border fortress for some time. When his punishment was complete, Puming was summoned by imperial edict and released from prison. Then he transmitted miraculous law, explained the nature of emptiness in his sermons, and opened the ritual area (*daochang*).[23] This legend was obviously modeled on that concerning Luo Qing and his scriptures *Five Books in Six Volumes*. This information seems to be missing from other sources on Puming's life, but the claim for the imperial sanction certainly served to attract high-ranking believers. We can assume the real existence of such high-ranking followers, which explains the printing of the Yellow Heaven Teaching scriptures, including *Baojuan of Benefiting Living Beings*, as a considerably expensive woodblock. This text also mentions the line of Puming's female descendants, who became leaders of the Yellow Heaven after Puming's death.

According to *Baojuan of Benefiting Living Beings*, Puming's recognition by the court happened the same year he died. Other internal sources of the Yellow Heaven say that Puming started preaching and produced his scripture, *Puming baojuan*, in 1558, and died around 1562 or 1563.²⁴ Thus the version of *Baojuan of Benefiting Living Beings* differs from other *baojuan* of that religion dating to the sixteenth century. This discrepancy may be because *Baojuan of Benefiting Living Beings* was composed later than the actual lifetime of Li Bin, and its author did not consult earlier writings of this sect, such as *Puming baojuan*. This hypothesis is confirmed by several other details in the text.²⁵

There is a reference from the late seventeenth century by Confucian scholar Yan Yuan (1635–1704) that probably relates to the contents of this *baojuan*. He wrote about the beliefs of the Teaching of Yellow Heaven (in his transcription, the Way of the Imperial Heaven [Huangtiandao 皇天道]), which at that time was widespread in both the capital area and the countryside. Yan Yuan mentioned that the Yellow Heaven believers "took a shellfish [*luobang*] as their deity."²⁶ This phrase probably refers to the previous rebirth of Mulian as a shellfish described in *Baojuan of Benefiting Living Beings*. Though Yan Yuan did not write anything about the link between Mulian and the shellfish, he noted the importance of the Mulian cult in the system of beliefs of the Teaching of Yellow Heaven. Yan Yuan did not mention the name of *Baojuan of Benefiting Living Beings*, but he referred to its contents. His reference may serve as an indirect indication of the existence of this *baojuan* in the seventeenth century and thus proves my supposed date for this text.

There is also a later reference in government documents concerning persecution of the sects in the early nineteenth century to a text of the scripture of the Teaching of Yellow Heaven with a title close to that of *Baojuan of Benefiting Living Beings—Scripture (Sūtra) of Benefiting Living Beings* (Li sheng jing). This title was mentioned in connection with the discovery of the activities of Yellow Heaven sectarians in Shanxi, Wanquan and Huai'an counties, and Zhangjiakou town in Zhili (modern Hebei) in 1819–20. Officials testified that this scripture did not contain any rebellious slogans.²⁷ Wanquan, Huai'an, and Zhangjiakou were places where the Teaching of Yellow Heaven originated, and where it was also discovered by Li Shiyu in 1947. Thus sectarians used *Baojuan of Benefiting Living Beings* at the beginning of the nineteenth century in places where the Teaching of Yellow Heaven originally spread.

One can conclude that both *Dizang baojuan* and *Baojuan of Benefiting Living Beings* were compiled around the second half of the seventeenth century; however, sectarians continued to revere them as important scriptures in the later period. Both were presumably used by sectarian groups in several places in northern China at the beginning of the nineteenth century; they were still in use in the middle of the twentieth century when modern scholars discovered them among scriptures of the groups of the Vast Yang and Yellow Heaven teachings. Both texts contain valuable information about the history of the Western Mahāyāna and Yellow Heaven teachings, although sometimes it contradicts information from other sources.

THE FORMAL CHARACTERISTICS

Dizang baojuan and *Baojuan of Benefiting Living Beings* have the usual decoration of the woodblock editions of *baojuan* from the end of the sixteenth to the beginning of the seventeenth century. Both are printed as accordion-style folded books with illustrations on the frontispieces and at the end of the texts. Illustrations in *Dizang baojuan* show Bodhisattva Dizang with the Ten Kings of Hell and the scene of the encounter of Mulian and his mother in front of Avīci hell. Illustrations in *Baojuan of Benefiting Living Beings* show the assembly of representatives of three religious teachings of China. Both texts also have "dragon placards" at the beginning and images of the guardian deity at the end. We already have encountered similar images in the Hermitage manuscript of *Baojuan of Maudgalyāyana*; therefore, decoration of the woodblocks of the seventeenth century continued the tradition of early manuscripts though neither *Dizang baojuan* nor *Baojuan of Benefiting Living Beings* has illustrations in the main body of the text.

Structure of Texts

Both *Dizang baojuan* and *Baojuan of Benefiting Living Beings* are composed of two volumes (*juan*). Both texts are divided into sections with titles, called *pin* in the first case and *fen* in the second. There are twenty-four sections in *Dizang baojuan* and thirty-six in *Baojuan of Benefiting Living Beings*. Every section has a regular structure consisting of a combination of a passage of prose with several stanzas of verse in different forms. In *Dizang baojuan*, every section consists of a passage of prose, four lines of seven-character verse, a long ten-character verse, a hymn, four lines of five-character verse, and a couple of stanzas of arias with the indication of an aria melody name. There is a different combination of passages of prose and verse in

Figure 4.01. Frontispiece illustration of woodblock edition of *Dizang baojuan* (1679). Private collection of Li Shiyu. Photo by the author.

Baojuan of Benefiting Living Beings, but the forms of verse employed are similar to those used in *Dizang baojuan*. Every section begins with a prose passage that is followed by four lines of seven-character verse, a ten-character verse, a hymn, four lines of five-character verse, and several stanzas of arias. The authors/editors of both texts tried to follow the structure accurately, but there are occasional variations in the sequence of verses with different meters in the sections.

As we already have observed in the case of *Baojuan of Maudgalyāyana*, division into sections and the rigid structure repeated in every section are features characteristic of *baojuan* since their early period of development. However, there is also a conspicuous difference between *Baojuan of Maudgalyāyana* on the one hand and two later *baojuan* texts about Mulian on the other: the latter two use more aria melodies than the first. At the same time the structure of *Dizang baojuan* and *Baojuan of Benefiting Living Beings* is typical of *baojuan* of the middle period. Thus, one can see continuity of special features of form in *baojuan* of the fourteenth to seventeenth century; it obviously is related to the continuity of their performance characteristics and forms a part of

Dizang Baojuan and Baojuan of Benefiting Living Beings

Figure 4.02. Frontispiece illustration of woodblock edition of *Dizang baojuan* (1679). Private collection of Li Shiyu. Photo by the author.

their register in the terms of Foley's "word-power" theory. At the same time the register in each text is quite individual and allows considerable flexibility in the consequence of forms.

Ritual Elements

The introductory and concluding parts of *Dizang baojuan* and *Baojuan of Benefiting Living Beings* are very important for our proper understanding of the religious context and ways of functioning of these texts. The introductory parts of both are even more elaborate than those of *Baojuan of Maudgalyāyana*. For example, in *Dizang baojuan*, the introduction consists of an invocation to the Kings of Hell and the Three Treasures of Buddhism, two lines of seven-character verse dedicated to the Three Treasures, a four-character verse, a seven-character verse, a prose narrative part, another seven-character verse, a second invocation of the Three Treasures, a *gāthā* on opening *sūtra* (*kaijingji*), a prose passage, four lines of seven-character verse, a ten-character verse, *baojuan* title, a hymn on burning incense (*juxiangzan*), and invocations to various buddhas and bodhisattvas.[28]

The same is true for the concluding parts of both texts. For example, the conclusion of *Dizang baojuan* consists of four lines of five-character verse; a seven-character verse on gratitude for the ten mercies (heaven and earth, sun and moon, emperor, water and soil, etc.); four lines of five-character verse; and a text for the transfer of merit of the Pure Land (*huixiang Jingtu wen*), which, in its turn, comprises invocations to Buddha and bodhisattvas, a mantra, a penitence for the sins of humankind, the wish that everybody will be reborn in the Pure Land, and the invocation to Bodhisattva Dizang and his *Prajñā-pāramita*.[29]

If we compare them with the introductory and concluding parts of early *baojuan* texts (including *Baojuan of Maudgalyāyana*), we discover that their structure became much more complex and varied although many basic elements continued to be used. The same standard elements appear in the introductory and concluding parts of other middle-period *baojuan*, for example, *Puming baojuan*.[30] This comparison with *Puming baojuan* demonstrates that by the sixteenth to seventeenth century the elaborate introductory and concluding parts were typical of the works of this genre.

The introductory and concluding parts of *Dizang baojuan*, *Baojuan of Benefiting Living Beings*, and other middle-period *baojuan* texts constitute a dense frame of religious formulas. The standard components of these parts were connected with rituals of "opening sūtra," incense burning, and invocation of deities in the introduction; and those of transfer of merit, expression of ten gratitudes, and seeing-off deities at the end of the text. Their exact wording could be different, however; there was no standard order in which these elements follow each other in different texts, and the number of prose and verse parts in the introduction and conclusion is different in every *baojuan*.

The prose parts of the introduction in *baojuan* focus on the main ideas of the text (prose introduction to *Baojuan of Benefiting Living Beings*) and introduce the story of Mulian (in *Dizang baojuan*) before entering into the main body of the text. The introductory and concluding elements in these *baojuan* texts, if analyzed in the terms suggested by Foley, represent the performance arena of *baojuan*, reflected in the written texts. In the case of *Dizang baojuan* and *Baojuan of Benefiting Living Beings*, this performance arena is at the same time the ritual setting of the recitation of the sectarian scriptures. The establishment of this performance (and simultaneously the ritual) arena specifies the type of communication that would be carried out during the performance—the religious message of deliverance.

Verses and Arias

Verses in both *Dizang baojuan* and *Baojuan of Benefiting Living Beings* usually amplify and embellish the events that are introduced in the prose parts. In this respect, their usage is similar to that of verses in *Baojuan of Maudgalyāyana*. At the same time, in both texts new episodes of the story are sometimes introduced in verses.[31] Therefore, the verse passages in *baojuan* were used not only for description but also for narration. To put it another way, if the verses are removed, the course of narration is broken. This is a special feature of register of these texts, compared with the earlier specimen of the genre.

In both *Dizang baojuan* and *Baojuan of Benefiting Living Beings*, seven- and five-character verses imitate the classical Chinese model of the new style poetry as in other *baojuan* of the middle period. In *Baojuan of Benefiting Living Beings*, longer seven-character verses are called *gāthās*, similar to several *baojuan* of the end of the sixteenth to seventeenth century. Their structure, however, differs from that of verses in Buddhist scriptures. In the Chinese translations of Buddhist scriptures, *gāthās* may have a different number of characters per line: four, five, six, or seven. Furthermore, the length of *gāthās* differs even within one scripture. In *baojuan* of the middle period, *gāthās* have standard seven-character meter and usually consist of sixteen or twenty lines.

The influence of classical new style poetry is obvious in several aspects of five- and seven-character verses in both *Dizang baojuan* and *Baojuan of Benefiting Living Beings*: it includes caesura and rhyme in every even-numbered line (in the first line the rhyme was optional). The rhymes in the verses of *Dizang baojuan* and *Baojuan of Benefiting Living Beings*, however, are not accurate. For example, in verses of different-meter syllables with the front and back nasal finals often are rhymed. Furthermore, the same characters are used twice for rhyme; this is not acceptable in the classical new style poetry. These two features of rhymes are also characteristic of verses of different forms in *Puming baojuan*.[32] Therefore, it is safe to assume that these characteristics of verse were quite common in *baojuan* of the middle period. In addition, Chinese scholars noticed both of these peculiarities of rhyme in lyrics and arias; the nature of arias as a popular genre was considered one of the reasons for this phenomenon.³³ Both seven- and ten-character verses in *baojuan* surely were set to a certain melody. These types of verses, although superficially resembling classical poems of the *shi* genre, are closer to lyrics and arias that were written to fit into a certain melody. The special features of their rhymes, therefore, resemble those of lyrics and arias.

The texts of both *Dizang baojuan* and *Baojuan of Benefiting Living Beings* used a large variety of aria motifs. There are thirty-one arias in *Dizang baojuan* with twenty-eight different titles. In *Baojuan of Benefiting Living Beings*, the corresponding numbers are thirty-nine and thirty-nine. This is quite typical of *baojuan* of the middle period. In his statistics based on the study of fifty-two *baojuan* of the sixteenth to seventeenth century, Che Xilun listed 232 different aria names. Forty-seven among them are used more than four times; 176 are used from one to four times.³⁴ Most of the aria names in *Dizang baojuan* and *Baojuan of Benefiting Living Beings* correspond to those listed in the classical catalogues of arias. Among arias used in *Dizang baojuan*, twenty-four motif names are in the *Register of Arias of Kangxi*; for *Baojuan of Benefiting Living Beings*, there are twenty-six. Some of the aria names, however, indicate strong links with sectarian ideology. They are unknown in the collections of arias and, as Che Xilun has argued, were invented or modified from common arias by the sectarians.³⁵ In the case of the two texts under discussion, such melodies are "Song of Stepping on the Path" (Ta dao ge) and the "Lament of returning home" (Gui jia yuan) in *Baojuan of Benefiting Living Beings*. Their names point to the ideas of spiritual cultivation and reunification with the Unborn Mother.

In addition to the arias, in *Dizang baojuan* there are two examples of popular songs: the "Melody of falling lotus petals on the appearance of the [true] nature in twelve palaces" (Shier gong nei chu xing lianhuale) and the "Song on realization of nature through forty-eight vows" (Sishiba yuan jian xing ge).³⁶ *Lianhuale* (usually known as *lianhualao*) is a genre of popular storytelling known since the Song dynasty. Initially, the term referred to the songs performed by beggars with the accompaniment of bamboo clappers; later their melodies were occasionally used in dramas.³⁷ Thus the author of *Dizang baojuan* employed popular melodies to transmit sectarian ideology. These songs described the inner elixir practices. Both songs have seven-character meter; however, they stand in places in the text that usually are occupied by arias. Scholars have pointed out these characteristics of sung passages with similar titles in other *baojuan* texts of the sixteenth to early seventeenth century.[38]

Although some arias are used twice in the same text, several musical units may be composed of a number of different arias. These musical units are called "sets" or "cycles" (*taoshu*). Different types of arrangements of arias are used in cycles in both texts;[39] and all of these types have been detected in other *baojuan* of roughly the same period.[40] Therefore, *Dizang baojuan* and *Baojuan of Benefiting Living Beings* demonstrate the same variety of arias and forms of their cycles that are found in other *baojuan* of the middle period.

A comparison of several arias from *Dizang baojuan* and *Baojuan of Benefiting Living Beings* with the classical schemes of arias collected in the manuals of theatrical prosody, such as *Register of Arias of Kangxi*, shows that the structure of arias in the two texts mostly corresponds to the standard schemes.[41] This indicates that verses for arias in *baojuan* were sung during the texts' recitations with accompanying music, similar to that used for classical examples of arias (now in many cases lost). At the same time, several peculiar types of sung passages are used in both *baojuan* under question that usually do not occur in the classical tradition of drama and "detached arias" (*sanqu*). The sung portions of both *baojuan* constitute an important part of the register of their performance; on the one hand, this register relies on the musical poetry adopted by the elite, and, on the other, uses folk music forms.

Language and Formulas

Both *Dizang baojuan* and *Baojuan of Benefiting Living Beings* are written in simple classical Chinese. A considerable number of colloquial phrases, however, appear in these texts. For example, they use many auxiliary words common in modern Mandarin, so they certainly were related to the spoken language of that time.[42] Both *Dizang baojuan* and *Baojuan of Benefiting Living Beings* use Buddhist terminology extensively. There are also a lot of terms from the inner elixir theory. These peculiarities of vocabulary may be explained by the nature of the sectarian teachings with which both *baojuan* were affiliated. On the other hand, there are few allusions to classical literature in the texts. There are several in the text of *Dizang baojuan*: "the mercy of moistening grass" (*zhan cao en*) and "repaying [the mercy] by hanging down reins" (*chui jiang bao*).[43] They come from the classical literature of the fifth to sixth century but were used widely in the later period.⁴⁴ The use of allusions in *Dizang baojuan* creates a more refined style of text as compared to that of *Baojuan of Benefiting Living Beings*. The author of *Dizang baojuan* also showed some knowledge of Buddhist scriptures, which is not as evident in the case of *Baojuan of Benefiting Living Beings*.

Both texts are full of formulaic expressions. The most important formulas serve as introductions to the prose and verse passages. In both *baojuan*, prose passages in almost every section start with the expression "[let us] tell [how]" (*shuo*). This formula is commonly used throughout the text of *Baojuan of Benefiting Living Beings*. In *Dizang baojuan*, there are also variations of this formula: "[let us] narrate" (*biaoshuo*), "the story goes like this" (*hua shuo*), "in the text it is said" (*wen zhong biaoshuo*), and "that which I heard" (*gai wen*). *Baojuan of Benefiting Living Beings* usually employs the formula "the *gāthā* says" in front of the seven-character verses. Both texts also use other narrative formulas, such as "we shall not discuss, [let us] narrate further [about]" (*bu ti, zai biao*) or "let us set this aside for the moment, now we shall discuss" (*zanqie fangxia, you tiqi*). These formulas speed up the narrative flow and introduce a new action and, therefore, imitate the manner of a storyteller. Their function is to produce the simulated context of the performance in the written text or, in Foley's terms, to mark the rhetoricized performance arena in the performance-style texts.

Formulas other than introductory ones are also found in these two *baojuan*. Formulaic expressions often are used in both prose and verse parts of the texts, for example, such customary descriptions as "disordered as [stalks] of hemp" (*luan ru ma*), "rejoiced without end" (*huanxi bujin*), and "tears pouring" (*lei fenfen*). This formulaic style is close to that of real folklore. It is unclear, however, whether this style demonstrates the connection of *baojuan* with the oral literature or if it is merely the imitation of the storyteller's manner in the texts compiled or edited by literate authors. Even judging by these few examples, the formulaic expressions usually consist of three or four characters. This makes it easy for them to fit into the meter of the seven- and ten-character verses (with the schemes four-three or three-three-four syllables in a line). The use of these meters is the same as the mechanistic function of formula in folklore—it is efficient for the quick composition of verse lines—which was stressed by the proponents of the Formulaic theory of oral literature.⁴⁵

At the same time, in both *baojuan* texts, the formulas not only have a mechanistic function but also serve as a means of conveying deep cultural meaning, leading us out of the confines of individual written texts. This is the "stock material" that can be traced to the sūtras, *bianwen*, and related literature. The examples of this are the repeated phrases of the type: "When one son leaves the family, nine [generations] of ancestors ascend to heaven" (*Yi zi chu jia, jiu zu sheng tian*; or "When one person studies the Path, nine [generations] of ancestors ascend to heaven," *Yi ren xue Dao, jiu zu sheng tian*); "Sins are [heavy] as hills and mountains" (*Zui ru qiu shan*; or "She committed sins heavy as Tai mountain," *Zao zui zhong ru Taishan*; or "She committed sins [heavy as] a mountain," *Zao zui ru shan*); "He broadly produced favorable [karmic] links" (*Guang jie liang yuan*). In a condensed manner, these formulas represent important Buddhist notions that were popularized by Buddhists among commoners in China: the concepts of karmic causation and retribution, and the Buddhist interpretation of filial piety. For a long time, these ideas had been associated with the story of the Mulian family: his pious father and sinful mother. In *Dizang baojuan* and *Baojuan of Benefiting Living Beings*, as in the earlier works, these concepts apply not only to the Mulian family but also to the audience/readers for whom Mulian serves as an example. In the case of these two texts, they were the followers of the sects. These examples demonstrate that the formulas (stock expressions) played an important role in both texts by connecting them with the long tradition of the literature on Mulian in China.

The rich musical repertoire of both *Baojuan of Benefiting Living Beings* and *Dizang baojuan*, frequent correspondence of aria meters to the classical schemes, use of colloquial language, rarity of literary allusions, and variety of formulas reveal that they were intended for performance and reveal the connections of these texts to folk storytelling. The people who compiled or edited both *baojuan* tried to make them suitable for oral performance by retaining the above-listed features in the published texts. At the same time, the register of *Baojuan of Benefiting Living Beings* and *Dizang baojuan* is considerably different from that of *Baojuan of Maudgalyāyana* in terms of new forms of verse (ten-character verses and greater variety of aria melodies), narrative function of verses, and the nature of pictorial devices. These differences demonstrate the evolution and variety of formal characteristics of the genre.

THE MULIAN STORY DEVELOPMENT

The core story of Mulian rescuing his mother from hell occupies a limited amount of space in both *Dizang baojuan* and *Baojuan of Benefiting Living Beings*: a part of the introduction and section 1 in *Dizang baojuan* and sections 3–7 in *Baojuan of Benefiting Living Beings*.⁴⁶ The details of the story are very compressed in both texts. For example, *Dizang baojuan* does not even give the secular name of Mulian and the names of his parents. In this text, the events in Mulian's family before Mulian became a monk are summarized in several sentences about the assembly of Buddha. Nevertheless, most details of the core story of Mulian rescuing his mother correspond to those in the earlier versions of this story, such as *Bianwen of Mahāmaudgalyāyana*, *Sūtra of Mulian*, and *Baojuan of Maudgalyāyana*. In both *Dizang baojuan* and *Baojuan of Benefiting Living Beings*, Mulian liberates his mother with the help of magic objects presented by the Buddha: a treasure and a pewter staff (Skt. *kakkara*) with nine rings in *Dizang baojuan*, and a brocade cassock, a staff, and a bowl (Skt. *patra*) with sacred water in *Baojuan of Benefiting Living Beings*.⁴⁷ A staff and bowl presented by Buddha also appear in all the earlier texts mentioned though the exact set of objects Buddha gives to Mulian varies in different versions of the story.⁴⁸

The more detailed retelling of the Mulian story in *Baojuan of Benefiting Living Beings* also contains some minor details similar to those of earlier Buddhist versions. These are, for example, the names of Mulian's parents, Fu Xiang and Liu Qingti; Mulian's secular name, Fu Luobo (transcribed as 傅羅鉢 in this text); the division of family property into three parts; the trade journey of Mulian to the Jin state; and the meditation of Mulian during which he came to know that his father had been reborn in heaven but his mother had been reborn in hell.⁴⁹ All of these details also appear in *Bianwen of Mahāmaudgalyāyana* and *Sūtra of Mulian*.⁵⁰ Thus both *baojuan* followed earlier popular versions of the Mulian story.

However, there is a significant difference between *Dizang baojuan* and *Baojuan of Benefiting Living Beings* on the one hand, and the earlier texts (*Bianwen of Mahāmaudgalyāyana*, *Sūtra of Mulian*, *Baojuan of Maudgalyāyana*, and *Baojuan of Maudgalyāyana-2*) on the other, which concerns the investiture of Mulian as Bodhisattva Dizang (literally "Earth Womb," Skt. Kṣitigarbha) in both later texts, as well as the insertion of the story of the earlier rebirth of Mulian as a shellfish in *Baojuan of Benefiting Living Beings*. Furthermore, in both *Dizang baojuan* and *Baojuan of Benefiting Living Beings*, the story of Mulian and his mother is just an introduction to other story lines that are connected with the propagation of sectarian teachings and occupy most of both texts.

Stories of Rebirths and Salvation

In both *Dizang baojuan* and *Baojuan of Benefiting Living Beings*, the story of Mulian is related to the cult of Bodhisattva Dizang, savior of souls in hell. In both texts, the connection between Mulian and Dizang is made on the basis that while Mulian was liberating his mother, other souls escaped from Avīci hell. *Dizang baojuan* says that Mulian set free 84,000 souls. They had not yet redeemed their sins, but they were reborn in the earthly world. Buddha Śākyamuni gives Mulian the task of gathering these souls and leading them to salvation. He bestows on Mulian the title of Bodhisattva Dizang, the Governor of the Underworld (Youming Jiaozhu). Buddha says:

> With the help of my treasures you opened the gates of the hell. You rescued your mother, so that she escaped from the Sea of Suffering. However, now the principle of Heaven has been lost. Eighty-four thousand souls have escaped. This fact caused blame from the Celestial Buddha. Now I shall send your mother to the Palace of Peace and Convalescence (Anyanggong), where she will enjoy happiness. However, you will go to gather all those souls. [And then you and your mother] together will arrive at the great summit on the Numinous Mountain.[51]

In this way, *Dizang baojuan* explains the role of Mulian as an underworld functionary. The type of salvation to which Mulian-Dizang leads the souls is defined in sectarian terms. For example, the verse in the text says: "Dizang will take the toil of gathering all the souls, // [And lead them] to return to the Primal source, to come Home."[52] These terms, "returning to the Primal source" (*huan yuan*) and Native place (Home of True Emptiness, *Zhenkong Jiaxiang*), were metaphors for salvation in sectarian teachings.[53] The Numinous Mountain (Skt. Gṛdhrakūṭa, Ch. Ling(jiu)shan, Vulture Peak), mentioned in the passage, is a Buddhist term; according to Buddhist scriptures, it was a place in India where the Buddha held sermons and is considered the eternal abode of the Buddha. At the same time, in Chinese sectarian mythology, it is equated with celestial paradise of the Unborn Mother.[54]

Among the elect (*dangren*) who were rescued by Dizang from the sufferings of the earthly world are six protagonists whose stories are narrated in *Dizang baojuan*. These are the pious son, the woodcutter Xiufu (Perfecting Happiness) from Dingzhou (modern Hebei); his eighty-one-year-old mother, Ms. Cheng; sinful Dai Wen from the town of Jiaxing (modern Jiangsu); his wife, Ms. Ye; a neighbor of Dai Wen, a rich man named Fugui (Wealthy and Honored—obviously a self-revealing name), addressed as "squire" (*yuanwai*);[55] and his wife, Ms. Bai. Dai Wen, who originally was an idle person, gambler, and unfilial son (section 6), takes the major role in the story. As he had not agreed to return the debt to Fugui, he was taken to the underworld by the order of Yanwang (section 7). Dai Wen toured hell (section 8) and was sentenced to be reborn as a mule in Fugui's household (section 9). He was allowed, however, to return to his former, still unburied body after Ms. Ye repaid her husband's debt to Fugui (section 10). Later, all the protagonists reach the realm of the Unborn Mother with the help of Dizang and the sectarian teachers (sections 11, 13–24).

All of the protagonists, including Mulian's mother, are in reality reborn bodhisattvas and inhabitants of the heavens. Mulian's mother is a rebirth of Bodhisattva Mahāsthāmaprāpta (Ch. Dashizhi); Ms. Cheng as Bodhisattva of Immeasurable Meaning (Ch. Wujinyi pusa); Xiufu as the fourth of the Heavenly Kings (Tianwang); Fugui as Sudatta, Householder Merciful for Orphans (Anāthapiṇḍada; Ch. Jigu zhangzhe); Ms. Bai as Bodhisattva Meilian; Dai Wen as the first among Five Hundred Arhats; and Ms. Ye as the last Bodhisattva among the inhabitants of the Twenty-four Heavens.[56] Some of the deities listed here are well-known in the pantheon of Chinese Buddhism. For example, Mahāsthāmaprāpta (One who obtained great powers) usually is portrayed in Buddhist scriptures as the attendant of Amitābha along with Avalokiteśvara. He uses his great powers to help living beings quit the lower paths of rebirth and come to the Pure Land. Heavenly kings are protectors of the world and Buddhist law who guard the four directions on the sides of Sumeru Mountain. The fourth among them, Vaiśravaṇa (Ch. Duowentian), is the guardian of the northern direction. Sudatta was a pious layman from the city of Śrāvastī in India. Buddhist scriptures tell about his mercy toward orphans and lonely people, hence his title; he is also known for donating the famous Jetavana garden to Buddha Śākyamuni. Five Hundred Arhats are the disciples of Buddha; and Twenty-four Heavens mean the gods (Skt. *devas*). Bodhisattva of Immeasurable Meaning (Skt.

Akṣayamati), who is believed to be able to observe and comprehend all of the actions of cause and effect, also appears in several major Buddhist scriptures.[57] The only deity in this passage that I was not able to identify in Buddhist sources is Bodhisattva Meilian.

Mulian's mother is said to have been banished from the celestial realm because she was lazy at studying scriptures; she had to live in the mundane world for five hundred years. Therefore, the author/editor of *Dizang baojuan* employed a story line of banished celestial inhabitants in order to link the traditional story of Mulian with sectarian beliefs. Protagonists, as deities convicted for mistakes who had to redeem themselves through spiritual training, suited perfectly the main idea of sectarian mythology in the sixteenth to seventeenth century. This was reflected in both *Dizang baojuan* and *Baojuan of Benefiting Living Beings*; most people were the children of the Unborn Mother who had lost their way in the mundane world and needed to return to their true parent with the use of determined spiritual practice.

The stories of characters in *Dizang baojuan* appear to be typical of sectarian *baojuan* of the sixteenth to seventeenth century, if we consult the classification of Sawada Mizuho. He divided the majority of *baojuan* into two groups according to the type of story line: karmic causation (*yinyuan*, usually spiritual cultivation during several rebirths) and reincarnations in the mundane world (*linfan*). The second type included two categories of protagonists: deities who were banished from the heavens and had to redeem their sins, and deities-saviors. The first category was quite common in other genres of Chinese literature but was modified in *baojuan* in order to propagate sectarian ideas of spiritual cultivation. The second was connected closely with the sectarian beliefs of the advent of deities who would save pious people.[58] *Dizang baojuan* combines all types of these stories. The story of Mulian, which in its basic form can be characterized as the story of karmic causation, was enriched by the inclusion of stories of reincarnation in the mundane world. In addition, stories of both categories of the second type according to Sawada's classification are found in this text.

Similar stories of reincarnation and universal salvation can be found in *Baojuan of Benefiting Living Beings*. According to this text, more than eight million souls whom Mulian set free from the underworld together with his mother are still entangled in the mundane world and hell. In order to rescue all of them, Mulian volunteered to be Bodhisattva Dizang.⁵⁹ This part is similar to the text of *Dizang baojuan*. The following part, however, is completely different from the text of *Dizang baojuan*. Although it also tells about the salvation of the elect, it does not contain stories of specific people. Surprisingly, Dizang is not among the main deities acting in *Baojuan of Benefiting Living Beings*. The main protagonists of the text are Ancient Buddha Master of Medicine (also equated with Amitābha: Yaoshi-Mituo), Buddha Governing the World (Dangyang Fo), Master of Accomplished (literally "Round") Perception (Yuantong Zhu), and Buddha Prabhūtaratna (Duobao Fo). Most of these figures are prominent in Chinese Buddhism. For example, Master of Medicine is the Buddha governing the eastern pure world of Lapis-lazuli (Skt. Vaidūrya), an analogue of the Pure Land of Amitābha. He is known for his power to heal believers. Buddha Governing the World is a title of Buddha Śākyamuni in Buddhist texts. Master of Accomplished Perception is a usual title of Avalokiteśvara (Guanyin). Prabhūtaratna is also Buddha-governor of one of the pure worlds in the East.

The interesting and special feature of this *baojuan* text is that all these deities (and Dizang as well) are at the same time identified with Buddha Puming, the title of the founder of the Teaching of Yellow Heaven. Thus all numerous divine figures in this text are included in the system of specific sectarian teaching centered on the belief in the Unborn Mother. The fascinating lines of associations and identifications of the main deities and their symbols are characteristic of the sectarian *baojuan* of the sixteenth to seventeenth century. The supreme deity was supposed to have many guises and was referred to by various names.⁶⁰

Numerous deities acting in *Baojuan of Benefiting Living Beings* certainly belong to the second category of the second type of *baojuan* stories in Sawada's classification. Puming, in all his guises, and his acolytes descend to the world to save the elect. Puming as Buddha Governing the World opens the competition in shooting with bows for the elect, thus testing their accomplishments in religious training (sections 18–22); Sudhana holds a banquet for the elect who are winners of the competition (section 23);⁶¹ Buddha Governing the World creates the magical Silver City as the abode for the elect (section 24); Buddha Governing the World bestows the treasure of "sweet dew" to profit all living beings (sections 25–27); Reverend Pūrna opens the celestial treasury and bestows gifts on the elect (section 31); and so on.⁶² There are also several episodes not as easily connected with the teaching of Puming: for example, scenes in which the King of Empty Skandhas (Yunkong wang) asks Reverend Lion (Shizi zunzhe) to give up his head as an offering to test his ability of self-sacrifice and then gives Reverend Lion sacred knowledge together with the Buddhist canon (Skt. Tripitaka) in three parts (sections 14 and 15).[63] This, however, should be inspired by the stories of self-sacrifice in order to obtain the true teaching in the Buddhist canonical scriptures.

Thus, in both *baojuan*, the story of Mulian, which was not originally a story of reincarnation, was modified presumably under the influence of that type of story in sectarian texts. Mulian-Dizang was turned into the savior not only of his mother but also of other predestined individuals. Furthermore, in *Dizang baojuan*, the sectarian way of salvation is illustrated by the concrete examples of several people who are protagonists of additional story lines.

In contrast, another usual aspect of the Mulian story in the earlier versions, namely the journey through the underworld, is abbreviated in *Dizang baojuan* and *Baojuan of Benefiting Living Beings*. Unlike *Bianwen of Mahāmaudgalyāyana*, *Sūtra of Mulian*, *Baojuan of Mahāmaudgalyāyana*, and later *baojuan* about Mulian, these texts devote little space to the description of different compartments of hell. Dai Wen's journey through hell in *Dizang baojuan* is very basic—the text merely names different compartments of hell that he observed; furthermore, it is narrated in verses.[64] Similar enumeration of different divisions of hell, which in this case are distributed between the Ten Kings, appears in *Baojuan of Benefiting Living Beings*.[65] The naming of the compartments of hell certainly serves the goal of terrifying the audience. Apparently the audience was familiar with the detailed view of each hell.

Dizang baojuan and *Baojuan of Benefiting Living Beings*, without a doubt, refer here to texts that described all the compartments of hell, similar to *Baojuan of Maudgalyāyana*, its later Non-Interference Teaching recension of the sixteenth through the seventeenth century and other *baojuan* texts, dealing especially with hell. This abbreviated description of hell and the abbreviated account of Mulian family's life serve as a reference to other texts of the *baojuan* genre and possibly to pieces of other storytelling genres and dramas that deal with these episodes at length. Both cases are a link to other texts, which constitutes one of the peculiarities of traditional oral literature and its derivatives. The audience could reconstruct a whole episode from an abbreviated one by recalling more detailed scenes from performances of other *baojuan* or dramas. In Foley's terms, these episodes in *baojuan* represent the communicative economy of performance reflected in these texts.

Returning Escaping Souls

The theme of returning escaping souls that we encounter in *Dizang baojuan* and *Baojuan of Benefiting Living Beings* had a significant impact on the further development of the Mulian story in Chinese popular literature. The episode in which souls escape from the hell opened by Mulian and must be recollected by the religious figures was a significant change in the history of the development of the Mulian story; this is traceable to *Drama Exhorting Goodness* by Zheng Zhizhen.[66] This episode is well developed and thus plays an important role in the later *baojuan* about Mulian. According to Chinese scholars of drama, this episode entered into the *baojuan* around the eighteenth to nineteenth century under the influence of Mulian dramas. The well-developed motif of souls escaping from hell and being returned appears in *Golden Rules*;[67] in this play eight million souls are re-collected by Zhong Kui, an important exorcist deity in China.[68] Contents of the seventeenth-century *baojuan* prove, however, that this motif appeared in the texts of this form much earlier than originally proposed. The details of this episode in *baojuan* texts are also different from those in *Drama Exhorting Goodness* and *Golden Rules*.

In the majority of drama scripts, the duty of returning souls is fulfilled by Zhong Kui, and in most late *baojuan* texts (nineteenth century) by Huang Chao. In both *Dizang baojuan* and *Baojuan of Benefiting Living Beings*, Dizang gathers the souls. In contrast to the later texts, the function of Dizang is not to return them to hell but to save them from the sufferings of the mundane world and hell—an idea that fit well into sectarian ideology.

Previous Rebirth of Mulian

Baojuan texts of the seventeenth century also enriched the story of Mulian with an episode of the previous rebirth of Mulian not found in earlier narratives. In *Baojuan of Benefiting Living Beings* we find the story of the spiritual cultivation of Mulian in his previous rebirth as a shellfish in the sea. Because of the shellfish's accomplishments, Ancient Buddha sent it to be reborn in the form of a man.[69] On the one hand, this modification of the story of Mulian fits into the first type of stories characteristic of the early *baojuan* in Sawada's classification (see earlier in this chapter). On the other hand, the previous rebirth of Mulian as a shellfish is missing from the majority of other *baojuan* and folk dramas.

Nevertheless, it does occur in the Chenhe drama of Hunan, *Prehistory of Mulian*. The details of the story in this drama are quite different, however, from those of *Baojuan of Benefiting Living Beings*. Archat Guizhi (Cassia Branch) is sent to be reborn in the earthly world by the Buddha because mundane thoughts arose in his head. He is reborn as a white shell that can weep. Fu Xiang, amazed by this creature, saves it from some fishermen and brings it home. Ms. Liu, though, thinks that this shellfish is a demon and orders a servant to kill it. Then Guizhi enters Ms. Liu's womb and is born as a man (the future Mulian).[70] A similar episode of Mulian's rebirth as a shellfish also appears in a *qi* drama (*qiju*) of Hunan and the "outline version" and "forty-eight-volume" versions of Sichuan drama.[71]

The difference between the stories of the shellfish in *Baojuan of Benefiting Living Beings* and the Chenhe and Sichuan plays is in their motif type. In *baojuan*, it is a story of spiritual cultivation (type one in Sawada's classification); in local drama, it concerns an exiled heavenly being (type two, category one, in the same system). Nevertheless, one can still observe the similarity of the *baojuan* text of the seventeenth century with the local drama, as concerns this detail. The similarity of the lore centered on the Mulian story in such distant places as Hebei, Hunan, and Sichuan is remarkable.

Unfortunately, the real dates of the Chenhe and Sichuan dramas are unknown, so it is hard to say whether the story of Mulian's rebirth as a shellfish first appeared in *baojuan* or the local drama. Furthermore, it has been argued that the perception of Mulian as being a deity's reincarnation is implicit in the drama script by Zheng Zhizhen.[72] Even though Zheng Zhizhen's version does not have the episode of the shellfish rebirth, it refers to the miraculous birth of Mulian. In this drama Fu Xiang does not have children until the age of forty. Mulian is born only after Fu Xiang goes to Hangzhou, where he takes vows, which has been considered reference to Mulian reincarnations. Fu Xiang's taking vows apparently implied the cessation of sexual relations with his wife. Therefore, Mulian should have been born in a miraculous way, as folk redactions of the drama presented it. Zhu Hengfu proposed that the episode with the shellfish already existed in drama by Zheng Zhizhen's time, but Zheng Zhizhen excluded it from his edited version.[73]

Whether or not this hypothesis is true, the episode of the shellfish is not found in the current script of *Drama Exhorting Goodness* by Zheng Zhizhen. Taking into consideration the early date of *Baojuan of Benefiting Living Beings* (the seventeenth century), I disagree with the conclusion that this episode first appeared in local drama. The earliest text in which this episode occurs is *baojuan* of the seventeenth century. It is not clear, though, whether *baojuan* could have influenced Hunan and Sichuan dramas.

Although the story of Mulian as narrated in *Dizang baojuan* and *Baojuan of Benefiting Living Beings* is similar to versions created up until the sixteenth century, it was significantly transformed then and resembles story lines typical of sectarian *baojuan*. At the same time, the similarity of several details in the Mulian story can be seen in these *baojuan* and later play scripts (especially local dramas). In terms of the two *baojuan* under question, the influence of drama is not evident, as opposed to later *baojuan*. Apparently these episodes are part of the lore related to the Mulian story that appeared both in early *baojuan* and drama (recollection of souls) or are details that at first appeared in *baojuan* and then influenced local drama (Mulian's previous rebirth as a shellfish and his investiture as Dizang). This certainly sheds doubt on the usual conclusion about the primary nature of drama and its influence on *baojuan*.

Conflation of Mulian and Dizang

Bodhisattva Dizang is one of four major bodhisattvas in Chinese Buddhism, along with Wenshu (Mañjuśrī), Puxian (Samantabhadra), and Guanyin.[74] Although it has been argued that Dizang evolved from a pre-Buddhist Indian earth goddess, Pṛthivī, he rarely appears in the early art or literature of India.[75] Dizang became popular in Central Asia and China because of his special role as the savior of souls of the dead.[76] This role was described in the *Sūtra of the Original Vow of the Bodhisattva of the Earth Sanctuary* (Dizang pusa benyuan jing, Skt. *Kṣitigarbha-praṇidhāna-sūtra* [?], hereafter abbreviated as the *Sūtra of the Original Vow*).[77] It was composed around the eighth to ninth century and is the major source of the hagiography of Dizang in China.[78]

Though the *Sūtra of the Original Vow* describes four previous rebirths of Bodhisattva Dizang, it does not conflate his image with that of Mulian. By the Ming and Qing dynasties, however, Mulian often was identified with Dizang. It is not certain why this identification took place. Mulian was most likely treated as a reincarnation of Dizang because there are two stories in the *Sūtra of the Original Vow* (sections 1 and 4) about previous reincarnations of Dizang as women famous for their filial piety: the Brahman Woman (Boluomen nü) and Lady Bright Eyes (Guangmu nü). The stories of the Brahman Woman and Lady Bright Eyes are very close to the canonical version of the story of Mulian rescuing his mother. Both ladies were devout Buddhists who liberated the souls of their sinful mothers from Avīci hell.[79] Based on the close correspondence of the plot, these stories and the story of Mulian likely influenced one another.[80]

In different versions of the Mulian story in popular literature (drama and *baojuan*), the connections between Dizang and Mulian are complex. They cannot be reduced simply to the fact that the story of Mulian rescuing his mother became incorporated into the popular hagiography of Dizang. Chinese scholars have differentiated at least five types of relations between Dizang and Mulian in popular literature: (1) the title of the Supervisor of the Underworld Bodhisattva-King Dizang is bestowed upon Mulian in drama on Mulian in ten volumes from Sichuan and in *Precious Account of Mulian*; (2) Mulian and his father become acolytes of Dizang (guardians of the Teaching) in *Baojuan of Three Rebirths*; (3) Dizang appears on the stage in the role of savior or critic of the protagonists in several regional dramas about Mulian, including the drama of Putian county in Fujian; (4) Dizang is summoned to the stage and receives offerings as an introduction to Mulian dramas in Jiangxi; and (5) the drama about former rebirths of Dizang was performed on the same occasion with the Mulian drama in Gaochun county of Jiangsu before 1946.[81]

The connection of Mulian with Dizang, however, dates to an earlier period. It is also confirmed in *Overview of the Origins of Spirits, Sage Emperors and Buddhas of Three Teachings* (San jiao yuanliu sheng di fozu sou shen da quan, hereafter *Overview*), an anonymous work of the sixteenth to early seventeenth century, so it is slightly earlier than *Dizang baojuan*. In the section on Bodhisattva Dizang in *Overview*, it says that Fu Luobo (Mujianlian) was appointed by the Buddha as the Supervisor of the Underworld. This account also mentions the story of Mulian rescuing his mother and establishing the Ullambana ritual.[82] Thus *Overview* represents the beliefs that underlay the composition of *Dizang baojuan* and were employed by sectarian leaders.

One of the major reasons why Huang Yupian described *Dizang baojuan* as a heretical work was this conflation of Dizang and Mulian. Huang Yupian emphasized that Mulian and Dizang came from different Buddhist scriptures and were never confused there. He quoted the *Sūtra of the Original Vow* and stressed that the Brahman Woman, not Mulian, was the previous rebirth of Dizang. Thus he concluded that this was an obvious error in the *baojuan* and so one could not trust the whole text.[83] It is clear that Huang Yupian relied on Buddhist scriptures, the officially adopted tradition, to criticize popular beliefs. His note on *Dizang baojuan* is valuable evidence of the demarcation drawn by a state official between intellectual and popular perception of religious stories.

At the same time, it is obvious that in *Dizang baojuan*, as well as in the Ming dynasty *Overview*, the story of Mulian was transformed in order to serve the mundane biography of Dizang in the popularized form of Buddhism. The purpose of such a transformation certainly was to bring the scriptural image of Bodhisattva closer to common people by relating him to the popular saint Mulian, whose biography as a layman already existed in the seventh to tenth century. This method of creating the mundane biography of a bodhisattva is not unusual in the history of Chinese Buddhism: recall the story of Princess Miaoshan, a previous incarnation of Bodhisattva Guanyin, or the story of Fu Luobo, who became Mulian. The story of Miaoshan offered a mundane biography of the Thousand-handed Great Merciful Guanyin, an esoteric form of the bodhisattva, which became popular in China during the Tang and Song dynasties.[84] Significantly, the story of Miaoshan became the subject of *Baojuan of the Incense Mountain* (Xiangshan baojuan), another very popular *baojuan* text dating to the early, presectarian period.

The unification of Mulian and Dizang, which presumably occurred during the Ming dynasty, also represented the domestication and development of Dizang's cult in China. While in the case of Guanyin, the purely fictional story of Miaoshan was employed, in the case of Dizang, the popular account of Mulian, originally another character from Buddhist scriptures, was used. This was the combination of two popular cults with primarily Buddhist origins.

CONCLUSION

In both *Dizang baojuan* and *Baojuan of Benefiting Living Beings*, the traditional Mulian story is adapted to sectarian cosmology and beliefs, centered on the cult of the Unborn Mother and related messianic prophecies. The authors (or editors) paid very little attention to the traditional core story of Mulian rescuing his mother, especially one of its central aspects: the journey through the underworld. Apparently the latter was well known to the audiences of these *baojuan* through other dramatic or storytelling pieces (as well as the visual representations of hell in Chinese popular art), thus demonstrating the intertextual connections of the printed versions of *baojuan*. On the other hand, such topics as the redemption of sins of the banished immortals, reincarnation of the divine messengers, and salvation of the elect, which betray the sectarian influence, became central in both texts.

One of the special features of the contents of *Dizang baojuan* and *Baojuan of Benefiting Living Beings* is the unification of Mulian's and Dizang's images and cults. This is not a particular feature of sectarian texts, as it is seen in an encyclopedia of popular religion of the seventeenth century and later dramas, which were not directly connected to the sects. This conflation, however, certainly represents popular beliefs, as it was criticized by a state official from the scriptural point of view.

In both *baojuan* of the seventeenth century, Mulian and Dizang appear in a sectarian context, revealed in the contents of the stories as well as in notes on the ritual setting, contained in the complex introductory and concluding parts, which are much more elaborate than those in *Baojuan of Maudgalyāyana*, and special singing passages. This enriched musical aspect of the texts, the smooth narration in prosimetric form, and colloquial language are characteristics similar to those found in oral storytelling that testify to the performative usage of *baojuan*.

CHAPTER 5

Beliefs and Practices in Sectarian *Baojuan*

Dizang baojuan is an important scripture of the Western Mahāyāna teaching. Despite its Buddhist appearance, ideas expressed in *Dizang baojuan* are quite similar to those propagated by the other Chinese messianic sectarian groups of the sixteenth to seventeenth century, such as the Yellow Heaven, Vast Yang, and Incense Smeller Teaching (Wenxiangjiao, or Eastern Mahāyāna Teaching [Dong Dashengjiao]) led by the powerful leader Wang Sen (1542–1619).[1] According to a recent classification, they were radically different from the Non-Interference Teaching, especially its form embodied in *Five Books in Six Volumes*, as they were based on messianic prophecies (which sometimes had political aspects, as the followers could try to realize these predictions), while the latter emphasized personal experience of enlightenment, developing the traditions of Chinese Chan.[2] Of course, this classification, devised by the modern scholar, is conventional, and there was significant cultural exchange between the Non-Interference Teaching and later sects. The story of Mulian, reinterpreted in these different traditions, is an example of themes shared among religious groups of that period.

As far as the teachings of the Western Mahāyāna can be reconstructed now with the use of internal sources (mainly *baojuan*) of the sixteenth to seventeenth century, we can conclude that it shared the common sectarian myth of the Unborn Venerable Mother (not present in the early writings of the Non-Interference Teaching). Many sectarian teachings of that period portrayed all of humankind as children of the Unborn Venerable Mother who were banished to the earthly realm and endured suffering. Later on, Mother, out of her compassion, sent messengers to convert people and help them reunite with her in a paradise-like realm. The most important among these messengers were Buddhas who reigned during three temporal periods: Dīpamkara (Ch. Randeng), Śākyamuni (Ch. Shijiamuni), and Maitreya (Ch. Mile). Sectarian patriarchs depicted themselves as the reincarnations of these and other Buddhas.[3] In the Western Mahāyāna Teaching these were successive abbesses of the Baoming temple, mentioned in the previous chapter.

One can find direct references to the Unborn Mother and the succession of the three Buddhas in *Dizang baojuan*. It mentions Dīpamkara and Śākyamuni; Maitreya does not appear in this text, but it is possible that Amitābha, who is mentioned in the text several times, performs the role of the future Buddha.[4] For example, one of the concluding verses in this text says:

> Amitābha leads the believers outside of the tree worlds.
> When a child sees his mother, he/she escapes disasters forever.
> Unborn Venerable Mother is very pleased in her heart,
> And the child starts talking with a smile, when he/she sees the Mother.[5]

Many symbols of salvation in *Dizang baojuan*, such as the passage to paradise in the Dharma boat and the abode of the Unborn Mother in the astral body, called the Palace of Dipper and Cow (Douniugong, Ursa Minor and Altair), are the same as in the major sectarian scriptures of the sixteenth to seventeenth century.[6]

Furthermore, the author of *Dizang baojuan* expressed belief in the superiority of his community's teaching, which is also characteristic of the Chinese sects of the same period.[7] The text says:

> Seventy-two patriarchs came to the mundane world.
> They destroyed the deviant teachings and established the orthodoxy.
> They sat on the Dharma boat and traveled on the Sea of Suffering.
> Only then they saved predestined persons of the miraculous sounds.[8]

Thus only the elect will reach the paradise of the Unborn Mother, while others will be left in the Sea of Suffering. The passage to paradise is possible only with credentials (lit. contract, *hetong*) that followers presumably receive from the sectarian leader. In paradise, the attendants of the Unborn Mother "check and verify their names," "register them in the lists of the elect," and "write their names on the golden board."[9] This bureaucratic structure of paradise that requires the same procedure is also depicted in other sectarian *baojuan* of the same period.¹⁰

A special feature of the sectarian beliefs revealed in *Dizang baojuan* is the cult of the Queen Mother (Wangmu), who is portrayed in this text as the counterpart (or another guise) of the Unborn Mother. The Queen Mother meets the saved protagonists in paradise and invites them to the Feast of Peaches (Pantaohui).¹¹ It is clear that the text here refers to the Queen Mother of the West (Xi Wangmu) and her peaches of immortality from the "curling peach tree." Since at least the Han dynasty (206 BCE–220 CE), the Queen Mother of the West as the hostess of a paradise-like realm was venerated in China. Her cult was popular in the late imperial period, and there are other *baojuan* of the same time in which the Queen Mother of the West was also equated with the Unborn Mother, suggesting that the cult of this female deity may be the antecedent of the sectarian cult of the Unborn Mother.¹² Whether or not this hypothesis is true, the link between the Queen Mother of the West and the supreme sectarian deity, emphasized in *Dizang baojuan*, makes an important point of interchange between the sectarian teaching of the seventeenth century and mainstream Chinese religion.

Baojuan of Benefiting Living Beings represents a classical form of the Yellow Heaven Teaching: many of its details correspond to other scriptures of this religion of the end of the sixteenth to the beginning of the seventeenth century. The similarity of themes and symbols in *Baojuan of Benefiting Living Beings* and *Puming baojuan*, one of the major scriptures of this sect ascribed to Puming himself, is especially striking.

First of all, both *baojuan* share the general belief in the Unborn Mother, the sectarian patriarchs as her emissaries, and the cosmology of the three epochs in world development. The deities that appear in *Puming baojuan* also act in *Baojuan of Benefiting Living Beings*; and several details of their activities are the same. For example, both *Baojuan of Benefiting Living Beings* and *Puming baojuan* have scenes of Buddha Amitābha, seated in the Dharma boat, in his great compassion for the people entangled in the sufferings of the earthly world, floating on the Sea of Suffering and rescuing the elect.¹³ This scene certainly serves the metaphor of Puming's proselytizing because he is presented as the rebirth of Amitābha or Master of Medicine in both texts.

Another important common idea is the renewal of the world (close to the Western concept of millennium) after its destruction. In *Baojuan of Benefiting Living Beings*, the future world, where the elect will enjoy happiness and longevity, is governed by Maitreya; in *Puming baojuan*, it is ruled by the Ancient Buddha of Imperial Ultimate (Huangji Gu Fo).[14] Both texts say that the Buddha of the Future will preside over the Assembly of Nine-Petaled Golden Lotus (Jiuye Jinlian).[15] *Baojuan of Benefiting Living Beings* recounts that when Maitreya will govern "celestial signs," the south and north will exchange their places according to the turn of heaven.[16] *Puming baojuan* claims that even the measurement of time will be different in the world of the future; for example, there will be 810 days and 18 months in a year.[17] Although the details are different, both texts tell of radical change in the future. The future world is described as the ideal one; both texts say that people who survive will live 81 kalpas (or millennia) in this new world.[18]

Government officials regarded this kind of prophesy as one of the most dangerous heretical ideas. The establishment of the new world implied the destruction of everything in the previous one, including the existing government. For example, Huang Yupian selected the aforementioned passage about the change of time measurement from *Puming baojuan* for criticism in his book.[19] If government officials in the early nineteenth century, who obtained *Baojuan of Benefiting Living Beings* from sectarians, had the same text as the one available now, it is strange that they did not notice this deviant idea in it.

The elements of religious practice propagated in both *Dizang baojuan* and *Baojuan of Benefiting Living Beings* are also similar. Even apart from the common topic of the inner elixir, they require that followers observe the five precepts, derived from mainstream Buddhist practice,[20] and insist on strict vegetarianism.[21] Complete vegetarianism for believers had appeared in a number of Chinese religious movements since the early period, and it was not necessarily related to messianism and the Unborn Mother cult. However, it was usually regarded as a religious deviation by the authorities, and since the eleventh to twelfth century it was one of the major reasons used to accuse religious communities of heterodoxy.[22] In late imperial China, sectarian groups usually prescribed vegetarianism for their followers.[23] Therefore, it is no wonder that we find its propagation in both *baojuan* discussed here.

The ideas expressed in *Baojuan of Benefiting Living Beings* are characteristic of the early period of the Yellow Heaven Teaching. Thus both *Dizang baojuan* and *Baojuan of Benefiting Living Beings* are typical sectarian texts of the seventeenth century. Furthermore, the beliefs and practices advocated in both texts are not very different from each other.

COMPOSITION OF SECTARIAN TEXTS AND THEIR BUDDHIST THEMES

Both *Dizang baojuan* and *Baojuan of Benefiting Living Beings* provide important information on the composition of *baojuan* texts. *Dizang baojuan* claims that Patriarch Lü was the author of this text. It says that Lü "pronounced this true scripture with her mouth"; "Although [Patriarch] pronounced the scripture, she did not know characters, so we pay thanks to Fushan, who held the brush."[24] The text itself preserves the direct message of this illiterate patriarch. One of the ten-character verses says:

> I have left *Dizang [bao]juan*. There are many mistakes in it.
> I have never read sacred wise books and do not understand writing.[25]

Therefore, *baojuan* pronounces that Lü is the author of the oral text that was written down by her follower. However, this is not reliable information. If Patriarch Lü's name refers to the founder of the Baoming monastery, the text should have been composed in the fifteenth century. It is clear, however, that in its present form this text is the product of a later period. There are several facts that support this: the nun Lü presumably did not have any belief in the Unborn Mother, since Guiyuan likely developed this concept a century later; and, as the text of *Dizang baojuan* mentions the genealogy of the Western Mahāyāna leaders through the end of the sixteenth century, it could not have been written before 1590.

Thus the claim that *Dizang baojuan* was compiled and transmitted orally by Patriarch Lü is not feasible. A Western Mahāyāna sectarian follower (or teacher), Fushan or Fubao, was likely the author of *Dizang baojuan*. Apparently, the real author (or authors) of the text wanted to make it more authoritative by ascribing it to the figure venerated as the founding patriarch of the sect. One can also suppose that the compilers communicated with the spirit of Patriarch Lü with the use of a mediumistic technique. One such technique, the planchette writing (*fuji*), was used by sectarian groups as early as the seventeenth century and became especially widespread in the nineteenth to the early twentieth century.[26] Unfortunately, *Dizang baojuan* does not specify how this communication took place.

On the other hand, sectarians, including the author(s), perceived *Dizang baojuan* as a Buddhist scripture. At one point in the text the author refers to it as Tripitaka (Dazang). According to *Dizang baojuan*, its text was among scriptures stored at the legendary abode of Buddha: "True scriptures are only in the Monastery of Thunder Sounds [Leiyinsi]."[27] After Patriarch Lü had received the sacred knowledge of this scripture, she pronounced *Dizang baojuan* a "true transmission."[28] As in the case of true Buddhist scriptures, its original should have been in a foreign language, Sanskrit. Therefore, while Patriarch Lü was credited with transmitting *Dizang baojuan*, Fubao was said to have "translated" it. The lines of an aria say:

> Patriarch Lü transmitted the truth; it is not an unimportant thing...
> Only when Fubao translated scripture, it was completed.[29]

In addition to the claim that this text is the Buddhist scripture, the author(s) tried to prove it with references to the Buddhist canon. These references, however, do not show a true knowledge of Buddhist scriptures. At one point the author mentions a sūtra by its name, the *Sūtra on Repaying the Kindness [of Parents]* (Bao en jing), claiming that the Buddha pronounced it on the occasion of the salvation of Mulian's mother, but the *Sūtra*'s contents are not clarified. Thus it is not clear which sūtra it is.[30] The author of *Dizang baojuan* also was well aware that the story of Mulian came from the Buddhist scripture. In the introduction, he says: "I have heard that in Tripitaka one can find a case on the monk Mulian from the household of the Śāk[yamuni]'s Mahāyāna teaching rescuing his mother from hell."[31] Therefore, the author points to the sūtra that tells the story of Mulian, which should be the *Sūtra of Ullambana*, although he does not give the sūtra's name.

Here the scripture on Mulian from the canon is called a *gong'an* (case or paradox). Originally this term referred to a legal case or public notice, but the Chan school of Chinese Buddhism used it for the meditation device based on paradox that potentially can lead ordinary consciousness to enlightenment, more commonly known in the West by its Japanese pronunciation, *kōan*. The identification of the Mulian story as *gong'an* creates an interesting perspective on its interpretation as a paradox in the Chan tradition. In the case of *Dizang baojuan*, this interpretation seems well justified, as the story of Mulian in this text serves as a model for enlightenment and salvation by sectarian followers.

The filial piety that the Mulian story represents is one of the important ethical values in *Dizang baojuan* (as in *Baojuan of Benefiting Living Beings*); the preaching of it is ascribed to the Unborn Venerable Mother herself. Filial piety is one of the necessary conditions of a person's salvation:

> The Unborn Venerable Mother sits upright.
> It admonishes the multitudes of believers to repay the ancestors' mercies.
> If you do not repay the parents' mercies,
> Your fasting and chanting the Buddha's name are useless!³²

Based on such passages, we can conclude that though the author refers to the Buddhist source, he interprets the scriptural story in a specific sectarian way. Furthermore, as already noted, details of the Mulian story in *Dizang baojuan* are completely different from those of the canonical source but very close to those of the later popular versions. The author of *Baojuan* probably never read the original sūtra and thus did not invoke its name, while his knowledge of the story certainly came from popular lore. The treatment of the other stories in *Dizang baojuan* that came from the Buddhist canon also supports this conclusion. For example, *Dizang baojuan* includes the facts of hagiography of Buddha Śākyamuni, the founder of Buddhism: "They say: when our Buddha appeared in the world, he left the Imperial palace, he fled to the Snowy Mountains [Himalayas], where he endured austerities for six years."³³ Therefore, the text invokes the popular version of the Buddha's biography that was derived from canonical sources (including stories of his previous lives). On the other hand, in the same passage of *Dizang baojuan*, the story of the conversion of Śākyamuni by Lamp-lighting Buddha, Buddha of the Past, is narrated briefly.³⁴ This episode connects the material derived from the canonical sources with the central sectarian conception of the succession of three Buddhas.

Therefore, it is evident that the author of *Dizang baojuan* tried to support his text with Buddhist scriptural material. He tried to disguise the sectarian teaching with the central cult of the Unborn Mother as a popular interpretation of Buddhism. This approach is especially understandable if we recall that *Dizang baojuan* was affiliated with the Western Mahāyāna Teaching, in part based in the Buddhist monastery and trying to present itself as a special form of Buddhism (note its name). The mixture of sectarian and traditional Buddhist elements becomes the principle of the construction of the text of *Dizang baojuan*. Ming (and perhaps early Qing) nobility and the court accepted or just overlooked this peculiarity of the message of the Western Mahāyāna Teaching and its scriptures. They accepted these texts as those affiliated with Buddhism. By the beginning of the nineteenth century, however, this conflation of canonical and sectarian material in the scriptures of this teaching became obvious to the officials investigating the sectarian groups, so that Huang Yupian condemned it.

Baojuan of Benefiting Living Beings, on the contrary, does not explicitly refer to the Buddhist scriptures. Though, as was demonstrated, deities of Buddhist origin have a place in it, it usually does not employ stories that can be traced to sūtras, with the exception of the central story of Mulian and several secondary episodes derived from the Buddha's hagiography.[35] In the preface to *Baojuan of Benefiting Living Beings*, the author explicitly ascribes the core of the text to the founder of the Yellow Heaven sect and gives information on the composition of this *baojuan*, as in the case of *Dizang baojuan*. The preface says that when the Ancient Buddha was reincarnated in the earthly world (presumably a reference to the teacher Puming), he left "Precious Gāthā on Benefiting Living Beings" (Li sheng bao ji) in seventy-two lines to the anonymous author of *Baojuan of Benefiting Living Beings*. This *gāthā* had miraculous power that enabled the author to expel evil, attract auspiciousness, and fulfill all his wishes. Later the author amplified these seventy-two lines into thirty-six sections and, thus, compiled *Baojuan of Benefiting Living Beings*.[36] Therefore, Puming is credited with laying the foundations of the text of *Baojuan*.

Whether or not this is true, we need to note the importance of the short verses for the transmission of sectarian teachings and the composition of longer *baojuan*. Both *Dizang baojuan* and *Baojuan of Benefiting Living Beings* demonstrate the wide use of short verses that revealed the major religious ideas of a given religion in a condensed way. "Maxims in Six Lines" and "*Gāthā* in Four Lines" in *Dizang baojuan* apparently belonged to this type. Furthermore, *Dizang baojuan* quotes the text of the "Maxims in Six Lines" that were transmitted by Patriarch Lü: "Obey your parents. Respect your elders. Live in peace with neighbors. Educate your sons and grandsons. Be satisfied with your place. Do not do inappropriate things!"[37] This injunction repeats "Six Maxims" that were ascribed to the founder of the Ming dynasty, Taizu (r. 1368–1398), and were the original source of Kangxi's *Sacred Edict*.[38] It is clear that sectarian teachers associated with this *baojuan* did not compose this injunction themselves but borrowed it from government authorities and used it for the ethical education of their followers.

Since the end of the sixteenth century, this situation was not unusual for the sects, and the same "Maxims in Six Lines" were included in scriptures of other teachings. At the same time, these maxims do not contain anything connected with specific sectarian beliefs. They simply testify that sectarian teachers, who propagated deviant mythology, nevertheless accepted the ethics promoted by the state authorities.[39] In the case of *Dizang baojuan*, these ethics were represented by the maxims that were presumably the same as the *Sacred Edict* mentioned in this text.

"*Gāthās* in Four Lines," which are mentioned in both *Dizang baojuan* and *Baojuan of Benefiting Living Beings* but not quoted in these texts, were not of the same type as the "Maxims." They presumably contained sacred knowledge closely connected with sectarian eschatology. For example, *Baojuan of Benefiting Living Beings* mentions the "Way of Non-Interference in four lines" (si ju Wuwei) in connection with the inner elixir practice: "Preserve the Way of Non-Interference in four lines, exercise a circulation in orbit [*zhoutian*] during fire times [*huohou*]."[40] *Gāthā* in seventy-two lines, as pronounced by Puming, also may have belonged to the same category.

Both kinds of verses should have been very useful for sectarian teachers. They allowed them to transmit their teaching without employing printed (or written) materials that would have been very vulnerable during the intensive persecution of the sects. These rhymed verses were intended for memorization. Because the verses were transmitted orally, they also were suitable for converting illiterate people, which enabled the sectarian congregation to expand. Both *Dizang baojuan* and *Baojuan of Benefiting Living Beings* testify that in the seventeenth century sectarian teachings employed two types of literature: voluminous and detailed *baojuan* texts and brief chants.

In the seventeenth century the brief chants, transmitted orally, were part of initiation practices in the Non-Interference Teaching, which also relied on the recitation of Luo Qing's books as the main form of transmission.[41] In the modern scholarship there have been attempts to associate these two types of literature with different types of sects in the later period (Qing dynasty).[42] The materials of *baojuan* of the sixteenth to seventeenth century, however, show that both types could be used by the same groups. While scriptures (and especially those that used the familiar Buddhist subjects and ideas) could have been intended for a literate and well-to-do audience, the abbreviated verses helped popularize doctrine for illiterate people.

MULIAN AND THE INNER ELIXIR TECHNIQUE

Mulian's (and consequently Dizang's) images were modified to fit into the sectarian cosmology revealed in *Dizang baojuan* and *Baojuan of Benefiting Living Beings*. The first issue is the connection of these deities with the inner elixir technique discussed in both texts. They represent the inner elixir as one of the main religious practices of the groups with which they were associated. In *Dizang baojuan*, there is the phrase: "Religious cultivation should not go out one's interior,[43] if it goes out of the body, it is the deviant teaching."[44] *Baojuan of Benefiting Living Beings* regards an imperishable body—yang body (*yangshen*) or adamantine imperishable body (*jingang buhuai zhi ti*)—produced as the result of inner elixir practice as one of the crucial conditions of salvation in the future Dragon-Flower Assembly.[45] Inner elixir descriptions often appear in other sectarian *baojuan* of the sixteenth to seventeenth century, notably those of the Yellow Heaven and Western Mahāyāna teachings.

Inner elixir refers to a range of esoteric doctrines and practices that adepts use to transcend the individual and cosmological states of being. Its origins are obscure, but scholars have singled out several trends that have contributed to its development. These are classical Daoist texts, correlative cosmology, *Yijing* (Book of Changes) lore, meditational and physical disciplines of *yangsheng* (nourishing life), cosmological traditions of *waidan* (external alchemy), medical theory, Buddhist soteriology, and Confucian moral philosophy.[46] The adepts of inner elixir teaching imagined the process of transformation of their bodies as the initial formation of the elixir from the *qi* (here the most appropriate interpretation of this term is "secretions and essences") of the body. Inner elixir then transforms into an immortal embryo (*xiantai*). If nourished properly, this embryo grows into a new immortal body that substitutes for the perishable body of an adept. Sectarian teachers who produced *baojuan* that are analyzed here adopted this ultimate goal of the production of the immortal body.

Inner elixir techniques were also quite popular outside of the sectarian context, and during the sixteenth to seventeenth century mainstream schools of the inner elixir were already highly syncretic. Therefore, it is hard to clarify which tradition had greater influence on the sects and their *baojuan*. Although early systematic presentations of inner elixir date to the Tang dynasty, three major inner elixir traditions developed primarily between the tenth and fourteenth century. They became known anachronistically as the Zhong-Lü, Southern Lineage (Nanzong or, more accurately, the Golden Elixir, Jindan), and Northern lineage (Beizong, more accurately Complete Perfection, Quanzhen).[47] In the thirteenth to fourteenth century the most influential and widespread traditions of Southern and Northern lineages merged, and many authoritative figures in inner elixir claimed to have continued the Golden Elixir heritage but also revered Complete Perfection heritage. By the fourteenth century, the teaching of the three main inner elixir traditions circulated among literati interested in self-cultivation as well as among adepts wanting to practice a new technique in their local communities.[48]

Most modern scholars have argued that the Complete Perfection school was the most likely source of influence on the northern sects of the sixteenth to seventeenth century.[49] There are several reasons for this conclusion. First of all, Complete Perfection, just as did these sectarian traditions, developed primarily in the north.[50] Furthermore, the Yellow Heaven Teaching, which was especially fond of the inner elixir, used the name of Complete Perfection for itself.[51] One should note, however, that the situation with the Daoist schools in northern China in this period was quite complex: many schools were active there, and "Complete Perfection" was not used very accurately in application to the Daoist adepts by the laity.[52] Therefore, one cannot assume that the Complete Perfection school was the main source of influence on sectarian *baojuan* of the sixteenth to seventeenth century: the inner elixir terminology in *baojuan* often is related to the sources of other schools; however, this question is not of central importance here.

What is most important for the present analysis is the association between the inner elixir and the image of Mulian-Dizang in both *Dizang baojuan* and *Baojuan of Benefiting Living Beings*. Dizang *baojuan* ascribes the instruction of the inner elixir technique to Mulian himself, who "realized his [true] nature and elucidated his mind." This passage on the inner elixir, the longest and most detailed one in either *baojuan*, demonstrates this aspect of the Mulian-Dizang cult in the two texts:

> Mulian entered into meditation and returned to the palace.[53] He elaborated on this case. Listen to how I shall explain this path: "You need to perfect roots, take the pure ones[54] and change the dirty ones with them. When you tightly close the six gates,[55] from the head it will descend downwards. Arrows will hit the Middle Palace.[56] They will break and open the flowers of the heart.[57] With the sound of a crash [you will find yourself] in front of the Gate of Golden Lock.[58] One sound is going downwards: it will be a cry in the Cold Gate. With a sound of [rustling?] wild grass, you will be nurturing a treasure in the navel.[59] Then you will stop at the Elixir Field.[60] Yang energy of a son will calm down. Then you will pass the intersection of Three Paths.[61] Reed sprouts will pass through the ankles,[62] the marrow will hurt. In the Palace of Eternal Spring a sparrow hawk will be reborn. It will reach and move the River with Nine Curves. In front of the Lumbar Barrier, raise a document for inspection and go in. Inside the Dark Barrier, in front of the Ancient Peak Range, yellow wind blows. In front of the Jade Pillow Barrier,[63] in the Palace of Dipper and Cow,[64] there are peaches of immortality of the Queen Mother [of the West]. Eight Immortals are wishing longevity. The Star of Longevity of the Southern Pole is in the Palace of Curvy Stream. It is the different realm, on the Heaven. Our Buddha Respected by the World[65] has arrived and sat on the Heaven. [Bodhisattva] Dizang has sat down. [You have?] Amitābha in your heart. In front of a phoenix's nest a golden chicken transforms into phoenix. On the left side it is chilly. On the right side [you hear] sounds of thunder. Teacher and pupils, five persons, took out true scriptures. They came to the Eastern land [i.e., China] to convert and rescue wise and good [persons]. Every person has the steep mount of Emei.[66] In the steep creek of Eagle's Worry set a compass and look. In front of [a grove of] double trees[67] Venerable Mother has been waiting for a long time. When you pass through a bridge of a single log, both ends of it are emptiness. Be extremely attentive! In front of a crossroads, there is an intersection of the four forms of life.[68] The troubles of transmigration of soul: three are on the left, four are on the right. A crown prince holds three peaks, a stone girl has a headache. Sad and confused, close tightly six gates! You should not relax! As you enter and are on the way, [you will see] that bright light has emerged on the summit of Kunlun mountain. The Unborn Venerable Mother meets predestined persons. In the celestial realm they are meeting for the assembly, and they will be never born again![69]

This passage demonstrates that the inner elixir technique was represented in *Dizang baojuan* in an obscure way. Many stages of the process are not even named, so it is not clear what exactly is circulated. Lots of notions appear as allegorical images that I was not able to find in the reference literature. Furthermore, a mixture of physiological and mythical (cosmological) notions is apparent. Along with the terms related to the circulation of *jing/qi*, popular deities of Daoist and Buddhist pantheons such as Eight Immortals (Ba Xian), Longevity Star (Shouxing), Queen Mother of the West, Amitābha, and Dizang appear along with the Unborn Mother. The conflation of different plans is common for other sectarian texts. Several *baojuan* texts of the sixteenth century have demonstrated that "sectarian writings can have multiple layers of meaning and could, therefore, be understood in different ways by different readers."[70] In this passage, as in the similar passages in other *baojuan*, it is unclear whether the barriers and passages are located in heaven or within one's own body (or whether they replicate each other in both realms). Nevertheless, the general message of this passage is quite clear: the pious should follow the example of Mulian, who perfected the inner elixir technique. If they exercise their body and spirit, they will leave the cycle of rebirth and arrive in paradise with the help of merciful deities.

As for the portrayal of the inner elixir technique in both *baojuan* under question, it appears to be quite similar to the relevant descriptions in other *baojuan* of the sixteenth to seventeenth century. Such inner alchemy terms as the True Lead and True Mercury, Tiger of Yin and Dragon of Yang, and Baby Boy and Lovely Girl, which denote the secretions and essences of viscera, are abundant in both texts.[71] Modern scholars usually face the difficulty of understanding the actual practice of the inner elixir to which these *baojuan* refer. These references are fragmentary and scattered; none of the known sectarian *baojuan* explains the inner elixir theory in a coherent way, and it has been suggested that Daoist terms were evoked just for their numinous power.[72] However, although they did not give precise instructions in their texts, the authors of these *baojuan* did not necessarily have only superficial knowledge of the inner elixir. There is no doubt that the inner elixir technique belonged to the category of sacred knowledge. The teachers probably were not willing to put it into writing in these broadly disseminated texts, and ambiguity of notions and ideas is also characteristic of the texts belonging to the more mainstream Daoist traditions. For example, an authoritative study of the traditional Daoist vision of the body notes that "the symbolic vision of the body ... remains so full of logical contradictions, that it is useless to look for any 'system.' At the same time, fundamental themes recur with surprising regularity throughout all the descriptions of the inner landscape."[73]

A detailed textual analysis of *Dizang baojuan* and *Baojuan of Benefiting Living Beings* demonstrates that the inner elixir was one of the central concepts of their teachings. It appears in connection with the main deities and protagonists of the texts, and shows that the practical religious background of these texts was quite different from that of the early *Baojuan of Maudgalyāyana*.[74] Among other mentions, in *Baojuan of Benefiting Living Beings* the practice of inner elixir is ascribed to the shellfish, the former rebirth of Mulian. Because of this self-perfection, it was able to attain a human form in the next rebirth. The author praises the shellfish that was so assiduous in its self-perfection that it attained enlightenment and was able to "leave the [mortal] shell and return to the palace [of the Unborn Mother]"; in this respect, many people are inferior to it.[75]

The importance of the connection between Mulian and the inner elixir technique in the system of the Yellow Heaven Teaching is corroborated further by the external evidence on its religious practices. For example, in the seventeenth century Yan Yuan wrote about the mixture of Buddhist and Daoist elements in the Yellow Heaven Teaching in this way: "Like Daoists, they employ the techniques of 'expelling the old and taking in the new' and collection and refinement [of inner elixir]" [*tuna cailian zhi shu*], but they also call the received embryo the monk Mulian [*n.b.!*] and chant Buddha's name."[76] The ancient phrase "expelling the old and taking in the new" refers to the ways of controlling and regulating the breath to refine the *qi* (vital energy or pneuma); later it was associated with the inner elixir practice.[77] This passage proves that the Yellow Heaven Teaching adepts used the name of Mulian to define the immortal embryo.

The reason for the association of Mulian with the inner elixir practice that we encounter in the sectarian *baojuan* of the seventeenth century is obvious if we consider the status of this character in the canonical Buddhist tradition. In the sūtras, Mulian is portrayed as the Buddha's disciple who had the greatest magical powers. He possessed "six penetrations" (also called six "superknowledges" or "spiritual penetrations," Skt. *abhijñā*, Ch. *shentong*). This magical power allowed Mulian to penetrate boundaries of the visible world, fly to special realms, perform self-transformation, and so on. Scholars have suggested that this belief in the supernatural abilities of Mulian explains why the story of mother rescuing was ascribed to Mulian and no other Buddhist figure. Thus, one can explain the popularity of Mulian's image in China by his resemblance to a medium (or shaman in other terminology) who possesses numinous powers. Such religious experts were popular in China since remote antiquity; thus Mulian's image was especially attractive to the Chinese of later times.[78] The supernatural abilities of Mulian in the Buddhist canon should have served as the foundation of the sectarian perception of him as a practitioner of inner elixir.

Thus *Dizang baojuan* and *Baojuan of Benefiting Living Beings* add a new feature to Mulian's image in Chinese literature. Many sectarian *baojuan* of the sixteenth to seventeenth century depicted other deities as practitioners of inner elixir as well,[79] but the image of Mulian was especially appropriate for an exemplar of an adept of this teaching. This explains the use of the Mulian story in both *baojuan* discussed here and the presumable cult of Mulian among the followers of the Teaching of Yellow Heaven.

MULIAN AND SECTARIAN FEMALE DEITIES

Both texts present other sides of Mulian-Dizang's image that had special meaning in the sectarian context. For example, *Dizang baojuan* and *Baojuan of Benefiting Living Beings* treat the final meeting of Mulian with his mother as an analogy of the reunion of the elect (lost children) with the Unborn Mother. *Dizang baojuan* describes this reunion in the following terms: when Mulian broke the gates of the Avīci hell, at first he could not see his mother. He needed a special magical object to see her:

> Mulian took out the Xuanyuan Mirror[80] from his chest,
> Only then he illuminated the hell and saw our Mother.
> With both his hands he pulled the Unborn Mother,
> And unconsciously tears flowed out of both his eyes.[81]

Here, Mulian's mother is equated explicitly with the Unborn Mother. We also see a continuation of the theme and imagery in *Baojuan of Maudgalyāyana*; however, while in that text this reunion was portrayed in the Buddhist context, in *Dizang baojuan* it clearly serves the metaphor of salvation in sectarian terms.

The cult of Dizang also appears in a transformed way in the sectarian *baojuan*. Dizang was an important deity in the teachings of Chinese sects of the sixteenth to seventeenth century. Chinese sects borrowed this cult together with the conception of hell that became extremely important in the popular religion. In the case of *Dizang baojuan* and *Baojuan of Benefiting Living Beings*, the miraculous power of Dizang also is reinforced by the supernatural abilities of Mulian, as both deities merged into one.

There are other *baojuan* that contain evidence that Bodhisattva Dizang was venerated by the Western Mahāyāna and Yellow Heaven teachings, to which *Dizang baojuan* and *Baojuan of Benefiting Living Beings*, respectively, belong. These are *Baojuan Preached by Maitreya of Dizang and the Ten Kings* (Mile Fo shuo Dizang Shi wang baojuan; Che no. 746, ca. 1630), belonging to the Western Mahāyāna Teaching; and *Baojuan of the Ten Kings of Mount Tai, the Eastern Peak* (Taishan Dongyue Shi wang baojuan; Che no. 1120, first printing dated to 1636), belonging to the Yellow Heaven Teaching.[82] In both texts, as in *Dizang baojuan* and *Baojuan of Benefiting Living Beings*, Dizang is portrayed as a savior from hell and a leader to paradise.[83]

In *Dizang baojuan*, Bodhisattva Dizang is called Venerable Mother, thus he is equated with this supreme sectarian deity. For example, the text says: "In Jiaxing there is a Temple of Dizang, and inside sits a golden body (i.e., statue) of the Venerable Mother."[84] Apparently the group of Western Mahāyāna sectarians who composed *Dizang baojuan* imagined Dizang as one of the manifestations of their supreme female deity. The same situation can be found in several other sectarian texts; for example, *Baojuan of the Ten Kings of Mount Tai* also calls Dizang "Mother."[85]

Equating Dizang with the supreme female deity also was common with other Buddhist deities included in the pantheon of Chinese sects of the seventeenth century. For example, it is well known that several sects regarded Guanyin as the reincarnation of the Unborn Mother, and she appears with this title in several *baojuan*.[86] The cult of Dizang underwent a transformation similar to that of Guanyin in the sects of the seventeenth century. In the case of Dizang, however, this process included not only identification with the Unborn Mother but also feminization of the deity, who usually appears in male guise in the sources of popular Chinese religion in the late imperial period.

SECTARIAN *BAOJUAN* IN PERFORMANCE

Dizang baojuan supplies rare information about the ritual practices of the Western Mahāyāna Teaching. Its 16th section describes the celebration of Dizang's birthday by a religious community on the thirtieth day of the seventh moon. Though set in Jiaxing, we can suppose that it refers to northern China, where the Western Mahāyāna spread. According to the text of *Dizang baojuan*, pious laymen Dai Wen and Fugui sponsored the rituals in honor of Dizang in the old temple of Bodhisattva Dizang.[87] As this temple is called *miao* (shrine), not *si* (Buddhist monastery), it must have been a kind of local sanctuary not specifically connected with Buddhism. At the same time *Dizang baojuan* says that the patrons wrote an invitation letter to an abbot of a Buddhist monastery and invited Buddhist monks to perform the rituals. The listed rituals are of primarily Buddhist origin. These are recitation of scriptures, penitence, feeding of hungry ghosts, and salvation of all souls and ancestors in particular. The text of *Penitence of Emperor Wu of the Liang [Dynasty]* (Liang Wu chan) is mentioned specifically. This penitence, according to the tradition, was compiled by the Emperor Wu (Wudi, r. 502–549) of the Liang dynasty (502–557) in order to rescue his favorite concubine, Ms. Xi, who was reborn in the form of a dragon because of her sins. It became very popular in Chinese Buddhism and often was performed as part of funerary rite.

These rituals in *Dizang baojuan* are mentioned alongside the recitation of the "true scriptures" (*zhenjing*). These scriptures certainly denote *baojuan*, as the text of *Dizang baojuan* refers to itself using this term.[88] The accompanying rituals described in *Dizang baojuan* include burning incense, displaying images of deities (*zhima*), burning ritual money, reciting the text of petition (or report, *shuhewen*), and thanking and seeing off deities.[89] The paraphernalia and rituals accompanying the scripture recitation are the same (at least in name) as those employed in the modern performance of *baojuan* in the southern part of Jiangsu.

This description in *Dizang baojuan* supports the supposition that the Western Mahāyāna Teaching tried to legitimize itself as a form of Buddhism. In addition to using Buddhist deities and subjects in their scriptures, Western Mahāyāna followers performed rituals similar to Buddhist ones. It is possible that the Buddhist monks mentioned in the text were followers of this sect or somehow supported it. This aligns with information on the Western Mahāyāna, which most probably appeared and developed under the shelter of the Buddhist nunnery. In the seventeenth to eighteenth century true ordained Buddhist monks took part in the transmission of several sectarian teachings, and sectarian preachers could be disguised as Buddhist monks.[90] The central cult of the congregation associated with *Dizang baojuan*, however, was not Buddhist. While superficially the sectarians were worshiping the traditionally accepted Dizang, they were, in fact, worshiping the Unborn Mother.

The congregation described in *Dizang baojuan* also sought the support of local authorities, secular persons. According to the text, the elders of the town (sages) participated. One of the protagonists, Fugui, is the representative of this category of people in the text. Furthermore, the author of *Dizang baojuan* ascribed the publication of this text to Fugui's support: he sacrificed money for carving printing blocks so that the text could be disseminated broadly and "would help ten thousand kinds of creatures to leave the abyss [i.e., the cycle of rebirth]."[91]

Unfortunately, it is impossible to confirm if Fugui was a real person who supported the publication or if he was just a fictional character in *Dizang baojuan*. We can compare the account in *baojuan*, however, with the contemporary description of a Buddhist assembly in the novel *Pacification of the Demons' Revolt*, where the deviant Buddhist nun performs stories about Buddhist deities. The performances described in these two sources have many similar features. In both cases, they took place on a public occasion and local secular authorities participated in them (even as the sponsors of events). Therefore, we can conclude that the festival described in *Dizang baojuan* certainly represented the actual event that took place in a town in northern China.

There is also evidence that *Dizang baojuan* was indeed recited during community festivals in several places in northern China in the recent period. For example, old folk musicians in Laishui recalled that *Dizang baojuan* was performed during Zhongyuanjie in the first half of the twentieth century.[92] This festival also included the ritual of floating lights on the river (*fang hedeng*) as described in *Dizang baojuan*. Until the 1950s, followers of the Vast Yang Teaching at Puyintang in Yixingbu performed *Dizang baojuan* during major annual festivals, among which the 30th day of the 7th moon (Dizang's birthday) was very important.[93] In Laishui, *Dizang baojuan* has been performed during funerary rituals, which were important community events in the traditional society.[94] This is quite natural, taking into account the themes of this text, which talks about the ancestor's salvation and universal deliverance and invokes the Ten Kings.

Internal and external evidence (fieldwork reports) concerning the performance of *Dizang baojuan* reveals that sectarian groups intended to hold rituals openly for the broader community so that they would become dominant in the spiritual life of commoners. This is supported by the evidence in historical documents that Chinese sects in the seventeenth to eighteenth century were engaged in popular rituals that imitated Buddhist or Daoist rituals for the benefit of laity.[95] These practices were often meant to attract new followers to the sect. As seen in *Dizang baojuan*, sectarian followers tried to rescue all souls of the dead. This practice explains why the cult of Mulian-Dizang, savior of souls, became important in the scriptures of the Western Mahāyāna Teaching.

Other sects are also known for performing similar rituals. The members of the Vast Yang Teaching, in particular, were known for performing funerary rituals.[96] Since the seventeenth century at the earliest, the Yellow Heaven Teaching's followers performed public rituals for the salvation of the dead.[97] In addition, several sectarian *baojuan* of the middle period still are recited during funerary services in the Min county of Gansu and the Changshu city area of Jiangsu.[98] Apparently some sects were successful in capturing the minds of (i.e., deceiving) commoners. There was a close connection between sectarian practice and conventional religion to the degree that "one could substitute for the other."[99] Therefore, the religious practice's description in *Dizang baojuan* is a reliable piece of historical evidence.

CONCLUSION

The beliefs and practices revealed in both *Dizang baojuan* and *Baojuan of Benefiting Living Beings* were typical of the messianic Chinese sects of the sixteenth to seventeenth century. The understanding of universal salvation as the transfer to the paradise of the Venerable Mother—with the help of her divine emissaries and religious practices of complete vegetarianism and inner alchemy—are central in these texts, though both *baojuan* contain a significant amount of material that can be traced to orthodox Buddhist writings. Images of Mulian and Dizang also underwent significant transformation under the influence of these beliefs and practices: both became deities of salvation and compassion in the religious systems of the Yellow Heaven and Western Mahāyāna.

At the same time, *Dizang baojuan* describes the situation in which *baojuan* recitation turned from specifically sectarian ritual to an event intended for the broader community. This marks the beginning of the period in the development of *baojuan* genre when recitation of and listening to these texts separated from the specific sectarian ideology and became an act of popular devotion. Although *Dizang baojuan* certainly belongs to written literature, its orientation toward oral and ritual performance, as demonstrated in the analysis of its form, must have facilitated this process.

As for the modern cases of ritualized recitation, though Vast Yang Teaching followers in Yixingbu preserved the recitation of sectarian *baojuan* texts (including *Dizang baojuan*) in the middle of the twentieth century, they seemed to have been completely unaware of their sectarian origins.[100] The same is true for the modern believers in Laishui.[101] The question of what the influence of the message of salvation, especially concerning the inner elixir technique, was on the audience of the broader community who participated in the recitation of the texts similar to *Dizang baojuan* remains unanswered. In these cases described by Chinese scholars, the influence seemed to be minimal. The transformation of *baojuan* recitation from sectarian ritual into an event of popular devotion took place in virtually all the currently preserved traditions of *baojuan* recitation. *Dizang baojuan* provides important testimony of this process dating to the seventeenth century.

CHAPTER 6

Late Examples in *Baojuan of Three Rebirths* and *Precious Account of Mulian*

In their present form, *Baojuan of Three Rebirths* and *Precious Account of Mulian* were created in the nineteenth century. *Baojuan of Three Rebirths* probably was written down in the southern region, and many early editions of it were printed in the southern cities of Zhenjiang, Nanjing, Changzhou, Suzhou, and Shanghai (see appendix 2). On the other hand, *Precious Account of Mulian* seems to have its origins in Sichuan, but it also circulated in northern China. As almost nothing is known about the authors/editors of these two texts and their places of origin, an examination of the particulars of editions of each sheds light on their history.

THE HISTORY OF THE TWO LATE *BAOJUAN*

The earliest known edition of *Baojuan of Three Rebirths*, dated 1876, was printed by Baoshantang publishers of morality books in Zhenjiang. Nevertheless, it certainly was not the first edition of the text; as the cover says, it was made with newly carved woodblocks. There are eleven different editions of *Baojuan of Three Rebirths*, made from 1876 to 1925 (see appendix 2, III). They fall into two groups. The first (appendix 2, III, nos. 1–7) are woodblock editions of similar style, with one illustration showing three rebirths of Mulian and clear text in comparatively large characters. The second group (appendix 2, III, nos. 8–11) comprises modernized editions of the same text, executed with the use of a new technique, lithography. Although in lithographic editions the redactions in the text are minor, the text is printed in a very concise manner (apparently for the purpose of economy). The style of illustrations and calligraphy in the early twentieth-century editions is more refined than that in the late nineteenth-century editions. Furthermore, a lithographic edition of 1921 by Wenyi publishers (Wenyi Shuju) in Shanghai (in two volumes) has several illustrations on the frontispiece in the first volume (appendix 2, III, no. 9); the majority of the other editions have one. The difference between woodblock and lithographic editions illustrates the attempt of publishers to improve the form of the printed book, as the Shanghai publisher Xiyin did with other narrative *baojuan*. *Baojuan of Three Rebirths* too was printed in the series by Xiyin, with the acclaimed editorship of Chen Runshen (appendix 2, III, no. 10).

The production of the new embellished editions of *Baojuan of Three Rebirths* in the early twentieth century was a result of its popularity among the reading public in urban centers such as Shanghai at the beginning of the twentieth century. This text's popularity throughout the whole country is also indicated by: (1) the existence of abridged versions, such as *Complete Volume of Mulian Rescuing Mother and Obtaining the Way in Three Rebirths* (Mulian jiu mu san shi de dao quan ben; appendix 2, XV); (2) the production of typeset revised editions of this text; and (3) its use in different places in China. *Complete Volume of Mulian Rescuing Mother* is a concise version of *Baojuan of Three Rebirths*, with many details moved from the prosaic part into verses; it also exists in several lithographic editions of the early twentieth century by Shanghai publishers. *Baojuan of Three Rebirths* was reprinted several times as typeset editions in Taiwan and Hong Kong (appendix 2, III, nos. 13–15). This text was also transmitted in the form of manuscripts, apparently used by folk performers (appendix 2, III, no. 12).

Baojuan about Mulian, performed today in different regions of China (mainly recent manuscripts), are connected with late nineteenth- to early twentieth-century editions of *Baojuan of Three Rebirths*. The contents of the *baojuan* texts used in the Jingjiang, Changshu, Zhangjiagang, Suzhou, and Wuxi areas of Jiangsu (appendix 2, nos. IV–X, XIII) closely resemble those of *Baojuan of Three Rebirths*. There is some evidence that performers in these areas consulted late nineteenth- to early twentieth-century editions of this text when they compiled the manuscripts they used for performances. For example, storytellers-*fotou* in Jingjiang owned an edition of *Baojuan of Three Rebirths* by Shanghai Hongda Morality Book Publishers

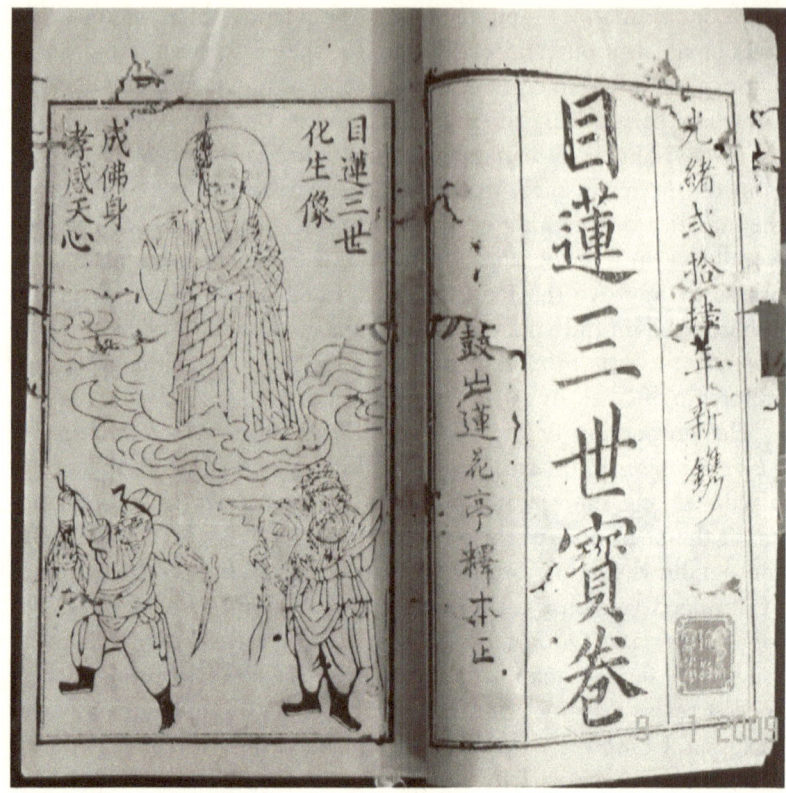

Figure 6.01. Frontispiece of woodblock edition of *Baojuan of Three Rebirths* (1898). Private collection of Li Shiyu. Photo by the author.

(appendix 2, no. III, 8). The contents of *Baojuan of the Pond of Blood* (appendix 2, no. XIII), performed in Jingjiang, prove that it certainly was based on this edition. Old editions of *Baojuan of Three Rebirths* from the end of the nineteenth to the beginning of the twentieth century also have been discovered in the possession of modern performers of *baojuan* in the Changshu area.[1] At the same time, local recensions of this *baojuan*, transmitted as manuscripts, can be much more elaborate than the older editions. For example, *Baojuan of Mulian Rescuing His Mother from Hell* (Mulian jiu mu diyu baojuan), still performed by the masters of scripture telling in Changshu (appendix 2, X), although it follows closely the plot of *Baojuan of Three Rebirths*, contains many new details. This elaboration in local texts has to do with their use in a ritual setting still preserved in Jingjiang and Changshu areas.

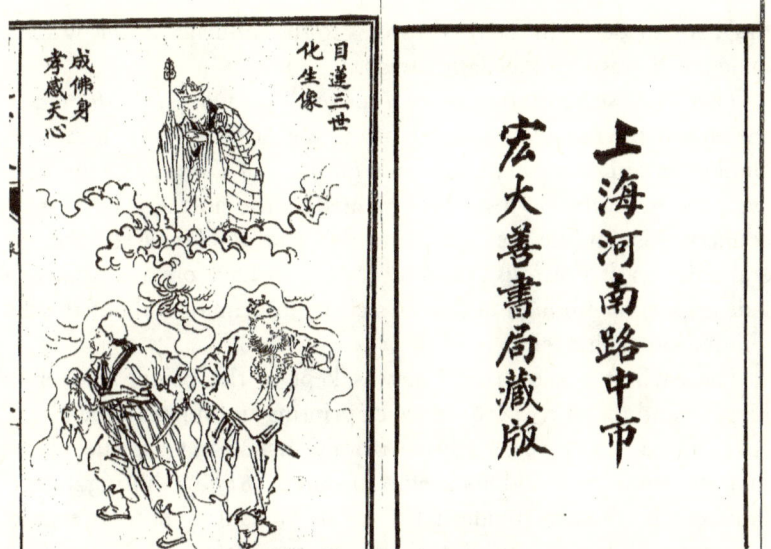

Figure 6.02. Frontispiece of lithographic edition of *Baojuan of Three Rebirths* (1922). Hongda Morality Book Publishers in Shanghai (Taiwanese reprint). Collection of and photo by the author.

In the twentieth century, *Baojuan of Three Rebirths* also was transmitted in the form of manuscripts in Hexi, and a modern recension was published in a collection of Hexi *baojuan* that lists only undated manuscripts of this text, though the preface to the collection cites the woodblock edition made in Changzhou in 1886.[2] This proves the hypothesis of the southern origin of this text, which was transmitted to Hexi as a printed edition. *Baojuan of Three Rebirths* has thus been circulated widely in different areas of China in the form of editions and manuscripts, and was adapted for performances in several areas of Jiangsu and Gansu.

Certain traits in the text of *Baojuan of Three Rebirths* also prove the hypothesis of its southern origin.[3] First, old southern editions refer to the subsidiary moralistic stories of rewards and retribution that are set in the area of Jiangsu but are excluded from the recension of this text from Hexi. These stories certainly belong to the local lore, and short references to them imply that *Baojuan of Three Rebirths* (at least in the latest recension) was compiled somewhere in Jiangsu. Second, the proximity between the story of the birth of Fu Luobu (Mulian) in *Baojuan of Three Rebirths* and local dramas of the Shaoxing area in Zhejiang also speaks for its southern origin. In addition, linguistic evidence in the text testifies to the influence of the Wu language of Jiangsu (or Zhejiang) areas.

There are several editions of *Precious Account of Mulian* from the end of the nineteenth to the beginning of the twentieth century. Unlike the contemporary editions of *Baojuan of Three Rebirths*, however, the majority of them were printed in the northern part of the country. Also unlike the editions of *Baojuan of Three Rebirths*, several editions of *Precious Account of Mulian* have prefaces that provide important (though not always clear) information about the dissemination of this text.

The earliest edition that I saw is kept in the Beijing University Library and dated to 1876 (place of printing unknown; appendix 2, XVII, no. 2);[4] however, a scholar from Gansu, Tan Chanxue, claims that she found a woodblock edition dated 1817 by Jintingguan of Jiankang prefecture (modern Gaotai in Gansu).[5] The existence of such early editions is quite probable, as the preface by Wang Zuoli dated 1881, appearing for the first time in the edition of the same year (appendix 2, XVII, no. 3), claims a long history for this text: "This [book] had been transmitted in the world for a long time. But because [Xia Yuqi][6] was afraid that [the copies] were already worn out and not in sufficient number, he wanted to carve anew the printing blocks to print and disseminate it broadly."[7] On the basis of another undated preface, which first appears in an 1892 edition (appendix 2, XVII, no. 5), one can conclude that the first printing indeed took place before the Second Opium War (1856–60). This preface says that "the original woodblocks were burned in the fire of war. I [anonymous sponsor of the edition—R. B.] could not help but grieve about it. Then after consulting with all my companions I undertook the new carving of blocks in order to disseminate it broadly and explain karmic causation." This indicates that the text appeared in printed form even earlier than *Baojuan of Three Rebirths*; however, both were circulated at approximately the same time in two different regions of China.

While the sponsors and editors of *Baojuan of Three Rebirths* are, in most cases, unknown (except for several early twentieth-century editions), both individuals and organizations that supported the publication of *Precious Account of Mulian* are listed in the prefaces and on the frontispieces of a majority of the editions. This provides interesting information about the history of printing and perception of this text. For example, the preface dated 1881 says that the new printing of the text was made possible with the help of more than twenty members of the philanthropic society Anrentang (Hall of Peace and Benevolence, location not provided). The main sponsor, Xia Yuqi, was a member of this organization. The reprint was aimed at the families of commoners, as sponsors believed that *Precious Account of Mulian* should encourage them to develop good thoughts and suppress evil intentions, and thus "bring commoners on the way of order."[8] The edition of 1893 was produced by the members of philanthropic society of Jishantang (Hall of Accumulating Goodness) in Dongguo village of Xinan township (*xiang*) of Daming county of Daming Prefecture of Zhili.[9] The moralistic aim is pronounced in the preface to the edition of 1892, probably written by one of its sponsors.

The prefaces of *Precious Account of Mulian* form an important ideological frame for the text. However, they still have not been used in the discussion of the oral literature connections, usage, and moralistic message of this *baojuan*.[10] Significantly, all the prefaces were written in more refined classical Chinese than the text of the story itself. Thus, the authors of the prefaces made claim to a higher cultural status than that of the supposed readership/audience of *baojuan*. This explains the simplicity of the literary style of the text.[11] The prefaces also indicate that this text was not simply a recorded oral version of the popular story. The texts were edited, and presumably more than once, as the preface of 1892 says that the publisher "visited famous scholars, who meticulously checked and revised the text, character by character and sentence by sentence."[12] Although that may be an exaggeration, the participation of literate people in shaping the modern redaction of the text is apparent.

According to these prefaces, people engaged in the reprinting of *Precious Account of Mulian* fall into two categories: sponsors, who gave money for the project, and editors, who revised the text. For the edition of 1881, those were Xia Yuqi and Wang Zuoli; in 1892, the anonymous head of the philanthropic society and local scholars; in the edition dated 1898, Hu Sizhen and Yinan Zi (Sage from the South of Yi [county], apparently the same person as Qingyang Shanren [Hermit of Qingyang], Mr. Guanwu (Guanwu shi), called the proofreader of the text), along with the corrector, Zhiyi Zi (Sage Who Understands Oneness).[13] Unfortunately, I was not able to find any details about the social and cultural background of these persons so far.

In the 1898/1899 edition the presence of the sectarian element is evident. The author of the preface dated 1899 and the editor, who used religious pseudonyms instead of real names, certainly represented the sectarian teaching of the Great Way of Former Heaven (Xiantian da dao), which constitutes the ideological background of *Precious Account of Mulian*. Yinan Zi, also called Hermit of Qingyang, is also known as the editor of the sectarian *baojuan—Baojuan of the Golden Elixir and Nine-Petaled Lotus of the Imperial Ultimate Period [that Leads to] Rectifying Belief, Reverting to the Real, and Returning to [Our] True Home* (Huangji jindan jiulian zhengxin guizhen huanxiang baojuan; Che no. 369), printed in 1909.[14] This text was ascribed to the Ninth Patriarch Huang (Huang Jiuzu) of the Great Way of Former Heaven, also known as Huang Dehui (1624–1690).[15]

While the prefaces of 1881 and 1892 stress the didactic function of the text, regarded as exhorting commoners to goodness, the author of the preface of 1899 treats it as an object of primarily religious devotion. This preface is written in the form of four-character verses. It speaks about the salvation of the elect (*yuanren*), familiar to the reader from *baojuan* of the seventeenth century—*Dizang baojuan* and *Baojuan of Benefiting Living Beings*—and "immortal roots, Buddha seeds" (*xiangen Fozi*), as well as their ancestors. Ancient Buddha welcomes them to the "boat of mercy," which can rescue them from entanglement in the net and abyss.[16] These terms, as well as "enlightened teacher," "Ancient Light in Mysterious Pass" (Xuanguan guguang), Emperor of the Un[limited] (Wu Huang), and Ancient Buddha, certainly represent the sectarian discourse. This discourse is well justified as the ideas that these terms represent appear in the text of *Precious Account of Mulian* itself. They also are the same as, or close to, those encountered in the sectarian *baojuan* of the seventeenth century.

The title of Ancient Buddha is applied to Mulian-Dizang, featured in this text. The author of the preface proclaims that Ancient Buddha will descend to the mundane world (China in particular) once again. Those who follow his teaching will be saved.[17] Therefore, the author of this preface not only instructs people to imitate Mulian in their behavior, as also seen in other prefaces, but transmits the ideas of sectarian mythology and eschatology. The 1899 preface reflects the sectarian affiliation of this *baojuan* text, which is not properly discussed in the existing research. It also demonstrates that the same text of *baojuan* was used by literati, who supported orthodox values, and sectarians.

Prefaces to *Precious Account of Mulian* also provide information on the range of the text's dissemination. Although not all the geographical names are easy to decipher, it is clear that the text of *Precious Account of Mulian* was disseminated in northern China.[18] The language of the text itself, however, bears traces of Sichuanese origin. There is one word in the text that certainly comes from one of the Sichuan topolects, *yuanba* (or *yan4pa1* in the topolect of Chengdu City) 院坝 (more common 院壩), "inner yard."[19] This word has a local flavor as it defines a peculiar trait of traditional Sichuan architecture. Like *Baojuan of Three Rebirths*, the story of Mulian in *Precious Account of Mulian* has received considerable influence from a local variant of Mulian drama—Sichuan drama in this case. As in *Baojuan of Three Rebirths*, however, the major part of the text is written in standard language. It is probable that the local pronunciation was added during the oral performances of this text.

In the modern period, *Precious Account of Mulian* continued to be disseminated in Sichuan (appendix 2, XVII, no. 10), which also testifies to its connection with Sichuan; but it was also copied and performed in Gansu and transmitted to Qinghai (appendix 2, XVII, nos. 4, 12); the new folk recensions of this text were also created there.[20] Judging from the available editions of the two texts, *Baojuan of Three Rebirths* and *Precious Account of Mulian* were circulated in two different regions of the country and therefore represent two regional traditions of *baojuan* in China.

PUBLICATION OF BAOJUAN AND PHILANTHROPIC ACTIVITIES

The publishers of *Baojuan of Three Rebirths* and *Precious Account of Mulian* represent the cultural background against which these texts circulated. Judging from the information in the editions of both texts, their publication usually was supported by philanthropists and their organizations. Several philanthropic societies in different locations printed *Precious Account of Mulian* at the end of the nineteenth century; although they are not easy to locate in historical sources, presumably they were typical of organizations of this kind in the late Qing dynasty period. These philanthropic societies were multifunctional in the late Qing period, and the free-of-charge distribution of the morality books (including *baojuan* of the late period) was only one of their usual activities. Members of philanthropic societies often printed morality books on their own or ordered printing from commercial publishers.[21] The printing of *Precious Account of Mulian* certainly was accomplished in this way although the specific places of printing often are not known.

In the case of *Baojuan of Three Rebirths*, special morality book publishers produced most of its available editions. They were printed at different times by Baoshantang in Zhenjiang, Yidezhai in Nanjing, Peibentang in Changzhou, and Yihuatang and Hongda Morality Book Publishers in Shanghai (see appendix 2). All these publishers were well-known for printing morality books; they also produced a variety of *baojuan* titles.[22] Although morality book publishers also had commercial intentions, the price of books was minimal. Publishers, being philanthropists themselves, encouraged other philanthropists to buy multiple copies of these books so that they could distribute them free of charge and therefore earn religious merit.[23] Several modern editions of *Baojuan of Three Rebirths* were circulated through the network of morality books in mainland China and continue to be distributed through this network in Taiwan and Hong Kong.

Thus the printing of *baojuan* occurred openly at the end of the Qing dynasty and early Republican period, as it constituted part of the philanthropic activities of the gentry. Some editions of the two *baojuan* under question were produced by well-established gentry associations or publishers related to them. Publishers and printers of these texts treated them as didactic materials. Editors (and therefore sponsors) of *Precious Account of Mulian* even, unintentionally or intentionally, ignored the sectarian ideology of this text, simply presenting it as a type of morality book. The 1899 preface by a sectarian teacher, however, demonstrates its obvious use in the sectarian network.

It is also well known that in the late period of Qing and the beginning of the Republic, some sects acted under the guise of philanthropic societies and distributed morality books. At the same time, the gentry participated in sectarian movements. It may be difficult to distinguish between philanthropic societies and sectarian organizations that published *baojuan*, especially since there is little precise information about them. It is very important for our understanding of the late period in the history of the *baojuan* genre to realize that both sectarians and gentry moralists could use the same texts. Both groups relied on different aspects of the text. This dual function also is implicit in *Baojuan of Three Rebirths*.

FORMAL CHARACTERISTICS

Structure

Baojuan of Three Rebirths is divided into three volumes (*juan*); however, the narration in *Precious Account of Mulian* is not divided into volumes. Each part of *Baojuan of Three Rebirths* corresponds to one of the three rebirths of Mulian, making this a special feature of the text. The first *juan*, dedicated to the usual story of Mulian, familiar to us from earlier texts, is disproportionately large compared to the other two, and the main part is a detailed description of Mulian's travel through the various departments of hell in search of his mother.

In *Baojuan of Three Rebirths* and *Precious Account of Mulian*, there is no division into small narrative units (sections). This feature is typical of *baojuan* of the late period and differentiates them from texts of the middle period. In both *Baojuan of Three Rebirths* and *Precious Account of Mulian*, however, there is a regular pattern in the episodes dealing with Mulian's journey in the underworld. In *Baojuan of Three Rebirths* the entire journey is divided into twenty-four episodes that look very similar. Every episode begins with a description of a special compartment of hell where Mulian sees the suffering of sinners and the functioning of its bureaucratic mechanism.[24] These compartments are the Pass of Demons, the Tower of the Mirror of Sins (or Karmascope), the Mountain of Broken Money, the Pavilion of Stripping Clothes, the Pool of Cold Ice, the Mountain of Sacred Chicken, the Place of Transformation into Cattle, the Cauldron of [Boiling] Oil, the Pool of Blood and Filth, the Mountain of Slippery Oil, the Tower of Looking at [One's] Native Place, the City of [Those] Driven to Death, the Hell of Saws, the Hell of Cutting Out Intestines, the Mountain of Knives, the Hell of Iron Presses, the Village of Fury Dogs, the Hell of Grinding in Mortars, the Hell of Burning on Pillars, the Hell of Millstones, the Estate of Auntie Meng (Meng Po Zhuang), the Bridge of Irreparability (Naihe Qiao), the Wheel of Rebirths, and Avīci Hell (City Enclosed in Iron, Tiewei Cheng). As Mulian passes through the stages of hell, he asks the demon-guard about the function of each place. The guard answers Mulian in the form of eight lines of seven-character verse (*gāthā*), describing the sins for which the souls received a certain kind of retribution. Two later elements of the pattern do not occur in every episode but also are quite frequent: (1) a verse pronounced by Mulian with sighs on the destiny of sinners and the moral injunctions for the people of the earthly world and (2)

Mulian's inquiry about his mother's fate and another verse describing Mulian's sorrow.

The narrative line in *Precious Account of Mulian* is based on another principle: hell is structured around Ten Courts, nine of which Mulian passes through, and he talks with each of the kings of hell.[25] Accordingly, each narrative episode includes prose and ten-character verse parts about each of the courts. Thus the popular concept of the Ten Courts of hell seems to be treated differently in *Baojuan of Three Rebirths* and *Precious Account of Mulian*. Nevertheless, the regular structure of episodes containing the description of hell is a common feature in both texts. On the one hand, it presents a continuation of the specific features of form in the texts of the middle period; on the other, it is certainly connected with the traditional concepts of the departments of hell (appearing on both the textual and pictorial levels).

Introductory and Concluding Verses

Baojuan of Three Rebirths and *Precious Account of Mulian* both have introductory and concluding verses, though they are not as elaborate as in the texts from the fourteenth and seventeenth centuries. Their introductory poems deal with the ideological setting of the narration but do not have much to do with the story line. *Baojuan of Three Rebirths* starts with eight lines of seven-character verse:

> Light and shadow—as you only bend your fingers[26]—fly like a thrown shuttle;
> As long as your killing mind does not die, what are your thoughts about?
> This world of dust with its lure in the end turns into an illusion—
> Make sure to carefully polish this mysterious secret!
> Never say that Our Buddha is far under the Western Heaven;[27]
> If you want to see the Western Heaven it is right before your eyes.
> If you ask for the road the distance is a hundred thousand miles—
> And your desire to get it by merits accomplished is like clouds and smoke.[28]

The verse talks about the main ideas underlying the narrative: all phenomena of the earthly world are perishable and illusory. It is not necessary to make a pilgrimage to see the Buddha; we only need to realize our potential for enlightenment. These ideas, as well as the metaphors used to express them, are in accord with the popular understanding of Buddhist doctrine and the ideas of the Chan school in particular.

At the same time, a hint on the full prohibition of killing as a religious precept, implying strict vegetarianism, that is the essence of the moralistic meaning of the story, appears here as well.

The first verse in *Baojuan of Three Rebirths* is followed by a *gāthā* on opening the sūtra. Although it is not labeled with this term in the text, it is similar in vocabulary and meter to the type of verses in *baojuan* of the early and middle periods. It reads:

> I am raising high in my hands a stick of true incense,
> The teacher ascends the platform, preaches the Law, and opens the sūtra.
> All men and women in this hall, please listen with the quiet thoughts.
> Fortune will come, your years extend, and there will be no disasters![29]

Precious Account of Mulian also opens with an introductory verse, but just one in this case. It is a lyric (*ci*) with the tune of "Moon above the Western river" (Xijiang yue diao):

> In this world good and evil produce two kinds of retribution.
> If you look at this—there will be no distortion.
> Even in the dark room you will not be ashamed by your blanket and shadow.[30]
> Attentively study [this rule]!
> Deities observe you constantly.
> If you commit sins, you will suffer a lot from evil retribution!
> If you gather virtues, you will stand in the rank of immortals!
> Retribution is always clear—whether in the distance or nearby,
> Not a few fail to recognize even half a point of this![31]

In general, this poetic introduction corresponds to the first verse of *Baojuan of Three Rebirths*.

The verses used in the introduction of these two late *baojuan* about Mulian basically fall into two categories: the first one belongs to the type of *gāthās* on opening the sūtra or hymns on burning incense (second verse from *Baojuan of Three Rebirths*). They are very technical and mark the beginning of recitation or opening of the performance arena. The *gāthā* on opening the sūtra seems to be a standard element in the texts of late *baojuan*. It repeats, with the modification of some lines, in the majority of texts.[32] In the modern traditions of *baojuan* performance in Hexi and Jiangsu, similar verses are included.[33]

The second type presents some ideological background to the text. Just as with verses of the first category, however, they are also quite uniform and are not connected specifically with the contents of each individual text. In the case of *Baojuan of Three Rebirths*, both types of verses are present; in the published version of *Precious Account of Mulian*, however, only the verse of the second type is used. As we have seen in the previous chapters, *gāthās* on opening the sūtra and hymns on burning incense as well as the verses and arias of ideological setting appeared in early *baojuan* and were used continuously in the middle period. Thus the introductory parts of late *baojuan* continued the tradition of early examples of the genre.

Concluding verses in both *Baojuan of Three Rebirths* and *Precious Account of Mulian* reiterate the results of Mulian's deeds and underscore the religious lessons of both texts. They are longer and more varied compared to the introductory verses in the same texts. For example, the concluding part of *Baojuan of Three Rebirths* consists of verses of different meters: at first a seven-character verse in forty-two lines, then six lines of five-character verse and four lines of seven-character verse, ending with the invocation of bodhisattva-mahāsattva, transferring to the Land of the Ultimate Joy (or Pure Land).[34] Concluding verses of both texts promise religious salvation for those who follow the propagated doctrines and wish good fortune to the members of audience. Therefore, in these verses, there is a continuation of the transfer of merit and gratitude rituals used in the *baojuan* of the early and middle periods.

At the same time, the introductory and concluding parts in *baojuan* of the nineteenth century are considerably simplified compared to the texts of the sixteenth to seventeenth century. At first glance, this tendency can be explained by the fact that the ritual setting common for the early *baojuan* weakened in the nineteenth and twentieth centuries, especially when the published texts of *baojuan* became the subjects of amateur performance and individual reading. Printed texts, however, do not necessarily reflect the tendency to simplify the accompanying rituals in the real practice of the contemporary *baojuan* performance.

A modern performance of the similar *baojuan* texts dealing with Mulian in southern Jiangsu (Jingjiang and Changshu) is helpful in clarifying this point. First, in these places, *baojuan* texts about Mulian are performed together with other texts of both ritual and narrative quality (see the prologue). Second, *baojuan* performances there always start and end with rituals that have the main function of inviting deities to descend to the meeting and sending them off; special texts of prayers are sung in conjunction with them. Special introductory and concluding ritual verses are also sung by the performers at the beginning of *baojuan* about Mulian in both Jingjiang and Changshu traditions.[35] There are similar terms and practices mentioned in *baojuan* texts of the sixteenth to seventeenth century. Thus printed texts of late *baojuan* do not represent in full measure the establishment of the performance arena (in Foley's theory of "word-power"). Many elements of this belong to the oral sphere of *baojuan* performance, and printed texts reflect only a small part of the actual performance.

Verses

Verses in *Baojuan of Three Rebirths* and *Precious Account of Mulian* are used to repeat the contents of the previous prose section as well as introduce new facts, just like *baojuan* of the seventeenth century discussed in the preceding chapters. They also reflect the emphasis on the direct speech of characters, which is often found in the late *baojuan*. The performance of *baojuan* in the late nineteenth to early twentieth century often involved dividing the text into roles, which were sometimes even marked in the written texts.[36] The performer imitated the voices of his characters, as happens in many other genres of storytelling in China.[37] This division of roles represents the dramatization of *baojuan*, which is an important sign of its performative mode (or register in Foley's theory of "word-power"). Usually there is no indication of role division in the texts of *Baojuan of Three Rebirths* and *Precious Account of Mulian*. It certainly existed, however, in text recitation, as demonstrated by performances of similar texts in Jiangsu. Here again we encounter an element of the register of the oral text (in terms of Foley's theory) that is lost in the written transcription.

It is important to note here that *Baojuan of Three Rebirths* uses many different forms of verse. There are seven-, five-, four-, and ten-character verses as well as several arias. Thus this text does not fit into the standard characterization of late *baojuan* by earlier scholars who regarded them as works with less variety of verse meters compared with *baojuan* of the middle period.[38] Nevertheless, in *Baojuan of Three Rebirths* one can find the predominance of seven- and ten-character meters that was noted as standard for the late *baojuan*. There are altogether ninety-two seven-character verses and eight ten-character verses in this text. By contrast, four- and five-character verses (as well as a seven-character antithetical couplet [*duilian*]) appear in the text only once each.

The verses with the seven-character meter usually are called *gāthās* in the *Baojuan of Three Rebirths*. In the second and third volumes of the text, however, virtually the same kind of verse is referred to as either *shi* or lyrics (*ci*).[39] This proves that, on the popular level, there was not much distinction in meter between religious Buddhist poetry and classical forms of verse. As in the case with the seven-character verses in the middle-period *baojuan*, the so-called *gāthās* in *Baojuan of Three Rebirths* absorbed some rules of classical *shi* poetry. Nevertheless, the seven-character meter poetry there is not restricted by as many rules as the new-style *shi* poetry (the same as in the texts of the middle period). For example, inaccuracy and even irregularity in rhymes are common.[40] Compared with *Baojuan of Three Rebirths*, *Precious Account of Mulian* has less variety of verse meters. The most often used meters are ten-character and seven-character. Unlike *Baojuan of Three Rebirths*, ten-character verses predominate in the text of *Precious Account of Mulian*. Many characteristics of meter and rhyme in these two types of verses are similar in these two *baojuan* texts, however.[41]

The material of *Baojuan of Three Rebirths* and *Precious Account of Mulian* demonstrates that arias and similar sung passages continued to be used in the late *baojuan* texts. Although scholars have argued that there is less variety of arias used in the late *baojuan* compared with the early ones, even claiming that the only aria form widely used in the late texts is "Crying during five [night] watches" (Ku wu geng),[42] this statement is not correct with regard to the texts discussed here; in *Baojuan of Three Rebirths* several arias appear, although their names usually are not marked. These are traditional "Crying during five [night] watches" and "Repaying ten mercies" (Bao shi en), two Daoist arias (*daoqing*), and one aria of unknown tune.[43]

The first two arias are recognizable immediately because of their standard structure as reflected in their names. These arias are divided into couplets, the numbers of which correspond to the names of the arias (with some additional couplets). For example, in "Crying during five [night] watches" each couplet starts with the number of the watch (or mercy, respectively): "in the first watch," "in the second watch," and so forth.[44] Both arias seem to be connected with the old forms of folk songs that already existed during the Tang dynasty. Records of tunes with a similar structure were discovered among the Dunhuang manuscripts.[45] At the same time, the scheme of the "Crying during five [night] watches" aria does not correspond to that given in the *Register of Arias of Kangxi*. The aria name "Repaying ten mercies" does not appear in *Register of Arias of Kangxi* at all. Both facts indicate that these two arias (at least in their form in *baojuan*) stood outside the classical tradition of the musical culture of the arias and apparently were sung with the use of folk melodies. "Crying during five [night] watches" is sung with the use of local melodies in the performance of *Baojuan of Mulian* and *Baojuan of the Blood Pond* in the Changshu and Jingjiang areas.[46] The inclusion of arias of this kind in the text of *Baojuan of Three Rebirths* is certainly proof of the text's connection with the tradition of folk music.

Another form of popular singing included in *Baojuan of Three Rebirths* is *daoqing* (lit. "Daoist tunes"). In *Baojuan of Three Rebirths*, *daoqing* tunes are sung by an old mother and a girl, in fact, the transformed Bodhisattva Guanyin and her attendant, who try to seduce Mulian during his journey to the Western Heaven.[47] *Daoqing* apparently originated in songs performed by wandering Daoist priests. These tunes emerged around the time of the Tang dynasty and constituted a tradition similar to that of *bianwen* and *baojuan*, the difference being that *daoqing* had primarily a Daoist background.[48] *Daoqing* had both singing and storytelling forms and a long tradition of written derivatives; some literati imitated their form. The meter and rhyme schemes of the *daoqing* pieces in *Baojuan of Three Rebirths* correspond to those of ten *daoqing* compiled by Zheng Xie (assumed name Zheng Banqiao, 1693–1765), a scholar from Jiangsu.[49] Although the *daoqing* by Zheng Xie are obviously the product of the literati culture, Chen Ruheng noted that they were quite close to folk music. Imitations of *daoqing* by Zheng Xie were very popular in China among commoners and professional storytellers.[50] The similarity between *daoqing* by Zheng Xie and those included in the *Baojuan of Three Rebirths* shows that the author/editor of *Baojuan* reproduced the standard pattern of the *daoqing*-aria genre.

The musical aspect of *Precious Account of Mulian* appears to be less varied than that of *Baojuan of Three Rebirths*. In this text there is also one lyric with the indication of its motif, "Moon above the Western river." This lyric form appeared quite early in the history of Chinese literature and was already popular during the Song dynasty. The melody with the same name also is occasionally used in *baojuan* of the sixteenth to seventeenth century. The meter of this lyric in *Precious Account of Mulian* is very close to that of classical examples.[51] The lyric was sung to a certain melody that still is preserved in the *baojuan* performances in Hexi, which inherited several aria tunes from the sixteenth and seventeenth centuries.⁵²

Therefore, both *Baojuan of Three Rebirths* and *Precious Account of Mulian* were connected with the culture of popular music, a feature noted in the analysis of the form of *baojuan* texts of the early and middle periods. The musical forms in late *baojuan* were closer to folk music than the arias in the early ones, which were modeled after the examples held in high esteem by literati circles. Although there is less variety of aria names than in the texts of the sixteenth to seventeenth century, these musical pieces continued to play an important role in the performance register of *baojuan* of the late period.

Language

In the language of *Baojuan of Three Rebirths* and *Precious Account of Mulian*, the mixture of classical and colloquial elements in the texts of the early and middle periods continued. Although *Precious Account of Mulian* displays a simplicity of language and lack of literary allusions (common in the texts of higher status),⁵³ several references to classics are evident, for example, "Fair, fair, cry the ospreys" (Guan ju, the name of the first song of the *Book of Songs*, ca. eleventh to seventh century BCE) and the famous phrase from the *Analects* (ca. fourth to third century BCE), ascribed to Confucius: "While your parents are alive, do not travel far."⁵⁴

Baojuan of Three Rebirths contains even more classical quotations and allusions. For example, in the argument on fasting between Ms. Liu and her brother Liu Jia, both use quotations from *Meng Zi* (Mencius), the classic ascribed to the Confucian philosopher Meng Ke (ca. late fourth to early third century BCE), to substantiate their views.⁵⁵ In this way, the author, using the words of his character, tries to reconcile the Confucian notion of benevolence (*ren*) with the Buddhist precept of nonviolence. It is no wonder that most of the citations come from *Meng Zi*, as it was one of the books with which traditional primary education started. There are more allusions to high literary tradition in *Baojuan of Three Rebirths*, which can be traced to the classical texts.⁵⁶

On the one hand, the appearance of classic quotations and references in *baojuan* texts can be explained by the influence of the drama about Mulian.⁵⁷ In its standard form, edited by literati, this drama belongs to the higher level of entertaining literature and thus possesses a more refined style than most *baojuan*. On the other hand, many expressions and figures were subjects of popular sayings, songs, and prints disseminated at many levels of society, so they naturally linked *baojuan* to the folk culture. Occasional historical and literary references substituted the stories from the Buddhist scriptures seen in *baojuan* of the seventeenth century. This is a sign of the further immersion of *baojuan* genre into the popular culture of China during its late period of development.

The language of late *baojuan* about Mulian contains a number of formulas. The most conspicuous, as in the case of the seventeenth-century texts, are prose- and verse-introductory formulas. To mark the turning point in the narrative, the authors/editors of both texts employ the formula of "[Let us] not talk about . . . , we shall tell [now] about" (*bu ti, que [dan] shuo*): for example, "[Let us] not narrate how Mulian was searching for his mother, we shall tell [now] about Bodhisattva Guanshiyin in the Grove of Purple Bamboo in the Southern Sea" in *Baojuan of Three Rebirths*.[58] In both texts, there are variations of this standard introduction that create the so-called rhetoricized register imitating that of oral storytelling. The verse-introductory formulas in *Baojuan of Three Rebirths* and *Precious Account of Mulian* are not as uniform as the prose-introductory ones. In *Baojuan of Three Rebirths*, the most common formula is "There is the *gāthā* to prove this; listen to what I shall say" (*you ji wei zheng, ting wo daolai*). In *Precious Account of Mulian*, verse-introductory formulas usually consist only of the variations of the second part of the formula most common in *Baojuan of Three Rebirths*: "Listen to what I shall say [pronounce, etc.]."[59] As in the case of the texts of the seventeenth century, the function of formulas in *Baojuan of Three Rebirths* and *Precious Account of Mulian* is not limited to the introduction of prose and verse passages. Formulaic expressions often are used to describe the emotions, actions, scenery, and other details. Many set expressions pertaining to the subject of the story can be traced to the early texts dealing with the story of Mulian, including the earlier *baojuan*.

The special features of the form of both *Baojuan of Three Rebirths* and *Precious Account of Mulian* demonstrate that both texts were connected closely with the local popular culture. Commoners certainly were the targeted audience, and both texts absorbed or imitated (considering the supposed editing by literati) some elements of folk (oral) literature. In comparison with *baojuan* about Mulian from the seventeenth century, the continuity of tradition in *Baojuan* of *Three Rebirths* and *Precious Account of Mulian* in terms of use of similar verse forms, standard introductory and concluding verses, colloquial language, and formulas is obvious. The display of images during the performance, discussed in the next chapter, also is similar to the pictorial entourage of the texts of the earlier period. At the same time, there are notable changes in the register and performative context of these texts, such as the disappearance of the division of the narration in the standard-patterned sections, simplification of the recorded elements of ritual setting, traces of the dramatization of the performance (division into roles), decrease in the variety of verse meters and the music of sung passages, arias approaching folk music culture, inclusion of metaphors and allusions widespread in the mainstream literary tradition, and traces of the influence of local language and culture. These changes more likely represent the evolution rather than the sudden transformation of the genre in terms of its formal characteristics; these paralleled the changes in the presentation and perception of the story line shared by the *baojuan* texts discussed here.

SPECIAL FEATURES OF THE STORY LINE

Both *Baojuan of Three Rebirths* and *Precious Account of Mulian* are examples of the complexly developed form of the Mulian story compared with *Baojuan of Maudgalyāyana* of the fourteenth century and later texts of the seventeenth century, *Dizang baojuan* and *Baojuan of Benefiting Living Beings*. The development of the core story of Mulian with the addition of new episodes is different in the two groups of *baojuan*, dating to the seventeenth and nineteenth centuries. While in *Dizang baojuan* and *Baojuan of Benefiting Living Beings* the episode of Mulian rescuing his mother is included in the stories of sectarian preaching and salvation, *Baojuan of Three Rebirths* and *Precious Account of Mulian* are focused on the events leading up to and the future development of the story itself.

In addition, *baojuan* texts of the nineteenth century represent a new way of interaction between drama and prosimetric literature on the subject of Mulian. We already have noted several common episodes in *baojuan* of the sixteenth to seventeenth century (*Baojuan of Maudgalyāyana-2, Dizang baojuan*, and *Baojuan of Benefiting Living Beings*) and the Mulian drama, but both *Baojuan of Three Rebirths* and *Precious Account of Mulian* demonstrate a much closer connection with Mulian dramas than do the earlier texts. Chinese and Western scholars of *baojuan* have long noticed this quality of the texts and unanimously interpreted it as the influence of drama on *baojuan*, such as the influence of Zheng Zhizhen's recension of drama on *Baojuan of Three Rebirths* and the interchange of content between *Precious Account of Mulian* and the Mulian drama, including its local recensions.[60]

Indeed, there is a close similarity between the development of the main story line of Mulian rescuing his mother from hell in *Baojuan of Three Rebirths* and *Precious Account of Mulian* on the one hand and Zheng Zhizhen's recension of the drama on the other. There are many episodes common to *Baojuan of Three Rebirths*, *Precious Account of Mulian*, and *Drama Exhorting Goodness* not present in *baojuan* of the fourteenth and seventeenth centuries (*Baojuan of Maudgalyāyana*, *Dizang baojuan*, and *Baojuan of Benefiting Living Beings*). These include Ms. Liu taking a vow to keep the fast together with Fu Xiang; the ascension of Fu Xiang on the crane to heaven after his religious merits are completed; Mulian's uncle on the maternal side, Liu Jia, persuading Ms. Liu to break the fast while her son is on a business trip; the sudden death of Ms. Liu at the moment when she takes a false oath of being innocent in the inner garden; the extended description of Mulian's journey to the West in search of Buddha's help; and the trick with transformations performed by Bodhisattva Guanyin and her attendant Sudhana (Shancai) when they turn into an old mother and a daughter to seduce Mulian to stay at their home as a son-in-law rather than rescue his mother. *Precious Account of Mulian*, furthermore, contains three more episodes in common with the drama that are absent from *Baojuan of Three Rebirths*: the capture of Mulian by the robbers on his return from his trade journey and their subsequent conversion by Bodhisattva Guanyin; the return home of Ms. Liu's soul after her death to ask Mulian for help; and the transformation of Ms. Liu into a dog before her final ascension to heaven.[61]

Both *baojuan*, however, especially *Baojuan of Three Rebirths*, present a concise version of the core story line. Because *Baojuan of Three Rebirths* is shorter than Zheng's recension of the drama, it omits some details that are developed in *Drama Exhorting Goodness*. Because Zheng's recension already was an abbreviated version of folk performances, *Baojuan of Three Rebirths* represents an even further abbreviation of the original performances. For example, the name of the servant Yili appears only once in *Baojuan of Three Rebirths* in connection with his report to Ms. Liu about Mulian's return.[62] In *Drama Exhorting Goodness*, however, Yili is a prominent character, as he embodies loyalty, one of the main moral values preached.[63] Therefore, it is clear that the audience/readers of the text were assumed to be familiar with this character, probably from a drama or another storytelling performance. This is an example of the communicative economy, in Foley's theory of "word-power": it refers to the metatext of the oral tradition. In *Precious Account of Mulian*, on the contrary, the origin of even minor characters is described in detail. This may serve as one of the signs of the connection with the local Mulian dramas that often are more detailed than Zheng's recension.

Furthermore, both *Baojuan of Three Rebirths* and *Precious Account of Mulian* obviously refer to the dramatic performances of the Mulian story in another episode where they address the "double burden" (*shuang tiao*) dilemma.[64] It is certainly borrowed from dramatic versions and describes how Mulian carries the spirit tablet of his mother (or her ashes in *Drama Exhorting Goodness*) and the sūtras on the ends of a pole. The scenes with "carrying a pole" are often performed in the course of full-fledged Mulian drama or as a part of funerary service in southern regions. This scene is noteworthy for the dramatic quality of expression of Mulian's problem: he does not know to which object he should give preference (and hence the aim).[65] This refers to scenic movement (changing ends of a pole) and certainly gives dramatic expression to the story of Mulian in *Baojuan of Three Rebirths*. In spite of the differences in length and details, it is significant that both *Baojuan of Three Rebirths* and *Precious Account of Mulian* relied on the previous knowledge/emotional expression of the audience, which should have been familiar with dramatic performances.

Prehistory of Mulian

Baojuan of Three Rebirths and *Precious Account of Mulian* include the so-called prehistory of Mulian and sequel of the Mulian plot systems (see chapter 2, "Dramatic Versions"). Both texts invoke a previous rebirth of Mulian and his next rebirth(s), and thus develop the story in both directions. The themes, however, are different. *Precious Account of Mulian* concentrates on the details of the life of four generations of the Fu family (Mulian's ancestors), and *Baojuan of Three Rebirths* presents in detail the next two rebirths of Mulian.

Therefore, both texts represent two characteristic tendencies in story development. As precursor and sequel to the Mulian story, they do not appear in Zheng's recension of the drama. These details of narrative vividly demonstrate the connection of both *baojuan* with more lengthy local variants of the Mulian drama.

Precious Account of Mulian tells the story of the Fu family, beginning with the great-grandfather of Mulian, Fu Tiandou, who served the Liang dynasty emperor Wu. Next comes the story of Mulian's grandfather, Fu Chong, and his father, Fu Xiang. This account of three generations of the Fu family proves the Sichuan origin of this text, which I have already suggested on the basis of linguistic evidence. Many details of the plot are the same in *Precious Account of Mulian* and the major "broad" versions of Sichuan drama: the "outline" and "forty-eight-volume" versions.[66] At the same time, the plot of both *Precious Account of Mulian* and the Sichuan dramas is very close to the drama *Fu Tiandou*, from Putian county in Fujian.[67] Chinese scholars regard the Putian version of the Mulian drama as one of the earliest extant multiple acts dramas on this subject. They consider the similar versions of Mulian's prehistory (in several places in southern China) to be the traces of the legacy of the original *nanxi* of Mulian. According to their theory, the original was disseminated from southeastern China to other regions.[68] In this case, the similarity between the contents of the Putian and Sichuan dramas is logical. *Precious Account of Mulian*, therefore, represents a continuation of the early development of the Mulian plot in dramatic versions.

We can still assume, however, that *Precious Account of Mulian* was modeled after Sichuan folk drama in particular. There are some minor details that link this *baojuan* text and local Sichuan drama. For example, both texts put special emphasis on the episode of the marriage of Mulian's mother, Liu Siniang. From oral tradition, as well as from the written sources, it is known that it was performed in detail in Sichuan, including the moving of the bridal palanquin enacted in the course of the performance.[69] *Precious Account of Mulian* also describes this episode in detail.[70]

In *Precious Account of Mulian*, the private life of the Fu family is closely connected with historical events at the end of the Liang dynasty. These events are presented in a fantastic way; for example, the death of Emperor Wu is explained as the result of karmic retribution. According to this *baojuan*, Emperor Wu was a woodcutter in his previous rebirth and obtained good karma by sheltering a statue of Buddha in a dilapidated temple; thus he became emperor in the next life. Because once as a woodcutter he killed many monkeys, in his rebirth as the emperor, he was killed by the rebellious general Hou Jing 侯景 (pronounced similarly as *houjing* 猴精 "monkey spirit"). Mulian's great-grandfather, Fu Tiandou, trying to help the emperor by bringing a supply of food to the besieged city, was killed by rebels.[71] *Precious Account of Mulian* also includes the story of Bodhidharma (Damo), who is proclaimed the teacher of the Great Way of Former Heaven and came to southern China in an unsuccessful attempt to convert and presumably rescue Emperor Wu.[72]

The inclusion of the story of Emperor Wu in *Precious Account of Mulian* also should be connected with local dramas. Several local variants of the Mulian drama in southern China include a story about Emperor Wu.[73] Most dramas focus, however, on the episode of Emperor Wu rescuing his concubine Ms. Xi from a bad rebirth. This story forms an obvious parallel with the later story of Mulian and his mother. On the other hand, this story of Emperor Wu and Ms. Xi is not elaborated in detail either in *Drama Exhorting Goodness* or in *Precious Account of Mulian*. The mention of Emperor Wu in *Precious Account of Mulian* is another sign of the intertextual connection of *baojuan* and local drama. It also links the Mulian story with Chinese historical lore. This specific feature is common for the two late *baojuan* about Mulian analyzed here, as *Baojuan of Three Rebirths* contains a developed episode where Huang Chao is introduced as Mulian's rebirth.

Baojuan of Three Rebirths presents a completely different version of the story preceding the birth of Mulian. It says that a monk, who came to the house of the childless pious layman, Fu Xiang, was the previous reincarnation of Fu Xiang's son, Fu Luobo (Mulian). This monk asked for a turnip as alms and, immediately upon eating it, died in front of the door of Fu Xiang's house. At night, he appeared in Fu Xiang's dream and informed him that he was going to reward Fu Xiang by giving him a son. Fu Xiang then gave the name Turnip (Luobo) to his just-born son. Several local dramas in different areas used the pun on Mulian's secular name to describe his miraculous birth. In most versions, however, Ms. Liu became pregnant after she ate a miraculous turnip.[74]

The episode with the monk who ate the turnip also appears in one of the recensions of local Shaoxing drama, the "old libretto" of *Records of Rescuing Mother* (Jiu mu ji).[75] This drama presents a broader version of this variant of Mulian's prehistory. At first, Fu Xiang was a cruel landlord; in order to punish him, the Jade Emperor sent two "destroying wealth stars," who were reincarnated as his sons Jinge and Yinge, and did everything to impoverish the Fu family.[76] Later, Fu Xiang, realizing his mistakes, reproached his sons, burned the fake scale with which they had cheated people, and turned to goodness. In order to reward him, the Jade Emperor took back the lives of Fu Xiang's sons, and Bodhisattva Guanyin ordered the Star of Joy and Truth (Xizhen Xing) to be reborn as another son of Fu Xiang, the future Mulian. The star deity first took the form of the monk who came to the house of Fu Xiang to ask for alms. Then the monk received the turnip that renters had brought to Fu Xiang. Upon eating the turnip, the monk drowned himself in a pond and became reincarnated as Fu Xiang's son.[77] Although some details of the two accounts in Shaoxing drama and *Baojuan* are different, many are the same. Therefore, *Baojuan of Three Rebirths* may have received influence from the local drama of Shaoxing or some adjacent areas. This matches perfectly with the details of the main dissemination of this text, both in written and oral forms, in modern Jiangsu and Zhejiang.

Future Rebirths of Mulian

Although the influence of dramatic discourse was very important in both *Baojuan of Three Rebirths* and *Precious Account of Mulian*, both texts preserve a certain degree of independence from the dramatic scripts. This independence first reveals itself in the close following of the basic story line. In both texts, additional episodes are tightly connected with the main story line, unlike in several other *baojuan* texts of roughly the same period, such as *Complete Version of [Bao]juan of Mulian* (Mulian juan quanji, first printing in 1877) (appendix 2, XIV) and the local Shaoxing recension of *Baojuan of Mulian* that represents a rewriting of a drama script (manuscript of ca. early twentieth century, appendix 2, V).[78]

In addition, the episodes of the next rebirth(s) of Mulian in *Baojuan of Three Rebirths* and *Precious Account of Mulian* are different from the concluding parts of the majority of drama scripts on Mulian, which usually do not contain these details. According to *Baojuan of Three Rebirths*, when Mulian opened the gates of Avīci hell, many souls imprisoned there escaped. In order to gather souls, Mulian had to be reborn twice as the leader of the rebellion, Huang Chao, and the butcher, He Yin. During his first rebirth, Mulian fulfilled the task of returning the souls who received rebirth in human form by killing eight million people. During the second rebirth, Mulian killed the same number of pigs and sheep. The tale of Huang Chao relates the Mulian story to Chinese historical lore.[79] The tale of the butcher, He Yin, a native of Chang'an (modern Xi'an, the capital of the Tang dynasty), who was converted by Bodhisattva Guanyin and succeeded in self-cultivation, brings the whole story closer to the everyday life of common folk—the supposed audience of *baojuan*.

The rebirth of Mulian as Huang Chao also appears in *Precious Account of Mulian*. Unlike the detailed account of his rebellion in *Baojuan of Three Rebirths*, however, *Precious Account of Mulian* relates the tale in several sentences: in order to gather eight million hungry ghosts who fled from hell, Mulian was ordered to be reborn as Huang Chao.[80] This text does not provide any significant details. Though there are local drama scripts that also portray Huang Chao as Mulian's rebirth, they are quite recent materials that postdate the editions of *Baojuan of Three Rebirths*.[81] Chinese scholars who have studied local dramas of Mulian usually interpret this shared episode as the influence of *Baojuan of Three Rebirths* on these dramas, although evidence is scant.[82]

CONCLUSION

Baojuan of Three Rebirths and *Precious Account of Mulian* represent late developed versions of the Mulian story, closely related to the local Mulian dramas of the central parts of China. The comparison of the form and contents of both late texts with *baojuan* of the middle period (*Dizang baojuan* and *Baojuan of Benefiting Living Beings*) demonstrates the simplification of the textual structure and musical aspect together with the strengthening of the narrative elements in their contents: both contain full-fledged stories of Mulian's life and deeds, including his own rebirths as well as his family genealogy (the second primarily applies to *Precious Account of Mulian*). The musical and ritual aspects, though much changed in comparison with *baojuan* of the seventeenth century, still play very important roles in the performance orientation of these texts. The latter is proved by the evidence of modern performances of similar versions of these *baojuan* in Jiangsu and Gansu.

The proximity of the story lines of *Baojuan of Three Rebirths* and *Precious Account of Mulian* with two different local versions of Mulian drama, namely Sichuan and Shaoxing, proves the connection of both texts to specific local culture and literature. Although in modern *baojuan* performances in Jiangsu *baojuan* about Mulian (very close to *Baojuan of Three Rebirths*) occupy a place similar to short dramatic scenes in the funerary rituals of southern China, in terms of content, they interacted with the multiple-act drama scripts that also had the ritual functions of exorcising malicious spirits and praying for a community's welfare.

Interaction with local dramas points to the connection of both *baojuan* with oral literature. The analyzed scripts of local dramas (if ever written down) were materials of theater groups discovered or reconstructed by modern scholars. These specific drama versions certainly were known primarily from performances. It is logical to suppose that authors/editors of *baojuan* borrowed the correspondent material from local oral literature. My analysis of the form of both texts also demonstrates the connection with the culture of commoners, seen in their language, musical aspect, and performance register. The primary target audience of these texts certainly was illiterate commoners; the simple language, popular tunes, dramatized scenes, and references to theatrical performances assisted their comprehension of the story. At the same time, *Baojuan of Three Rebirths* and *Precious Account of Mulian* possess a degree of independence from drama scripts that is most apparent in the religious ideology of these texts.

CHAPTER 7

The Religious and Performative Context of the Late *Baojuan* about Mulian

Precious Account of Mulian and *Baojuan of Three Rebirths* are notable for their clearly pronounced religious syncretism. For example, the author/editor of *Baojuan of Three Rebirths* urges the audience to read and worship the scriptures of all Three Teachings—Buddhism, Confucianism, and Daoism—advocating the syncretism of the major religious traditions of China. The text says that one should study the "great way of all-pervading unity, revealed by the Confucian school," as well as "the wise pronouncements of Daoists."[1] The first expression in this line is strikingly close to the name of the famous sect Way of Pervasive Unity (Yiguandao). This religion, however, certainly was formed later than the first known edition of *Baojuan of Three Rebirths* was printed.[2] Therefore, it likely refers to the famous expression in the *Analects* ascribed to Confucius: "My doctrine is that of an all-pervading unity"; this often appears out of sectarian context as well but was used as one of central concepts by the founder of Yiguandao.[3] Therefore *Baojuan of Three Rebirths* cannot be directly associated with this new religion.

Nevertheless, both *Precious Account of Mulian* and *Baojuan of Three Rebirths* are related to the sectarian teachings of the second half of the nineteenth century. At first glance, it seems that the instructions of both texts represent a combination of popularly interpreted Buddhist and Confucian ethics. Looking closely, however, one can find many ideas and terms of the sects. In both texts, the story of Mulian and the threat of hell were employed by the religious communities that stood outside of officially accepted religious institutions.

RELIGIOUS IDEAS IN TWO LATE *BAOJUAN*

Baojuan of Three Rebirths

In the case of *Baojuan of Three Rebirths*, the particular religious community with which this text was associated is unknown, but one certainly existed. Its goals and methods are pronounced mainly in the third volume of text, dedicated to the rebirth of Mulian as the butcher He Yin. Concluding verses of *Baojuan of Three Rebirths* promise the following afterlife reward for the people who follow the proper teaching:

> Stripped of your mortal name, you will be in the ranks of immortals;
> Registered to the Western Heaven, you will not be listed on earth.
> After they greet you beyond the heaven of Thirty-three,
> You will join the World-Honored One at the Dragon-Flower Assembly on the Numinous Mountain.[4]

The notions and places mentioned in this passage, such as "the ranks of immortals" (*xianji*), "registration" (*gua bang*) in paradise, and Dragon-Flower Assembly on the Numinous Mountain, were very important in the sectarian teachings of the sixteenth to nineteenth century and, as we have seen, made frequent appearances in *baojuan* of the seventeenth century dealing with the Mulian story.

Baojuan of Three Rebirths also mentions the supreme female deity, characteristic of Chinese sectarian movements from the sixteenth until the twentieth century. Another poem describes paradise in the following way:

> In the ranks of immortals and buddhas you will return to the Land of Ultimate Joy.[5]
> At the Dragon-Flower Assembly you will enjoy free and easy roaming,
> You will eat the fruit of immortals and drink the jade nectar,
> Never aging, eternal Queen-Mother will summon you there.[6]

The Queen-Mother is one of the female deities worshiped in different sectarian teachings. Here she probably is the combined image of the Unborn Mother, Queen Mother of the West, and Bodhisattva Guanyin. The last often appears in the text with the epithet "Old mother" and provides guidance for the protagonists.[7] As we have already observed in *baojuan* texts of the seventeenth century, these female deities often were conflated in the sectarian teachings. One can interpret this passage in connection with the expression "returning [to the true] home" (*gui jia*) that in the text is named as the ultimate goal of religious practice of this specific teaching.[8] It is certainly related to the old sectarian term "home of true emptiness," the abode of the Unborn Mother.

Baojuan of Three Rebirths presents details of the practices of the religious community that edited and disseminated it. There are direct admonitions included in the text and a description of the behavior of the "man of the Path" (*daoren*, i.e., righteous man) Wang Shan, who was the owner of the ritual paraphernalia store and a neighbor of He Yin.[9] Wang Shan, though, did not pass the test organized by Guanyin when he and He Yin followed the disguised Bodhisattva to the Western Heaven.[10] Despite his later apostasy, he can be regarded as an ideal practitioner of the teaching portrayed in *Baojuan of Three Rebirths*.

As for the religious prescriptions of *Baojuan of Three Rebirths*, first, the text urges followers to maintain vegetarianism and adhere to the principle of not harming any sentient beings. These principles are summarized in the concluding verses of *baojuan*:

> Just eat some pure and bland plants that bloom into flowers,
> Stop eating horsemeat or beef with the gamy smell of flesh.
> Whether these people are your friends or your relatives,
> Exhort them to be satisfied with their lot and recite the enlightening sūtras![11]

As an example of this, Wang Shan maintained a vegetarian diet from his youth, and every day he recited scriptures beginning in the early morning.[12] Maintaining a vegetarian diet is a common Buddhist practice, as it is connected with the principle of "not killing," one of the "five precepts" of Buddhism (the term also used in this text). However, in the mainstream tradition of Chinese Buddhism, vegetarianism, though desirable for monks and lay believers, was not a requirement for lay followers.[13] Wang Shan's vegetarianism, on the contrary, was especially severe; he even refused to drink a cup of tea offered by He Yin because the latter was a non-fasting person.[14]

Complete vegetarianism for laymen preached in *Baojuan of Three Rebirths* echoes the texts of sectarian teachings. However, participants of *baojuan* recitation in modern times in southern Jiangsu usually do not observe a vegetarian fast, even on the very day of the performance. On the contrary, meat offerings often are made during these assemblies. Their use is especially noteworthy in the case of funerary performances in the Changshu area that can include recitation of *Baojuan of Mulian*.¹⁵ Although they used modified recensions of *Baojuan of Three Rebirths*, clearly these communities did not adopt one of the practices propagated in it.

Second, the author/editor of *Baojuan of Three Rebirths* also advocated a community of lay believers. Its concluding verses proclaim that people should not abandon their original professions in order to get salvation.¹⁶ Thus so-called self-cultivation in *Baojuan of Three Rebirths* did not imply leaving family and society for monkhood. Furthermore, *Baojuan of Three Rebirths* encourages people to observe the civil laws (here called "law of officials" [*guanfa*]), which, considering the time of the composition of the text, meant imperial legislation. For example, the monk who converts He Yin (in fact, transformed Bodhisattva Guanyin) argues that one can follow both the Law of the Buddha and that of officials without any conflict. The explanation of what stands for the Law of the Buddha and the law of officials follows:

> You only have to keep to the fast, recite the name of the Buddha, and respect and revere Three Treasures. The father should be kind and the son should be filial; the older brother should be loving and the younger brother should be respectful; you have to live in harmony with your neighbors, and you have to be trustworthy in your contacts with friends; and you should not commit treachery, robbery, perversity, or adultery, or any other kind of evil and fraud.¹⁷

In this injunction, there is a clear mixture of Buddhist precepts with the popularly interpreted Confucian moral. The state (or official) moral law, as described here, is close to the *Sacred Edict* form that was adopted by sectarians in the seventeenth century.

Third, the transmission of the teaching represented in *Baojuan of Three Rebirths* supposedly took place through the work of religious teachers called monks in the text. These monks came to convert Fu Xiang to the true teaching; and a monk, the disguised Guanyin, converted He Yin and Wang Shan.¹⁸ It is doubtful that these wandering monks were indeed ordained clergy; they were likely sectarian teachers disguised as Buddhist monks. This situation is also in line with the historical reality of sectarian activities. In the organization of local sectarian communities, the direct teacher-disciple relationship had great significance.¹⁹ The author of *Baojuan of Three Rebirths* also stresses the importance of this contact through Mulian's explanation of the true teaching transmission to a hell guardian, who asks him for religious instruction. There the encounter with the teacher and acceptance of his religious guidance are crucial factors in the enlightenment and final salvation of the believer. Mulian says:

> When the enlightened teacher points [to the Path], the root of the Path sprouts.[20]
> When [you] penetrate Three Barriers, the Path opens its flowers.
> When you enlighten mind and see your nature, the Path forms its fruit.
> By each single movement and step, on this Path you return home.[21]

This short poem has rich religious meaning, presented with the clever use of similes and puns. It may point to one of the variants of inner elixir practice that continued to be employed by the sects in the nineteenth century. Such terms and phrases as "to point" (may refer to the opening of the Dark Barrier), Three Barriers (within the body), and "enlighten mind and see your nature" are occur frequently in sectarian writings. Some of them also have been used in seventeenth-century *baojuan* about Mulian. The sectarian term for returning home appears with a pun on the word *Path*, a universal metaphor for religious teaching.

Although this poem may have referred to the inner elixir practice as a part of the propagated special teaching, in another place, the author/editor of *Baojuan of Three Rebirths* severely criticizes the inner elixir practice. This passage describes practitioners of inner elixir as cheaters, "single monks and unattached priests who deluded people with their perverse way," who are sentenced to cruel punishment in hell. "They refined red lead as their greatest treasure and indulged in their lewd desires."[22] It is a clear reference to sectarian followers. The accusations that they were cheating people for money and being lewd are very similar to the usual government critique of heterodox teachings. Furthermore, like the author of *Baojuan of Three Rebirths*, at the beginning of the nineteenth century, government investigators employed the threat of hell, which was adopted by many sects, against sectarians themselves.[23]

Because *Baojuan of Three Rebirths* mentions inner elixir explicitly with negative connotations, the true attitude of the author/editor toward this technique remains puzzling. Also there remains the question of whether the community, which revered the text, actually practiced inner elixir. There can be different explanations for this dual attitude. Sectarians, with whom *Baojuan of Three Rebirths* was associated, may have intentionally concealed some aspects of their practice. The appearance of inner elixir terms, although vague, may have been an oversight or an intentional hint directed at initiates. The author/editor of the text certainly wished to represent his community as an orthodox one in terms of conformity to the state system and ideology. He could have adopted the government approach against deviant practices to present his teaching as officially accepted. Such a critique, however, was also a useful tool against competitors, teachers in other popular religious communities who here are called single monks and unattached priests.[24] We should recall the existence of inter-sect competition, which is revealed clearly in the *baojuan* of the sixteenth to seventeenth century. The material of *Baojuan of Three Rebirths* demonstrates that inter-sect competition found its expression in the late period *baojuan* about Mulian as well.

Fourth, along with the inner elixir technique, *Baojuan of Three Rebirths* criticizes some widespread mainstream religious practices. One is the burning of "otherworld money" (*mingqian*), imitation money burned in funeral rituals and believed to be transformed into the capital of the dead person in the other world. The critique of money burning is developed in the description of the Mountain of Torn Money in hell. According to a hell guardian's explanation, this mountain is formed of money that relatives had burned for their deceased in order to improve the soul's destiny in the otherworld. All this money, however, is "without any use." Only merits are useful in the underworld, otherwise "the poor would all perish, and the rich would escape."[25]

The image of the Mountain of Torn Money is certainly not an innovation in *Baojuan of Three Rebirths*. It appears, for example, in *Drama Exhorting Goodness* where it is formed from incompletely burned ritual money. In the drama, however, the Mountain of Torn Money exists along with the Golden and Silver Mountains, which consist of properly burned ritual money. Pious deceased receive this money for their expenses and ascend the Golden and Silver Mountains on their way to heaven.[26] This explanation encourages people to burn ritual money. In *Baojuan of Three Rebirths*, the Golden and Silver Mountains are not mentioned, which implies disapproval of the whole idea of burning money. This minor detail becomes very important in the interpretation of the sectarian affiliation of *Baojuan of Three Rebirths*. In modern ritual traditions in southern Jiangsu, on the contrary, burning of ritual money constitutes an important practice accompanying recitation of *baojuan* (including those about Mulian). This situation obviously contradicts the message in *Baojuan of Three Rebirths*.

Because of these minor and unclear details, it is hard to determine the sectarian affiliation of *Baojuan of Three Rebirths*. Nevertheless, the beliefs and practices advocated in this text are very similar to those of some modern Chinese sectarian movements. One is the Teaching of Dragon-Flower [Assembly] (Longhuajiao). This religion represents one of the later developments of the Teaching of Non-Interference (or Luo Teaching [Luojiao]). Together with other similar religions, the Teaching of Dragon-Flower is known commonly as the Teaching of Fast (Zhaijiao). In the late Qing period, it was active mainly in Fujian, and it still exists today in Taiwan.[27] By the nineteenth century several branches of the Teaching of Non-Interference included many messianic elements (Unborn Mother and Maitreya worship) as well as the religious practices of the inner elixir, apparently borrowed from other sectarian movements that originated in the sixteenth to seventeenth century.[28]

These religious movements, such as the Teaching of Dragon-Flower in particular, worship the Unborn Mother as the highest deity and preach sectarian millenarianism, and the main part of their practice is strict vegetarianism, hence the common name of modern branches of the Teaching of Non-Interference.[29] On the other hand, the followers of the Teaching of Dragon-Flower in Fujian and Taiwan have emphasized the Buddhist nature of their practices and also support Confucian ethics, so their organization may be interpreted as a Buddhist lay (vegetarian) movement. Nevertheless, it was a self-defined religion, which juxtaposed itself with other traditions. It had some particular practices, one of which is the refusal to burn ritual money.

Although the available data are insufficient for proving a connection between the Teaching of Dragon-Flower and *Baojuan of Three Rebirths*, many details are similar in the reconstructed worldview of the author/editor and target audience of *Baojuan of Three Rebirths* and the followers of the Teaching of Dragon-Flower: belief in the supreme female deity, terminology (the notion of the Dragon-Flower Assembly being crucial in both traditions), claim to be a Buddhist laymen community, acceptance of Confucian ethics, and accusation of money burning. *Baojuan of Three Rebirths* should have been affiliated with a religious community similar to the Teaching of Dragon-Flower within the broad spectrum of religions stemming from the Teaching of Non-Interference in southern China at the end of the Qing dynasty.

Furthermore, the historical evidence supports the connection between the local variants of *baojuan* about Mulian and this type of religion. For example, the traditions of *baojuan* performances in the Jingjiang and Changshu areas, which use the variants of *Baojuan of Three Rebirths*, were connected with the descendants of the Teaching of Non-Interference or the Great Vehicle.[30] In addition, the names of Patriarch Lü and Unborn Mother appear in the text of *Baojuan of the Blood Pond* from Jingjiang that was recorded by a local performer and published in a collection of Jingjiang *baojuan*.[31] This proves that this recension of *baojuan* about Mulian was formed under the influence of earlier scriptures related to a branch of the Teaching of Non-Interference (now irrevocably lost there). We can thus conclude that *Baojuan of Three Rebirths* had a certain sectarian affiliation even though its specific ideas were not realized in the modern *baojuan* performances in Jiangsu.

Precious Account of Mulian

Unlike *Baojuan of Three Rebirths*, *Precious Account of Mulian* clearly indicates the name of the religious community it was affiliated with: the Great Way of Former Heaven. This was an influential sect that formed around the middle of the nineteenth century and was apparently the important precursor of the famous Way of Pervasive Unity. It still exists in Taiwan, some areas of Fujian, and in the countries of Southeast Asia. The Great Way of Former Heaven probably represents the later development of the Teaching of Non-Interference, adopting the messianic elements of the Unborn Mother religions of the late imperial period.[32] *Precious Account of Mulian* says that the Great Way of Former Heaven was the religion preached by Bodhidharma in China (which obviously is a late sectarian legend) and adopted by Fu Xiang and later Mulian during their two successive pilgrimages to Hangzhou. Mulian receives this "secretly transmitted" teaching from the abbot of the Monastery of the Light of Wisdom (Huiguangsi) in Hangzhou.[33]

As we have seen, *baojuan* of the seventeenth century do not appear to be coherent and detailed representations of the essentials of the sectarian teachings with which they were affiliated; *Precious Account of Mulian* is even less so. Nevertheless, judging by scarce details, *Precious Account of Mulian* indeed represents the teaching of the Great Way of Former Heaven. In this text, Bodhidharma is called the thirty-second western patriarch; this corresponds to the legendary line of teaching transmission adopted by this religion.[34] The notion of the elects who form the religious community, called the original "seeds of Buddha's root" (*Fogen zhongzi*), is also present.³⁵ This idea continues the tradition of the sectarian teachings of the sixteenth to seventeenth century. The procedure of salvation explained in the episode of the transmission of the teaching to Mulian is also strikingly similar to that described in the sectarian texts of the seventeenth century. It includes submission of a report to the Venerable Mother and opening of the aperture of Emptiness of the Former Heaven.³⁶ The second is a type of initiation technique, known as the opening of the Dark Barrier (Xuanguan) in the traditions of the Great Way of Former Heaven and the Way of Persuasive Unity. A believer may become an immortal/Buddha if his soul leaves the body from the space between the eyes (Dark Barrier). The Dark Barrier is dotted by the teacher at the time of initiation.³⁷

Furthermore, there are constant references to self-cultivation (*xiulian*, *duanlian*), which included the inner elixir technique; the notion of "golden elixir" (*jindan*) also appears in the text several times. The same term was crucial in the scripture of the Great Way of Former Heaven, *Baojuan of the Golden Elixir and Nine-Petaled Lotus of the Imperial Ultimate Period* edited by Qingyang hermit Yinan Zi, who also edited *Precious Account of Mulian*. The injunction given to Mulian by the abbot of the Monastery of the Light of Wisdom in the form of a lyric "Moon above the Western river" also mentions several terms of the inner elixir, such as tiger and dragon, lovely girl and baby boy.³⁸ This passage has an important place in the story line as it forms the summary of the future experiences of Mulian, including his descent to hell, the liberation of his mother's soul, and the transformation of hell into the city of lotuses. Significantly, in this verse, Mulian's journey to the West is equated with the spiritual path to salvation, ending in the paradise-like realm called the Cloud mountain (city). Thus the story of Mulian is interpreted in the context of sectarian teaching, similar to *baojuan* of the seventeenth century. Just like *Dizang baojuan* and *Baojuan of Benefiting Living Beings*, *Precious Account of Mulian* presents inner elixir practice as the crucial condition of the success of Mulian's undertaking.

Nevertheless, the author/editor of *Precious Account of Mulian* also propagated ethical principles traditionally connected with Confucian teaching. These frequently are summarized under the terms of "five constants" (*wu chang*, or "five moral principles" [*wu lun*]), which usually designate five cardinal virtues (father's justice, mother's mercy, elder brother's friendliness, younger brother's respect, child's filiality;

or benevolence, justice, propriety, wisdom, and loyalty) and appeared in antiquity in the literature of the Confucian school. As in *Baojuan of Three Rebirths*, the author/editor of this text also insists on the necessity of adherence to the state law. This is an obvious attempt to represent the teaching preached in *Precious Account of Mulian* as legal although it may not have been so from the government's point of view. So far, the belief in the deity-progenitor Venerable Mother, the propagation of the inner elixir practice, the adherence to traditional ethics, and other religious ideas included in *Precious Account of Mulian* are in line with the outlook of the Great Way of Former Heaven.

Sectarian or Mainstream?

Both *Baojuan of Three Rebirths* and *Precious Account of Mulian* reveal that some part of late narrative *baojuan* continued to be associated with sectarian teachings. To a certain degree, my observations undermine the conclusions of several scholars about the crucial shift in the *baojuan* genre when the intended audience changed from the secretly organized religious community to the broad circle of folk believers.[39] On the other hand, the spread of specific sectarian beliefs and practices certainly occupies less space in the *baojuan* of the nineteenth century compared with those of the seventeenth century. This presumably enabled these and similar texts to be transmitted and performed outside the sectarian context in southern Jiangsu and Gansu.

Nevertheless, both *Baojuan of Three Rebirths* and *Precious Account of Mulian* contain many aspects of sectarian discourse (belief in the Mother-deity, community of the elects, cultivation by the means of inner elixir, vegetarianism, simile of cultivation and Mulian's spiritual journey, itinerant preachers, and inter-sect competition) and therefore continue the tradition of sectarian *baojuan* on the same subject. As in *Dizang baojuan* and *Baojuan of Benefiting Living Beings*, the authors/editors of the late *baojuan* employed not only the popular story of Mulian but also the cult of Bodhisattva Dizang in order to ensure the salvation of the followers as well as their ancestors from hell.

It is no wonder that sectarians continued to employ the story of Mulian in *baojuan* of the nineteenth century. It served as the perfect illustration of their precept of fasting and vegetarianism. We can see this characteristic of the ideological background of the late *baojuan* about Mulian if we compare them with the Mulian drama scripts.

Already in the sixteenth century in *Drama Exhorting Goodness* the emphasis shifted from the Buddhist prohibition of killing to the propagation of Confucian values.[40] In this drama, underworld functionaries explain to Ms. Liu that the essence of her sins is not consumption of meat per se but the breaking of the oath to adhere to a vegetarian diet as well as her false oath of innocence taken in the inner garden just before her terrible end.[41] This implied an insult to the heavenly deities as well as a violation of her husband's will and deceiving her son. The latter sin contravened the cardinal Confucian female virtue known as "three-fold obedience" (*san cong*), explained in the ancient classics.[42] Both aforementioned episodes had an important role in *Baojuan of Three Rebirths* and in *Precious Account of Mulian*, apparently serving as a link to the Mulian dramas. On the other hand, late *baojuan* texts about Mulian preserve the initial emphasis on Buddhist values, adopted as basic by sectarians. It is particularly evident in *Baojuan of Three Rebirths* where the call for vegetarianism constantly appears in connection with Ms. Liu, numerous episodes in hell, self-cultivation of Wang Shan, and the penitence of the butcher He Yin. The concluding verses reiterate the admonition to eat only "plants that have flowers" and avoid even the smell of meat.[43] In this text, all consumption of meat leads to inevitable retribution through suffering in hell and/or future rebirth in the form of a bird or an animal.

The material of *Baojuan of Three Rebirths* and *Precious Account of Mulian* leads us to reevaluate the status of the late narrative *baojuan* that use subjects of mainstream religious traditions. There is extensive evidence of the sectarian affiliation of the late period *baojuan* of the Guanyin cycle and other popular deities.[44] The history of these texts has much in common with *Baojuan of Three Rebirths*; they were published by the same morality book publishers, including Baoshantang in Zhenjiang, Manao Sūtra Store (Manao Jingfang) in Suzhou, and Yihuatang and Hongda in Shanghai. As discussed earlier, it is difficult to distinguish between philanthropic societies and sectarian organizations that supported the production of late *baojuan*.

For example, religions of the Great Way of Former Heaven and the Way of Pervasive Unity have employed a vast variety of scriptures in the modern period. These include traditional morality books as well as those written or edited by sectarians.[45] The same situation might have taken place in the nineteenth century. For example, during the governmental investigation in 1820 of the religion of Mahāyāna

(Dashengjiao, precursor of the Blue Lotus Teaching [Qinglianjiao]) in Guizhou, officials apprehended a relative and follower of the sectarian leader, who at the same time held the rank of "senior licentiate" (gongsheng). Officials discovered that the so-called Mahāyāna scriptures that he kept at home were, in fact, Confucian, Buddhist, and Daoist scriptures together with some books exhorting loyalty and filiality ("morality books") and "vulgar" poems that had no words connected with revolt.[46] Therefore, mainstream texts with religious contents, potentially attractive to commoners, could appear in the sectarian context. Both *Baojuan of Three Rebirths* and *Precious Account of Mulian* can fall under the category of such morality books. Besides, there is a close connection between *Baojuan of Three Rebirths* (and similar texts) and folk rituals, as evidence from Changshu and Jingjiang demonstrates.

RITUAL ASPECTS OF TWO LATE *BAOJUAN*

Rituals of Salvation from Hell

Both *Baojuan of Three Rebirths* and *Precious Account of Mulian* contain detailed descriptions of hell. However, the organization of the underworld in these two texts is different. At first glance, the structure of hell in *Baojuan of Three Rebirths* seems to be different from that of mainstream traditions of China. It is not structured along the common conception of the Ten Courts. Instead, there are different executive compartments of hell. Nevertheless, the appellation "Ten Courts of hell" appears in connection with the name of Yanwang—"Yanwang of the Ten Courts."[47] The author uses Yanwang as the general name of judges in all Ten Courts. This feature makes the contents of *Baojuan of Three Rebirths* different from the mainstream accounts of the Ten Courts of hell, such as various versions of the Mulian drama; however, it continues the archaic tradition of hell representation found in the early *baojuan* texts, such as *Baojuan of Maudgalyāyana*.

Descriptions of hell in both *Baojuan of Three Rebirths* and *Precious Account of Mulian* certainly fit the ritual function of the assemblies where they were recited, and several recensions of *Baojuan of Three Rebirths* still are recited during religious assemblies that are aimed at the salvation of a woman's soul in Jiangsu. Today the most elaborate form of such ritual assemblies continues to exist in the *baojuan* performances tradition (telling scriptures) of the Changshu area (and neighboring Zhangjiagang). In Changshu, *Baojuan of Mulian* usually is incorporated into the funerary service for a woman (mother) held on the second day after her death. It is recited together with *Baojuan of the Great Vehicle of Non-Interference on Returning to Emptiness and Pointing the Way (of Soul)* (Dasheng Wuwei gui kong zhi lu baojuan), *Baojuan of the Ten Kings* (Shi wang baojuan), *Baojuan of Dizang* (Dizang baojuan), *Baojuan of the Earth God* (Tudi baojuan), and other texts dealing with the underworld and its deities.[48] The first text must originally have been related to one of the branches of the Teaching of Non-Interference, though it now appears outside of a sectarian context; the others are narrative texts, common in the Changshu tradition. *Baojuan of Mulian* is recited only at a woman's funeral; during men's funerals, performers recite *Baojuan of Explicating and Clarifying [Origins] of Hell* (Xiaoshi mingzheng diyu baojuan, abbreviated as *Baojuan of Hell*; Che no. 1357) instead. It is an early sectarian scripture that belongs to the Teaching of Returning to the Origin (Huanyuanjiao) that appeared at the end of the sixteenth century in northern China; its earliest printing dates to 1591.[49]

The recitation of *Baojuan of the Ten Kings*, which precedes that of *Baojuan of Mulian*, is heavily ritualized. It is accompanied by offerings to the Ten Courts of hell (known as *jiao dian* or *zhaigong Shi wang*), when the master of telling scriptures kneels in front of the altar and burns special memorials with the name of the deceased in order to ask for the mercy of the Ten Kings and save his or her soul from suffering in hell.[50] A similar program also is performed during a memorial day for a deceased person on the thirty-fifth day after his or her death (known as the "fifth seven" [*wu qi* 五七] in China) when the soul is believed to be at Yanwang's court.[51] On this occasion, however, *Baojuan of Mulian* usually is not recited.[52]

Recitation of the expanded recension of *baojuan* about Mulian in the Changshu area, called *Baojuan of Mulian Rescuing His Mother from Hell*, is accompanied by a special ritual. Masters of telling scriptures perform a ritual of worship of the deities of hell every time they finish the description of each hell compartment. Each section (*pin*) in the first volume of the text ends with the submission of the memorial to the ruler of each hell (*tong die*), the recitation of "mantra of returning to life" (*wang sheng zhou*), and chanting of a *gāthā*.[53] These *gāthās* have didactic contents related to the religious ideas that the text preaches. Thus the narrative about Mulian rescuing his mother is equated to the ritual recitation of the Buddhist scripture. Rituals performed during its recitation in Changshu closely imitate the salvational rites performed in conjunction with another "funerary" text, *Baojuan of the Ten Kings*.

A situation similar to the funerary performances of *Baojuan of Mulian* in Changshu exists now in the Gangkou area of Zhangjiagang, close to Changshu, though a much simpler variant of the text is used there.[54] In Min county of Gansu, *Baojuan of Mulian* (mainly recensions of *Precious Account of Mulian*) also still can be recited during funerary and memorial services (held for "Seven sevens" days).[55] Though in the Jingjiang area, unlike in Changshu and Min county, *baojuan* (including those dealing with the Mulian story) are not performed at funerals but rather for living people, the purpose is still to ease their lot in the afterlife. In spite of the differences in the contents and schedule of the religious assemblies, there are many similarities concerning the performance of *baojuan* with the Mulian story in the Changshu and Jingjiang areas.

First, it appears in the narrative context of other *baojuan* texts about popular deities. Thus the whole session of *baojuan* performance in both areas is very long and usually takes a day and night. In Changshu, the funerary *baojuan* performance usually lasts from 5 p.m. until 6 a.m. the next day. The performance that I witnessed in Jingjiang on April 13, 2009, lasted almost twenty-four hours. Second, these performances require the special setting that creates the religious atmosphere in which the texts are recited. The performance spot, called "hall for [telling] scriptures" in both Jingjiang and Changshu, usually is arranged in the hall of a rural house. There are hanging scrolls (sacred images) and small icons called *zhima*, representing deities summoned at the beginning of an assembly. In the Jingjiang tradition, performers-*fotou* usually use a permanent household altar with the deities' images, on which *zhima* and other paraphernalia are placed.

In the Changshu area, the masters of telling scriptures usually construct a temporary altar, called "Buddha's platform" (Fotai), in the form of a long table in the center of the room where they place *zhima* and offerings for the deities. During funerary and memorial services, this altar is adorned with a scroll representing Dizang. The performer and chorus, who sing the refrain of Buddha's name, sit around the table, facing this image. The performers also can adorn the performance spot with pictures of the Ten Kings. While traditionally ten scrolls representing each king of hell separately have been placed on

Figure 7.01. "Scripture hall" during the funerary performance of *baojuan*. Changshu, 2011. Photo courtesy of Yu Dingjun.

the side walls of the room, today performers usually hang one combined image of the Ten Kings on the side altar where the offerings for these deities are performed. It is likely that the detailed description of the compartments of hell in different *baojuan* about Mulian was substantiated with images (as is the case with other *baojuan* dealing with the hell themes). There is evidence that before 1949 performers of *baojuan* referred to images of heaven and hell to illustrate their story during public performances; for example, such a practice was common in Wuwei city in Gansu (also called "explaining morality books" [*jiang shanshu*]).[56] In modern practice in the Changshu area, storytellers display images during the performance but do not refer to them. The same situation existed until recently in *baojuan* performances in Hexi; there storytellers occasionally have displayed images of deities, hell, and heaven as ritual implements during performances.[57]

Therefore, modern performances of *baojuan* cannot be considered true picture storytelling. In this sense, they are very different from

Figure 7.02. Funerary performance of *baojuan*. Gangkou area of Zhangjiagang (Changshu), 2004. Photo courtesy of Yu Yongliang.

bianwen performances (as far as we can reconstruct the latter now). Thus the argument that visual aids in *baojuan* performances make them and *bianwen* related representatives of a single tradition of oral Buddhist narrative is not valid.[58] In order to explore the origin of images in *baojuan* performances, one should turn instead to the use of images in Buddhist and Daoist rituals. Displaying images of deities is common during these services, including modern funerary performances in several areas of China, but ritual specialists presiding over these services usually do not refer to them.[59] These images simply create the atmosphere of the performance, as in modern *baojuan* recitations.

Paintings of the Water-and-Land Service (Shuiluhua) in particular are close antecedents of the images used in *baojuan* performances. This ritual assembles and delivers all living beings of Water and Land, who are depicted in the paintings displayed during its performance.[60] This connection was pronounced in the terminology of *baojuan* performers themselves. For example, in the mid-twentieth century, followers of the Vast Yang Teaching in Yixingbu displayed images of the Ten Kings of hell during recitation of sectarian *baojuan* and called

Figure 7.03. Scroll of the Ten Kings, used during the funerary performance of *baojuan*. Changshu, 2014. Photo courtesy of Huang Zhiheng.

them "Water-and-Land" (Shuilu).[61] These images were of course different from the usual elaborate sets of Water-and-Land paintings and should be regarded as the folk response to the popular, but sophisticated, Buddhist ritual. Both, however, followed the same principle. The display of images of deities during a performance forms the visual part of the rituals of "inviting" and worshiping deities during the ritualized performance session. It also parallels the mode of illustration of middle- and late period *baojuan* texts with their pictures of deities and pantheons in front of and/or after the text.

Figure 7.04. Images of hells in lithographic edition of *Baojuan of Three Rebirths* (Shanghai: Wenyi Publishers, 1921). Collection of and photo by the author.

Though in most cases *baojuan* performances were not picture storytelling, visual aids still played an important role in establishing their performance arena. While listening to the oral narrative, the audience looked at the depiction of rewards and punishments of human deeds. These perfectly fit the extended descriptions of hell in

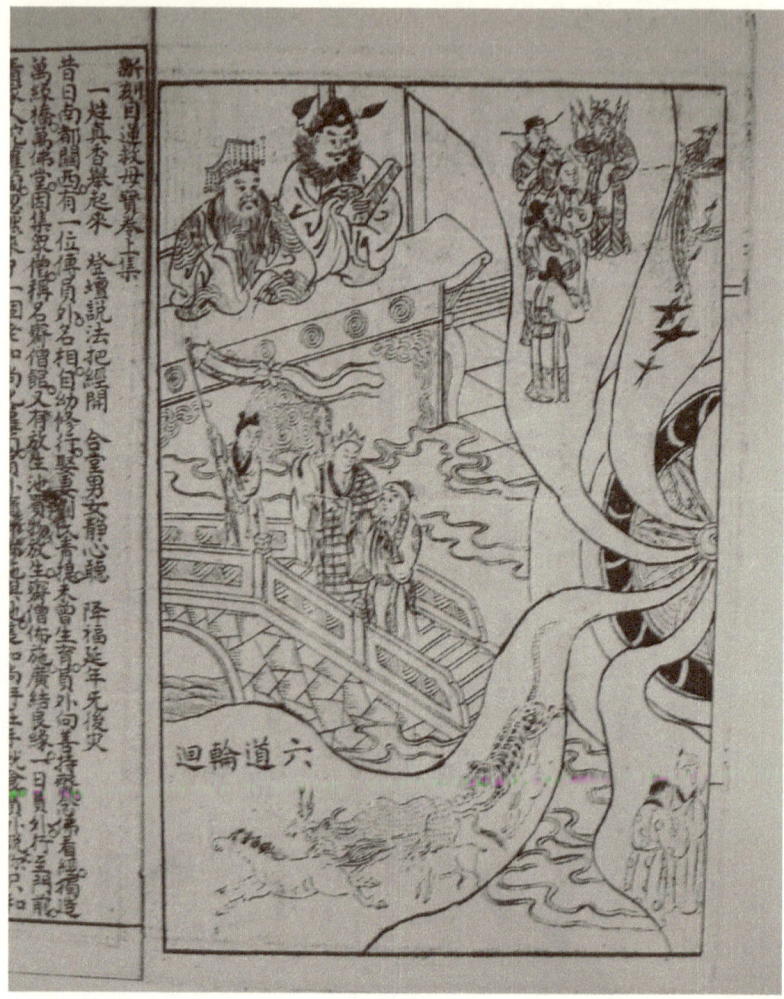

Figure 7.05. Images of hells in lithographic edition of *Baojuan of Three Rebirths* (Shanghai: Wenyi Publishers, 1921). Collection of and photo by the author.

Baojuan of Three Rebirths and *Precious Account of Mulian*. Similar images also appear in the old editions of both *baojuan*. For example, illustrations on the frontispiece of the Wenyi edition of *Baojuan of Three Rebirths* of 1921 (appendix 2, III, no. 9) depict two kings of hell, tortures of sinners, the Wheel of Rebirths, and Mulian rescuing his mother. These illustrations certainly represent traces of the practice of displaying images during performance. Individual readers could refer to them in the same manner as the audience of a professional performance could refer to the hanging scrolls.

The Blood Pond in Texts and Ritual

Both *Baojuan of Three Rebirths* and *Precious Account of Mulian* contain extended descriptions of the Blood Pond. For example, *Baojuan of Three Rebirths* says that women, who polluted gods with their blood, are sentenced to imprisonment in this pond. Their sin is breaking the confinement during the first month after childbirth:

> Before one month had passed, we walked into the family hall,
> Thus polluting the family's ancestors and the household gods.
> Before one month had passed, we walked into the kitchen,
> Thus polluting the Kitchen God and the visiting deities.
> Before one month had passed, we went to the riverbank;
> With our washing, we polluted the Dragon King's palace,
> And by drying the blood-stained clothes in the open air,
> We also polluted the sun, moon, and stars up in the sky![62]

Only pious deeds on the part of descendants, such as fasting and reciting scriptures, can save a woman from her sufferings in the Blood Pond. Thus this text refers to violating the taboo regarding postpartum confinement that is well known and still observed in China.[63] In many regions of China, however, people believe that once a woman gives birth she is destined to be imprisoned in the Blood Pond after death, regardless of whether she violates the taboo. This belief may be reflected in *Precious Account of Mulian*, which has a short description of the Blood Pond (also called the Blood River there) in just a few lines of verse and does not specify for which sins the female souls are suffering there. It merely names "impurity" as a reason for their confinement.[64]

The descriptions in both texts, though short and not very clear, are connected with the ritual of salvation of women from the Blood Pond. Rituals centered on the Blood Pond have been performed in connection with the recitation of *Baojuan of Mulian* in several areas of Jiangsu up to the present day. We have already observed an especially elaborate ritual of "breaking of the Blood Pond" performed in connection with the modern *baojuan* performances in Jingjiang.[65] It accompanies the recitation of the narrative text of *Baojuan of the Blood Pond*, also known as *Baojuan of Mulian*. Recitation of *Baojuan of the Blood Pond* takes place when a woman, for whom an assembly is held, reaches menopausal age. It is the final purification of a woman before the end of her earthly life. After the completion of purification, this woman is not allowed to enter the room where childbirth takes place so that she will not be polluted again. For this reason, most local women prefer to perform the ritual when they are sixty or seventy years old, after their daughters have given birth. In the case of "telling scriptures" assembly that I witnessed in Jingjiang the host woman was seventy-three years old. According to the old custom, the ritual of "breaking of the Blood Pond" should be performed three times in the course of three years for one woman, but today this prescription is not strictly observed: performing the ritual just once in a lifetime is considered sufficient. The culmination of the recitation of *Baojuan of the Blood Pond* is the symbolic emptying of the Blood Pond, performed by the descendants of the host woman (including her sons, daughters, daughters-in-law, sons-in-law, and grandsons-in-law). Breaking the hell prison, when all souls of deceased are liberated, also takes place before the end of narration.

Prior to the 1950s, similar rituals concerning the salvation from the Blood Pond that involved recitation of *Baojuan of Mulian* were performed in other areas of Jiangsu. Here, for the sake of brevity, we examine only the Changshu situation. Today masters of telling scriptures in Changshu also perform the ritual of salvation from the Blood Pond during funerals for women or during the "fifth seven" memorial service. In this case, however, they usually recite not *Baojuan of Mulian* but *Scripture of the Blood Pond* (Xuehu jing) and *Baojuan of the Blood Pond* (Xuehu baojuan).[66] The former is based on a short Daoist scripture on this topic, and the latter focuses on the description of sufferings in the Blood Pond. In Changshu, *baojuan* recitation, however, is not accompanied by the drinking of the red water as in Jingjiang. A parallel Daoist funerary service is performed for women there, which includes breaking the Pond of Blood and drinking the red water. Local residents regard this Daoist ritual as different from telling scriptures and have it performed at a different time (usually on the day that follows the night session of telling scriptures). We find a similar situation in Jingjiang: in that area, "breaking of the Blood Pond" should be performed for the same woman twice: once during her lifetime by the *fotou* and a second time during her funeral by the Daoists.

Thus the performances of *baojuan* about Mulian that promise salvation for women from the Blood Pond have important social meanings of family integration and moralizing instruction. In the Jingjiang area, the recitation of this text not only has a ritual (salvational) function but also has a consolatory meaning for the elderly women and didactic meaning for their descendants. In this respect, the episode concerning a female soul imprisoned in the Blood Pond that Mulian sees on his way through the underworld is especially noteworthy.[67] It cries out for her husband, children, and servants to help her get out of the pond. Her requests to her children are especially important because she fell into the pond primarily because of childbirth, and the children need to repay their mother for her sufferings and mercies. Naturally, the complaints of the women in the Blood Pond contain a description of major events and hardships in the life of women in traditional Chinese society, thus shedding light on the everyday life of a household.

Not only does the text of *Baojuan of the Blood Pond* in Jingjiang have many moralizing passages, the organization of the assembly that involves all members of the household helps bring together family members and sometimes even resolve conflicts between representatives of different generations. Most important, daughters-in-law can be reconciled with their mothers-in-law with the use of this ritual, as they also have to share the symbolic responsibility of the mother-in-law's purification and salvation. Once more they are reminded about the hardships their mother-in-law has endured and about their duty toward her, which can elicit a strong emotional response. Young women are also given hope that their own toil will be rewarded when their descendants perform the same ritual for them. In the case of Changshu, holding the funerary telling scriptures for a deceased mother, including texts about Mulian and the Blood Pond, works as a way to express filial piety and maintain social prestige. In modern China traditional-style funerals remain an important social event during which family and social ties are reestablished,[68] and the Changshu situation is no exception. Their inclusion in funerary rituals demonstrates the important social function of *baojuan* about Mulian and the Blood Pond.

The rituals of the Blood Pond performed in connection with *Baojuan of Mulian* have remarkably ancient foundations. As we have already seen, originally they were related to the Buddhist and Daoist rituals of the same meaning. However, in the case of telling scriptures in Jingjiang and Changshu, this ritual can be thought of as borrowed from sectarian teachings, a conclusion well substantiated by the use of Blood Pond imagery in *baojuan* of the sixteenth to seventeenth century. The rituals of the breaking of the Blood Pond must have been transmitted to these areas by the followers of a branch of Non-Interference (or Luo) Teaching, with which the initial spread of *baojuan* texts there was related. At the same time, the ritual of the salvation of deceased women from the suffering in the Blood Pond is an important part of the ritual practice of common folk in China, not necessarily related to sectarian practices.

The form of "breaking of the Blood Pond" in the Jingjiang tradition is similar to rituals performed by the Daoists or lay (i.e., non-monastic) Buddhist priests in southern China. For example, Daoist rituals of the Blood Pond in Shanghai and Suzhou (performed during female funerals) also include the drinking of red water from a bowl, symbolizing the Blood Pond, by a woman's descendants.[69] In other regions of southern China, such as Fujian, Taiwan, Sichuan, and Guangdong, a similar ritual is performed for deceased women, usually accompanied by dramatic scenes.[70] The symbolic destruction of Avīci hell by the *fotou* in Jingjiang is very similar to the destruction of objects, symbolizing hell in these ritual traditions. The appearance of the image of the Blood Pond in sectarian scriptures and rituals can be interpreted as the appropriation of mainstream religious practice by sectarian believers.

In the Jiangsu-Zhejiang region, the Blood Pond rituals were very widespread and took a variety of forms. Before 1949, the ritual of "breaking of the Blood Pond" in several areas of Zhejiang was performed with dramatic scenes on the subject of Mulian. These occasions included funerary rituals for individuals as well as full-fledged dramas staged for communal observances.[71] For example, the Daoists performed "breaking the filthy Blood Pond" with theatrical scenes of Mulian during funerals in Jiande county in Zhejiang.[72] These ritualized theatrical performances appear similar to the aforementioned enactment of the Mulian story during funerals in Fujian, Guangdong, and Taiwan. *Baojuan* performances in southern Jiangsu today certainly are the equivalent of such ritual dramas; the main difference is the use of storytelling instead of theatrical scenes.

At the same time, although in Zhejiang the Mulian dramas used to be quite popular, most places in southern Jiangsu do not possess well-developed traditions of the Mulian drama.[73] The only place with a well-known Mulian drama in Jiangsu is Gaochun county in the western corner of the province where several variants of the ritualized Mulian drama were staged before 1949.[74] The tradition of Mulian drama was transmitted to that place, however, from neighboring areas in Anhui, where Mulian dramas had been widespread since the Ming dynasty at the latest. Therefore, we can conclude that in several areas of Jiangsu, where *baojuan* about Mulian still are performed, they basically substitute for the ritualized dramatic performances common in the neighboring areas.

Exorcistic Meaning of Baojuan Performances

The recitation of *baojuan* dealing with the Mulian story is also used to ward off calamities and bring fortune. This is clearly stated in the introductory verse of *Baojuan of Three Rebirths* that promises long life and elimination of disasters (see chapter 6, "Formal Characteristics"). *Baojuan* texts about Mulian describe the exorcising of "lonely souls"; this is evident, for example, in the episode of Huang Chao, who collects the souls that flee from hell.[75] Although this episode was certainly borrowed from the historical novel that also deals with Huang Chao—*Romance of the End of the Tang and [History of the] Five Dynasties* (Can Tang Wudai shi yanyi zhuan, sixteenth or early seventeenth century)—it continues the motif of collecting escaped souls that appeared in the texts of the seventeenth century: *Dizang baojuan* and *Baojuan of Benefiting Living Beings*. It thus had complex origins. Furthermore, Huang Chao's image in both *Romance* and *Baojuan* is modeled on that of exorcist deity Zhong Kui.[76] This connection intensifies the exorcistic meaning of this episode.

Baojuan of Three Rebirths promises salvation of all "lonely souls," which are imagined as ghosts and thus very dangerous for living people in Chinese religion. Its concluding verse says that after recitation of the text all unattended souls "have perceived the Oneness," and "none of them abides in the land of springs," that is, the underworld or hell.[77] After the transfer of thus obtained merit, "each and every place turns into paradise."[78] Furthermore, in both *Baojuan of Three Rebirths* and *Precious Account of Mulian*, the figure of Mulian preserves connection with Bodhisattva Dizang, the savior of souls in hell. In the first case he turns into the Dizang's assistant; in the second, into Dizang himself. Thus these late recensions of *baojuan* still refer to the universal salvation of souls that is the goal of the Ullambana ritual around which the whole Mulian literature originally developed.[79]

The exorcistic meaning of late recensions of *Baojuan of Mulian* also appears in the modern performance traditions of *baojuan* in Jiangsu. For example, in the Changshu area *Baojuan of Mulian*

Rescuing His Mother from Hell is performed not only during funerals and memorial services but also during religious meetings with exorcist meaning. The exorcist ritual expulses "the Heavenly dog" (Tiangou), who is said to be the reincarnation of Mulian's mother in the local recension of *baojuan*, and is believed to devour fetuses and cause miscarriage. Masters of telling scriptures often send off the Heavenly dog after recitation of *Baojuan of Mulian*, when they chant the special spell.[80] Beliefs about the Heavenly dog (a malicious astral deity) have an ancient origin, which we do not have space to discuss here. In Chinese folk beliefs the shooting of the Heavenly dog usually is associated with Immortal Zhang (Zhang Xian), who also appears in *baojuan* texts of Changshu.[81] At the same time this belief and related exorcistic rituals were associated with the Mulian story in the local tradition.

The link of *Baojuan of Three Rebirths*, and its recensions now used in several areas of Jiangsu, with the performance of the salvational and exorcistic rituals, especially in comparison with similar traditions of the ritual Mulian dramas, leads us to a reevaluation of the ritual function of *baojuan* texts. Johnson, for example, has juxtaposed folk Mulian dramas and *baojuan* about Mulian (in this case, specifically *Precious Account of Mulian*) as "non-discursive, affective and experiential" ritual versus verbal art, deeply "involved with reason and social-political order."[82] Although this distinction is reasonable, it is not that clearly delineated in real-life performances. As we have seen in the examples of performances from Jingjiang and Changshu, *baojuan* about Mulian also have a deep kinship with ritual and thus possess emotional power similar to that of ritual drama. Rather than treat *baojuan* as espousing completely imposed values,[83] we should take into account their involvement with the religious beliefs and practices of common people in rural areas.

The influence of upper-class moralists and sectarian teachers who presumably edited and employed the texts of the late period *baojuan* is undeniable. The infusion of the influence of the elite is revealed, for example, in the borrowing of historical material from a novel for the episode of the folk exorcism. The function of the late *baojuan* about Mulian, however, should not be reduced to the purely didactic. It should be interpreted as a combination of didactic with ritual action; this aspect was not much different from that of the local Mulian dramas. The episodes of the soul's salvation and exorcism of escaped souls in these *baojuan* make them equivalent to ritualized dramas. Although the concrete presentation of salvation and exorcism in *Baojuan of Three Rebirths* can be different from similar episodes in drama, there is an interchange of motifs and ideas between these two categories of texts. The inclusion of ritual practice into text recitations constitutes a special feature of *baojuan* performances (including the local variants of *Baojuan of Three Rebirths*) in southern Jiangsu. This feature also enabled them to survive even during the times of anti-religious propaganda in the twentieth century.

CONCLUSION

Texts of both *Baojuan of Three Rebirths* and *Precious Account of Mulian* preserve signs of their sectarian affiliation. The sectarian ideas are not as pervasive and concentrated as in *baojuan* about Mulian of the seventeenth century, but we can detect non-standard ideology in the two texts. This challenges the usual classification of *baojuan* into sectarian and non-sectarian (narrative), as even narrative texts of the late period can be closely related to sectarian cults and practices. At the same time, the combination of fictional features with a weakened sectarian tinge presumably enabled both *Baojuan of Three Rebirths* and *Precious Account of Mulian* to be transmitted and recited outside of the sectarian context in modern China.

Other special details of the two texts' contents, such as the connection with popular rituals and exorcist practices, reflected the worldview similar to that of the broad circle of folk believers. For example, the connection of *Baojuan of Three Rebirths* and its modern variants with the rituals of worshiping the Ten Kings of hell, breaking of the Blood Pond, and exorcism enabled its variants to continue to be performed outside the sectarian context in several areas of southern Jiangsu. We have observed how a short episode in the description of the underworld in *Baojuan of Three Rebirths* developed into the full-fledged ritual action in live performances of *baojuan* in these areas, reminding us once again of the importance of performance context of *baojuan* texts. Some particular features of belief and practice expressed in *Baojuan of Three Rebirths*, however, were not adopted in the modern tradition of performance of its folk recensions.

In spite of the difference of contents, *baojuan* texts about Mulian of the nineteenth century as well as those of the seventeenth century fostered the idea of universal salvation and propagated the cult of Bodhisattva Dizang. This made both late *baojuan* perfect pieces for funerary services, and the recensions of *Baojuan of Three Rebirths* and *Precious Account of Mulian* have been recited for this purpose in Jiangsu and Gansu, respectively, up to the present day. Inclusion in the funerary rituals reflects the social and cultural significance of these texts. In addition to Buddhist-based soteriology, they also propagate the core values of traditional syncretic Chinese morality, which was adopted even by the sectarians of the Unborn Mother religions—the most ideologically deviant part of the Chinese population in the late imperial period. In this sense, *baojuan* recitation appears to be equivalent to ritual Mulian drama—both combine ritual action and didacticism.

On the other hand, because *Baojuan of Three Rebirths* and *Precious Account of Mulian* had moralizing content that was at least superficially in accord with the state ideology, they became acceptable tools of "civilizing" and teaching the commoners for educated moralists, who were, or at least pretended to be, unaware of their sectarian content. Both late *baojuan* can be seen as sectarian elaborations of a popular story that ultimately left the sectarian context and assumed the double role of didactic book and ritual performance.

Conclusion

Through the long process of evolution of the story of Mulian rescuing his mother in *baojuan* texts of different time periods, Mulian appears in different guises, yet the core of the story has remarkable continuity. Though unlike Tantric Buddhist deities Mulian is not depicted with many faces (and hands) in the artworks, he still possesses many guises, even if we limit the discussion to the *baojuan* texts. Still the survival of this originally Buddhist legend in the *baojuan* texts testifies to the persistence of traditional subjects in Chinese performance-oriented literature in vernacular literature. At the same time, this story was embellished in different ways and imbued with new meanings depending on the religious and cultural background in which individual texts were formed. Most of them are anonymous—created collectively by several authors/editors, who apparently also used oral materials extensively.

These texts demonstrate that *baojuan* about Mulian had origins in earlier popular literature and began to circulate in the fourteenth to fifteenth century, which was the early (or Buddhist) period in the history of this genre. The special features of texts of this period are embodied in *Baojuan of Maudgalyāyana*, which survived as two early manuscripts associated with the courts of the Northern Yuan and Ming dynasties. The commission of the 1440 manuscript of *Baojuan of Maudgalyāyana* by an imperial concubine testifies to the very early association of this type of literature with a female audience, particularly that of the elite society. The topic of female salvation (also associated with the special rituals aimed at women such as escape from the Blood Pond after death), central in this text, was especially appropriate for this type of literature. Elaborate illustrations of both manuscripts provided visual aids that assisted their double function of both performance script and reading material for less sophisticated/junior readers.

At the same time, a transformation of the traditional Buddhist subject is apparent in this early *baojuan* text about Mulian, compared with earlier versions of this story in Chinese popular literature, notably *bianwen* (transformation text) from Dunhuang and an apocryphal sūtra about Mulian. Starting with *Baojuan of Maudgalyāyana*, *baojuan* about Mulian incorporate sectarian ideas about merciful deities, a supreme female deity (later also progenitor) who can be interpreted as a predecessor of Unborn Venerable Mother of dissenting religions in the sixteenth to seventeenth century, syncretism of different religious beliefs and values, and community of the elects. These and related topics are much more developed in the later recension of *Baojuan of Maudgalyāyana* penned by a follower of Non-Interference Teaching around the sixteenth to seventeenth century; these became central in sectarian *baojuan* relating the Mulian story—*Dizang baojuan* and *Baojuan of Benefiting Living Beings* (ca. the seventeenth century). These texts present voluminous descriptions of the specific beliefs and practices of sectarian teachings in their developed form, most notably the cult of the Unborn Mother with its millenarian (and messianic) aspects and inner elixir technique. These beliefs and practices appear in additional story lines in these texts. They were connected skillfully, however, with the core of traditional Mulian story.

Many developments of the Mulian story—his miraculous birth, connection with Bodhisattva Dizang, and exorcistic and salvational role—that are found in *baojuan* of the seventeenth century also appear in the later local drama versions of the Mulian story. Because these are different from the well-known drama recension of the late sixteenth century by the literatus Zheng Zhizhen, *Drama Exhorting Goodness*, the interaction of *baojuan* and drama can be traced to the middle period of *baojuan* genre development. This demonstrates the influence of sectarian writing on the development of popular and oral literature in late traditional China and of sectarian teachings in Chinese traditional culture.

In late *baojuan* texts about Mulian, *Baojuan of Three Rebirths* and *Precious Account of Mulian* (both dating to the nineteenth century), interaction with drama and novels (or novels' oral renditions) became even more evident than in the texts of the seventeenth century. The connection with the local variants of both multiple-act and short scenes accompanying rituals (two types of the folk Mulian drama), mainly oral versions, is especially clear in these texts. For example, one can detect the connection of *baojuan* with the multiple-act dramas in the additional story lines dealing with the genealogy of Mulian's family and Mulian's miraculous birth. *Baojuan of Three Rebirths* also extensively employs historical material in an additional story line concerning the rebellion led by Huang Chao that comes from the novel *Romance of the End of the Tang and [History of the] Five Dynasties* (or its oral renditions), though it was reinterpreted in *baojuan* in the context of its ritual function.

The connections of the Mulian story with the rituals of salvation and exorcism, such as "breaking of the Blood Pond," appealing for pardon of the Ten Kings of hell, and expulsion of the unattended souls, which also appear in the texts of *Baojuan of Three Rebirths* and *Precious Account of Mulian*, reveal the ritual function of these texts and the genre as a whole in Chinese society. One can clearly observe this function in the modern performances of *baojuan* in southern Jiangsu during which the above-mentioned rituals are enacted. In this aspect, the performance of *baojuan* about Mulian is very similar to that of the short scene ritual drama performed during funerals in several regions of China.

In terms of formal characteristics, the changes in the performance register in the texts of the third (late) period if compared with early texts also represent the immersion of the *baojuan* genre into the popular culture of China. This tendency is revealed in the arias approaching folk music culture, the inclusion of metaphors and allusions of the mainstream literary tradition, and the traces of the influence of local language and culture.

Material from *baojuan* about Mulian also answers some questions concerning the history of the *baojuan* genre and its status in traditional Chinese society. The close analysis of texts from different periods leads to a reconsideration of the existing views about the history of this genre in Chinese and Western scholarship.

First, the material of the early *baojuan* manuscripts about Mulian demonstrates that the earliest narrative texts of this genre appeared around the fourteenth century. If we assume that the use of the generic name indicates the appearance of the genre, then *Baojuan of Maudgalyāyana* would be the earliest extant example of this genre.

The close antecedent of this text is the apocryphal sūtra about Mulian (ca. eleventh to the twelfth century), which in its turn is related to *bianwen* (ninth through the tenth century). *Baojuan of Maudgalyāyana* is linked to Buddhist proselytizing literature both in the subject matter (similarity with the apocryphal sūtra and penitence texts) and the formal characteristics (elements of ritual frame) of these texts. Therefore, the study of *baojuan* about Mulian helps clarify the problem of the antecedents of this genre, which is not settled in the previous scholarship. We can prove the connection between early *baojuan* narratives, apocryphal Buddhist scriptures, and their oral retellings, which one can also find in other early *baojuan* texts and their close antecedents. These Buddhist-type *baojuan* appeared earlier than the sectarian scriptures; however, in the sixteenth to seventeenth century the latter inherited many of its elements from the first.

Second, the appearance of sectarian ideas in *baojuan* about Mulian of the nineteenth century demonstrates the need for a reevaluation of the characterization of the late period of the genre development as "nonsectarian." We should not divide rigidly middle- and late period *baojuan* but rather treat them as a single genre with continuity in social and ritual meaning. Several narrative *baojuan* texts of the nineteenth to early twentieth century have a sectarian affiliation; for example, *Precious Account of Mulian* was clearly associated with the Way of Former Heaven. Sectarian ideas, however, are not as pervasive and concentrated as in *baojuan* about Mulian from the seventeenth century. Sectarians who composed (or edited) these texts also adopted conventional morality, a mixture of Buddhist and Confucian principles, which can make it hard to determine the exact affiliation of the text in the wide range of popular religious movements of that period (e.g., *Baojuan of Three Rebirths*).

The combination of fictional features with the weakened sectarian tinge enabled *Baojuan of Three Rebirths* and *Precious Account of Mulian* to be transmitted and recited outside of a sectarian context. Some apparently sectarian beliefs and practices in *Baojuan of Three Rebirths* were irrevocably lost in the modern traditions of the performance of its folk recensions in southern Jiangsu. The data extracted from the editions and manuscripts of *baojuan* texts, as well as from their modern performances, demonstrate the multifunctional nature of these texts and the genre on the whole. Their propagation of conventional morality and connection with popular rituals and exorcist practices made them attractive for upper-class moralists as well as rural religious communities.

Third, evidence from a *baojuan* text of the seventeenth century, *Dizang baojuan*, shows the interplay between sectarian practices and communal religious activities. The rituals it describes resemble those known from contemporary descriptions of *baojuan* recitation in the novel *Pacification of the Demons' Revolt* (seventeenth century) as well as the modern *baojuan* performances. One should treat this seventeenth-century passage as important testimony about the process of transmission from the middle to the late phase in the development of the genre and as evidence of conventionality in the periodization of the genre's history. Taking into consideration the demonstrated continuity in the formal characteristics of the texts, this process can be considered evolution, not a sudden transformation of the genre.

Fourth, *baojuan* texts represent the product of the interaction between written and oral traditions in Chinese literature. Such interaction is obvious in the origin of the material in *baojuan*, its organization, special features of the form and, therefore, the performance mode of these texts. Most of the texts analyzed include material of oral tradition as well as references to written classical literature. They were composed or edited by literate people but designed as scripts for oral performances. Many characteristics of the form of the texts, such as their ritual framing, a large variety of verses and singing passages, their connection with popular musical culture, and the inclusion of (or reference to) visual aids, indicate their orientation for performance. These characteristics vary from case to case, for example, in the form and order of verse passages and the nature and quality of images that accompany the written texts and/or their performances. The performances originally had a broad audience and appeared in varied social milieus; today they survive in the form of "cultural relics" in remote rural areas of several provinces of China.

At the same time, *baojuan* texts of different periods were multifunctional. The copies of written texts indicate that they could be used as scripts for professional or amateur storytelling as well as reading materials. The high aesthetic quality of the early manuscripts of *Baojuan of Maudgalyāyana* and the growing importance of the embellishment of the lithographic editions of the early twentieth century point to their use as reading material.

Baojuan texts are not specifically a part of folklore or written literature but are performance-oriented texts with a varying degree of interchange with oral folk literature. Scholars have noted many characteristics of folk literature in the written texts that had oral origins (either oral-derived literature or that composed as imitations of oral texts) in literary traditions other than Chinese that also appear in *baojuan* texts. The syncretic nature of the *baojuan* genre made it attractive to representatives of different layers of society, although later in the process of its development the audience narrowed and *baojuan* turned into "cultural relics." A similar process can be observed in the history of popular literature of the West in the early modern period, which provides a new perspective for interpretation of the history and function of *baojuan* texts in China. Its development should be understood as a process of constant and complex interaction of elite and popular, written and oral, mainstream and sectarian traditions of China.

APPENDIX 1: MAJOR TEXTS IN CHINESE LITERATURE DEALING WITH THE MULIAN STORY

Title	Date	Extant or Not
Sūtra of Ullambana, Expounded by the Buddha 佛說盂蘭盆經, trans. Dharmaraksha	4th c.	extant
Sūtra of Bowl to Repay Kindness of Parents 報恩奉盆經, anonymous translation	4th–5th c.	extant
Pure Land Ullambana Sūtra 淨土盂蘭盆經	ca. 600–650	extant
Commentary on the Sūtra of Ullambana 盂蘭盆經疏, Zongmi 宗密	ca. 830	extant
Bianwen of Mahāmaudgalyāyana Rescuing His Mother from the Underworld 大目乾連冥間救母變文	ca. 800	extant
Text Expounding the Sūtra of Ullambana 盂蘭盆經講經文	ca. 850	partially preserved
Yuanqi of Mulian 目連緣起	9th–10th c.	extant
Drama zaju 雜劇 Mulian Rescues His Mother 目連救母	12th c.	non-extant
Sūtra of Reverend Glorious Mulian 目連尊勝經	12th c.	non-extant

Title	Date	Extant or Not
Sūtra of Mulian Rescuing His Mother, Expounded by the Buddha 佛說目連救母經, in Korea known as *Sūtra of Great Mulian, Expounded by the Buddha* 佛說大目連經	Chinese edition of 1251, reprinted in Japan in 1346	extant
Drama *zaju* 雜劇 *Mulian Realizes Filial Piety and Rescues His Mother* 行孝道目連救母	ca. 13th–14th c.	non-extant
Penitence at Ritual Place of Mercy of Mulian Repaying the Basic 慈悲道場目連報本懺法	ca. 14th c.	extant
Baojuan of Reverend Maudgalyāyana Rescuing His Mother [and Helping Her] to Escape from Hell and Be Born in Heaven 目犍連尊者救母出離地獄生天寶卷	ca. mid-14th c.	partially preserved
Newly Compiled Drama Exhorting Goodness of Mulian Rescuing His Mother 新編目連救母勸善戲文 by Zheng Zhizhen	1583	extant
Southern drama 南戲 *Reverend Mulian* 目連尊者	ca. 14th–15th c.	non-extant
Baojuan of Reverend Maudgalyāyana Rescuing His Mother [and Helping Her] to Escape from Hell and Be Born in Heaven 目犍連尊者救母出離地獄生天寶卷, second recension	16th–17th c.	partially preserved
Records of Rescuing Mother 救母記	late 16th–early 17th c.	non-extant
Baojuan of Bodhisattva-King Dizang Governing the Underworld 地藏王菩薩執掌幽冥寶卷	ca. 1679	extant
Baojuan Expounded by Buddha of Benefiting Living Beings and Understanding of the [True] Meaning 佛說利生了意寶卷	17th c.	extant
Golden Rules Exhorting Goodness 勸善金科 (several recensions)	17th–18th c.	extant
Precious Account of Mulian Rescuing His Mother in the Underworld 目連救母幽冥寶傳	ca. 1817	extant

Appendix 1

Title	Date	Extant or Not
Baojuan of Mulian Rescuing His Mother in Three Rebirths 目蓮三世救母寶卷	ca. 1876	extant
Scenes in Beijing opera: *Mulian Rescues His Mother* 目連救母	ca. late 19th c.	extant
Tanci 彈詞 *Mulian Looks for His Mother* 母連尋母	ca. late 19th c.	extant
Folk recensions of *Baojuan of Mulian* in southern Jiangsu	ca. late 19th c.–early 20th c.	extant

APPENDIX 2: *BAOJUAN* TEXTS DEALING WITH THE MULIAN STORY

Abbreviations

Beijing University: Beijing University Library

Chinese Academy of Arts: Research Institute of Drama in Chinese Academy of Arts, Beijing

Fudan: Fudan University Library, Shanghai

Fu Sinian Library: Fu Sinian Library of Academia Sinica Institute of History and Philology (Taibei)

Harvard-Yenching: Harvard-Yenching Library of Harvard College Library (formerly in Patrick Hanan's collection)

Institute of Literature: Research Institute of Literature in Chinese Academy of Social Sciences (Beijing)

National Library: National Library of China, Beijing

Shanghai Library: Shanghai City Library

SOAS: School of Oriental and African Studies, University of London

Texts

I. *Baojuan Expounded by the Buddha of Benefiting Living Beings and Understanding of the [True] Meaning* (Fo shuo li sheng liao yi baojuan 佛說利生了意寶卷), Che no. 236. Undated woodblock edition (ca. seventeenth century). Library of the Chinese Buddhist Association (Beijing). Reprinted in *MMZJW*, 5:397–480.

II. *Baojuan of Bodhisattva-King Dizang Governing the Underworld* (Dizang wang pusa zhizhang youming baojuan 地藏王菩薩執掌幽冥寶卷), Che no. 160. Woodblock edition dated 1679. Chinese Academy of Arts. Copy dated 1710 in colophon. Reprinted in *MJBJ*, 110:501–95. Musical association of Southern Gaoluo village (南高洛村南樂會) of Laishui county of Hebei (not seen). Tianjin City Library.

III. *Baojuan of Mulian Rescuing His Mother in Three Rebirths* (Mulian sanshi jiumu baojuan 目連三世救母寶卷), Che no. 694; abbreviated as *Baojuan of Mulian* (Mulian Baojuan 目蓮寶卷).

1) Woodblock edition of 1876 by Baoshantang 寶善堂 in Zhenjiang. Alternative title—*Precious Staff of Perfection* (Xiuxing bao zhang 修行寶杖). Shanghai Library, Harvard-Yenching, Institute of Literature, Tianjin City Library.

2) Woodblock edition of 1885 by Yidezhai 一德齋 in Nanjing. Alternative title—*Precious Staff of Perfection*. Shanghai Library, Fu Sinian Library. Reprinted in *SWCK*, 352:199–305.

3) Woodblock edition of 1886 by Peibentang 培本堂in Changzhou. National Library; Taiwan National Library; Duan Ping (Lanzhou); SOAS.

4) Woodblock edition of 1886 by Leshantang 樂善堂 in Changzhou. Nankai University Library (Tianjin).

5) Woodblock edition of 1898, place unknown. Tianjin City Library, Li Shiyu (Tianjin). Reprinted in *BJCJ*, 27:240–394, and *MJBJ*, 111:134–72.

6) Woodblock edition of 1909 by Manao Sūtra Store 瑪瑙經坊 in Suzhou. National Library.

7) Woodblock edition of 1922 by Yihuatang 翼化堂 in Shanghai. Shanghai Library, Fudan, Beijing University.

8) Lithographic edition of 1922 by Hongda 宏大 Morality Book Publishers in Shanghai. Shanghai Library; Fudan; Institute of Oriental Manuscripts (Russia, Saint-Petersburg); Institute of Literature and Philosophy at Academia Sinica (Taibei); SOAS.

9) Lithographic edition of 1921 by Wenyi 文益 publishers in Shanghai (Che no. 689). With the alternative titles *Baojuan of Mulian Rescuing His Mother, Illustrated Baojuan of Mulian*. 2 vols. Shanghai Library, Fu Sinian Library, National Library, Institute of Literature.

10) Lithographic edition by Xiyin 惜蔭publishers in Shanghai, ed. Chen Runshen 陳潤身, undated (Che no. 689). With the title *Newly Compiled Baojuan of Mulian Rescuing His Mother* (Xin bian Mulian jiu mu baojuan 新編目連救母寶卷). Institute of Literature.

11) Lithographic edition of 1924 by Zhenyuan xiao shushe 振園小書社 in Shanghai, edited by Feng Guosheng 馮國聲 and He Zhizhang 賀知章. Fu Sinian Library.

12) Manuscript in two volumes (Che no. 686). Copied by Lu Heqing 陸蕭卿 (or Lu Wenhuan 陸文煥) in yichou 乙丑year (1925?). Shanghai Library.

13) Reprint of the Hongda edition by Mingfeng publishers 明豐印刷所 in Gangshan town 岡山鎮 of Gaoxiong county in Taiwan, 1975; on behalf of the Buddhist hall of Complete Happiness 福全佛堂 in the same town. Author's collection.

14) Modern (typeset) edition with the title *San shi yinguo Mulian jiu mu* ([Story of] the karmic links of three rebirths on Mulian rescuing his mother) 三世因果目蓮救母. Taizhong: Ruicheng chuju 瑞成書局, 1980 (reprinted in 2010). Author's collection.

Appendix 2

15) Modern (typeset) edition by Dahua Yongji publishers 大華永記 in Xianggang in 1980. Author's collection.

16) Modern edition; Duan Ping 1992a, 2:911–80.

17) Modern edition; *Jingjiang baojuan* 2007, 1:379–405.

IV. *Baojuan of Mulian* (Mulian Baojuan 目連寶卷), Che no. 686. Undated manuscript by the performer from the Suzhou area (first half of the twentieth century). Suzhou Museum of Drama.

V. *Baojuan of Mulian* (Mulian Baojuan 目連寶卷), Che no. 685. Undated manuscript from the Shaoxing area (ca. early twentieth century). Yangzhou University Library.

VI. *Baojuan of Mulian* (Mulian Baojuan 目連寶卷). Undated modern manuscript by the performer from the Wuxi area. Collected by author.

VII. *Baojuan of Mulian* (Mulian Baojuan 目連寶卷); an abbreviated recension of *Baojuan of Mulian Rescuing His Mother in Three Rebirths* (no. III), by performers in the Zhangjiagang area (multiple modern manuscripts), for the modern recensions, see *Heyang baojuan* 2007, 1:281–89; see also *Shashang baojuan* 2011, 2:1046–54.

VIII. *Baojuan of Mulian* (Mulian Baojuan目連寶卷). Undated modern manuscript by a performer from the Kunshan area. Collected by the author.

IX. *Baojuan of Mulian of the Great Vehicle* (Dasheng Mulian Baojuan 大乘目連寶卷). Manuscript copied by Wang Hezhang 王鶴章 in January 1988, place unknown. Copy in David Johnson's collection (Berkeley, CA).

X. *Baojuan of Mulian Rescuing His Mother from Hell* (Mulian jiu mu diyu baojuan 目蓮救母地獄寶卷). Manuscript by Yu Dingjun 余鼎君 from Liantang 練塘 township of the Changshu area, copied in 2004 (after the manuscript copied in 1909 by Yu Shengxing 余勝興), in 2 vols. Yu Dingjun.

XI. *Baojuan of Reverend Maudgalyāyana Rescuing His Mother [and Helping Her] to Escape from Hell and Be Born in Heaven* (Mujianlian zunzhe jiu mu chuli diyu sheng tian baojuan 目犍連尊者救母出離地獄生天寶卷), Che no. 691. Alternative title: *Baojuan of Mulian Rescuing His Mother [and Helping Her] to Escape from Hell and Be Born in Heaven* (Mulian jiu mu chuli diyu sheng tian baojuan目連救母出離地獄生天寶卷), abbreviated title: *Baojuan of Mulian*. Illustrated manuscript dated 1372; only last volume survived. National Library, formerly in Zheng Zhenduo's collection. Illustrated manuscript dated 1440; volumes 1, 3, and 4. State Hermitage Museum (Russia, Saint Petersburg); formerly in collection of Vladimir A. Desnitskiy.

XII. *Baojuan of Reverend Maudgalyāyana Rescuing His Mother [and Helping Her] to Escape from Hell and Be Born in Heaven* (Mulianlian jiu mu chuli diyu sheng tian baojuan 目犍連尊者救母出離地獄生天寶卷), Che no. 693. Another recension of the previous baojuan, sixteenth or seventeenth century. Undated manuscript; volumes two and three in Chinese Academy of Arts; formerly in Zheng Qian's collection.

XIII. *Baojuan of the Pond of Blood* (Xuehu baojuan 血湖寶卷). Undated manuscript by fotou Zhao Songqun 趙松群 from the Jingjiang area, undated. A recension by fotou Wang Guoliang 王國良 printed in *Jingjiang baojuan* 2007, 1:407–30.

XIV. *Complete Version of [Bao]juan of Mulian* (Mulian juan quanji 目連卷全集), Che no. 688.

1) Woodblock edition of 1877 by Manao Monastery sūtra publishers 瑪瑙寺經坊 in Suzhou. Shanghai Library, Fudan.

2) Woodblock edition of 1877 by Huikong sūtra publishers 慧空經坊 in Hangzhou. Shanghai Library, Harvard-Yenching.

3) Incomplete undated manuscript without title on the cover. Shanghai Library.

XV. *Complete Volume of Mulian Rescuing Mother and Obtaining the Way in Three Rebirths* (Mulian jiu mu san shi de dao quan ben 目連救母三世得道全本), Che no. 913.

1) Lithographic edition by Yinyu 殷裕 publishers, 1907. Beijing Normal University.

2) Lithographic edition by Yuanchang 元昌 publishers in Shanghai; undated (between 1912 and 1949). Shanghai Library.

3) Lithographic edition by Chunyin 椿蔭 publishers in Shanghai; undated (between 1912 and 1949). With the alternative title of *Complete Story of Mulian Rescuing His Mother in Three Rebirths with Illustrations* (Huitu san shi jiu mu Mulian ji quan zhuan 繪圖三世救母目蓮記全傳). Fu Sinian Library.

XVI. *The Monk Mulian* (Mulian seng 目連僧). Manuscript copied by Qian Peizhang 王培章 in January 1919; place unknown. Copy in David Johnson's collection (Berkeley, CA).

XVII. *Precious Account of Mulian Rescuing His Mother in the Underworld* (Mulian jiu mu youming baozhuan 目連救母幽冥寶傳), Che no. 690.

1) Woodblock edition dated 1817 by Jintingguan 金庭舘 of Jiankang prefecture 建康郡 (modern Gaotai 高臺 in Gansu). Tan Chanxue 譚 蟬 雪 (Gansu).

2) Woodblock edition of 1876 by Qingyuantang 清源堂; with preface dated 1876 and ascribed to Bodhisattva Dizang. National Library, Beijing University.

3) Woodblock edition of 1881. Chinese Academy of Arts, Wu Xiaoling (Beijing) (not seen).

4) Manuscript dated 1890 by Wang Yong 王鏞 from Jiankang prefecture 建康郡 (modern Gaotai 高臺 in Gansu). Printed in *Jiuquan baojuan* 2011, 3:295–327.

Appendix 2

5) Woodblock edition of 1892 by Zhang Junqing 張俊卿 from Yiyi 益邑. With an undated preface to the new edition (1892?). Fudan.

6) Woodblock edition of 1893 by association of Jishantang 積善堂; Dongguo 東郭 village of Xinan 西南 township of Daming 大名 county of Daming 大名prefecture of Zhili. With an undated preface (same as in 1892 edition) and preface by Wang Zuoli 王作礪 from Yinchuan 澱川, dated 1881. Fu Sinian Library, reprinted in *SWCK*, 352:5–196; Harvard-Yenching.

7) Woodblock edition by Hu Sizhen 胡思真 from Yan Nan 燕南 of 1898. Revised by Zhiyi Zi 知一子; edited by Qingyang shanren (Hermit of Qingyang) 青陽山人–Mr. Guanwu 冠五氏. With preface by Yinan Zi dated 1899; an undated preface (1892?); preface by Wang Zuoli dated 1881. Chinese Academy of Arts, National Library, Institute of Literature, Vena Hrdličková (Prague). Reprinted in *MMZJW*, 8:945–1001.

8) Woodblock edition of 1900 by Su Changtai 肅昌泰 from Gansu. Harvard-Yenching.

9) Woodblock edition dated 1918, reprint of the edition of 1898. National Library.

10) Undated woodblock edition owned by an actor from Zhongjiang 中江 county in Sichuan. Collected by Du Jianhua.

11) Incomplete undated manuscript of the first part of the text. Titled *Newly Continued Precious Scroll of Monk Mulian Rescuing His Mother from Underworld* (Xin xu Mulian seng jiu mu youming baojuan 新寶卷連僧救母幽冥寶傳). Beijing University. Reprinted in *BJCJ*, 28:115–203 and *MJBJ*, III:173–97.

12) Modern critical edition based on edition of 1876 in Xu Ming and Huo Fu 2007, 63–128.

APPENDIX 3: TRANSLATION OF THE FIRST
PASSAGE OF *BAOJUAN OF MAUDGALYĀYANA*
(MANUSCRIPT OF 1440)

In the city of the King's seat [Rājagṛha] there was an elder called Fu Xiang. His family was very wealthy: his camels, mules, elephants, and horses filled the mountains and covered the plain; true pearls filled the storehouses, with heaps of jade and piles of gold. The elder was fond of doing charity and fasting, and constantly practiced the *pāramitās*. The elder suddenly was struck by the grave illness and after several days he died. Husband and wife had only one son, who since his birth liked goodness. His name was Luobu. When Luobu saw that his father had died, he organized a vegetarian feast and a ritual assembly, buried his father in the mountains and maintained mourning for three years.

> When his mourning for his father ended,
> All the family storehouses and treasuries were completely empty.

> People busy themselves wasting their thoughts on account of profit,
> In vain they establish families, storehouses, treasuries, and granaries.
> They pile up rare treasures as high as mountains,
> But no matter how much money you have you cannot buy off death.
> Luobu remained in mourning for three whole years,
> Then he addressed his mother, saying "Listen to your son's words:
> When father was alive the family wealth flourished,
> Now the treasuries are empty and we lack money."

> All sentient beings crave profit, in vain they waste their minds, all their scheming is for nothing;
> Striving only for wealth and rank, they are not willing to cultivate themselves, and only focus on building their enterprise.
> Your children and beloved wife, when death comes knocking, which of them will be willing to die for you?

> The lifespan of a person does not reach hundred years,
> In vain you will store up myriads of coins.
> You may pile up treasures as prominent as mountains,
> But when death arrives it is all for nothing.

NOTES

PROLOGUE

1. This is the most common translation of the genre's name. Daniel L. Overmyer, however, suggests the term *precious volumes* instead (Overmyer 1999, 1). I use the Chinese names of the genres in transcription.
2. For the term *topolect*, see Mair 1989b.
3. Bender 2001, 104; Che Xilun 2009, 330–31.
4. Sangren 1987, 208.
5. For summaries of these stories, see Berezkin and Mair 2014, 5–10; Bender 2001, 121–24; and Lu Yongfeng and Che Xilun 2008, 63–68.
6. Che Xilun regards "sacred words" as a distortion of the name of the *Sacred Edict* (Shengyu 聖諭), the emperor's moral injunctions (Che Xilun 2009, 298); however, the exact wording of this element in the Jingjiang tradition does not support his hypothesis.
7. On this "prosimetric form" in Chinese literature, see Mair 1997.
8. *Jingjiang baojuan* 2007, 1:425.
9. Ibid., 1:427.
10. Ibid., 1:428.

INTRODUCTION

1. The first term is more usual for the southern part of China while the second one is common in the northern part of the country.
2. Sawada Mizuho 1975a, 28–38; Che Xilun 2009, 2–5.
3. Sects (or folk secret religions, Ch. *minjian mimi zongjiao*), which flourished in the sixteenth to seventeenth century (such as the Way [or Teaching] of Yellow Heaven [Huangtiandao], Western Mahāyāna [Xi Dashengjiao], Vast Yang [Hongyangjiao], and other teachings) were centered on belief in the deity-progenitor Unborn (or Eternal) Venerable Mother (Wusheng laomu), who can benefit and save people. These religions, however, also combined ideas of Buddhist, Daoist, and Confucian teachings. Modern scholars treat them as fully developed religious systems; see, e.g., Overmyer 1976; Ma Xisha and Han Bingfang 2004; and Seiwert and Ma Xisha 2003.

4. Zheng Zhenduo 1996, 478–513; Li Shiyu 2007a, 20–24; Overmyer 1999, 3–4. Overmyer calls the period of the thirteenth to the fourteenth century "pre-sectarian."

5. Sawada Mizuho 1975a, 26–27.

6. On the persecution of sects, see, e.g., Overmyer 1976, 26–32; Seiwert and Ma Xisha 2003, 209–210; Ma Xisha and Han Bingfang 2004, 1:126–28, 395–413; Liang Jingzhi 2004, 25–26, 283–85; Li Shiyu 2007b, 343–47.

7. Sawada Mizuho 1975a, 37; on morality books, see, e.g., You Zi'an 1999.

8. Liu Yonghong 2013a, 33–36; Liu Yonghong 2013b.

9. Tan Chanxue 1986; Duan Ping 1992b, 1–206; Che Xilun 2009, 279–333.

10. Yu Yongliang 1997; Fang Buhe 1999, 311–82; Bender 2001; Shi Lin 2010; Qiu Huiying 2010; Berezkin 2011a, 2011b; Yu Dingjun 2012; Satō Yoshifumi et al. 2011; Li Yu et al. 2010.

11. For example, scroll recitation in Zhangye city and Shandan county in Gansu was awarded this title at the state level in 2006; scroll recitation in Shaoxing at the state level in 2007; scripture telling in Jingjiang, scroll recitation in Jinxi (Kunshan), and in Tongli town (Wujiang, Suzhou) at the provincial level in 2007, 2009, and 2009, respectively.

12. Duan Ping 1992a; Fang Buhe 1999, 9–310; *Jingjiang baojuan* 2007; *Heyang baojuan* 2007; *Tongli xuanjuan* 2010; *Jiuquan baojuan* 2011; *Shashang baojuan* 2011. Because of the space limitations, the current study cannot include the complete bibliography of modern studies and editions of *baojuan*.

13. Xue Yibing 2000.

14. Liu Yonghong 2013a, 86–96.

15. Two transcriptions of his name are possible: 目連 and 目蓮.

16. On the development of the idea of hell (Skt. Naraka, Chin. *diyu*, literally "underground prison") in China, see, e.g., Sawada Mizuho 1968; Teiser 1988, 1994.

17. Its complete title is *Baojuan of Reverend Maudgalyāyana Rescuing His Mother [and Helping Her] to Escape from Hell and Be Born in Heaven* (Mujianlian zunzhe jiu mu chuli diyu sheng tian baojuan, according to another manuscript dated to 1440). Most scholars have used the title of *Baojuan of Mulian Rescuing His Mother [and Helping Her] to Escape from Hell and Be Born in Heaven* (Mulian jiu mu chuli diyu sheng tian baojuan, Che no. 691) that appears at the end of the 1372 manuscript. Hereafter, I provide the numbers of *baojuan* texts as given in Che Xilun's catalogue of *baojuan* (if the text is included there); see Che Xilun 2000.

18. See, e.g., Overmyer 1976, 162–93; Nadeau 1990; Overmyer 1999; Ma Xisha and Han Bingfang 2004; Li Shiyu 2007a; ter Haar 2014, 12–84.

19. Zheng Zhenduo 1996, 478–513; Sawada Mizuho, 1975a; Zeng Ziliang 1975; Overmyer 1985.

20. Grant 1989; Nadeau 1994; Dudbridge 2004, 47–56; Yu 2001, 293–352; Idema 2002, 2008a, 2008b, 2009.

21. Xu Yunzhen 2010.

22. The largest collections of *baojuan* reprints are *BJCJ*, *MJBJ*, and *MMZJW*.

23. Idema 2008a, 2008b, 112–59, 181–213; Idema 2009, 9–86; Idema 2015.

24. Chen Fangying 1983; Zhu Hengfu 1993; Liu Zhen 1997; Nomura Shin'ichi 2007; Wang Kui 2010.

25. Mair 1986–87, 1989a, 17–18; Teiser 1988, 43–107; Cole 1998, 80–102, 159–91; Johnson 1989; Zhu Hengfu 1993; Guo 2005; Dai Yun 2006; Wang Kui 2010.

26. Johnson 1995.

27. Grant and Idema 2011, 35–145.

28. The four latter texts are available in collections of reprinted *baojuan* published recently in China; see appendix 2. For an introduction to these texts and a summary of their contents, see, for *Baojuan of Maudgalyāyana*: Zheng Zhenduo 1996, 486–95; Liu Zhen 1997, 251–53; Che Xilun 2009, 72–77; for *Baojuan of Benefiting Living Beings*: Yu Songqing 1994, 205–11; for *Precious Account of Mulian* and *Baojuan of Three Rebirths*: Sawada Mizuho 1975a, 123–26; Chen Fangying 1983, 93–110.

29. The Gangkou town area of Zhangjiagang city, where I also conducted fieldwork, is situated mainly on the land separated from the ancient county of Changshu in 1962.

CHAPTER 1

1. E.g., Bordahl and Wan 2011.

2. For the English translation, see Roy 1993–2013.

3. *Xu Jin ping mei* 1990, 73:1005–35. On the *baojuan* performances in both novels, see Sawada Mizuho 1975a, 285–99, 81–82. In *Plum Flowers*, *baojuan* are presented as a form of Buddhist preaching, which probably testifies to the reception of these texts as mainstream religious writings during the end of the Ming dynasty.

4. On this text, see Che Xilun 2000, 53, no. 228.

5. *Jin ping mei* 1980, 728.

6. Li Shiyu 2007b, 355.

7. On the status of these performers in the context of Chinese ritual and performance culture, see Berezkin 2011b, 35–42.

8. Che Xilun 2009, 284.

9. *Jingjiang baojuan* 2007, 1:1.

10. Bender 2001, 111–12.

11. Lu Yongfeng and Che Xilun 2008, 437.

12. Satō Yoshifumi et al. 2011, 38.

13. On these genres, see Bender 2003 and Bordahl 1996.

14. Johnson 1995, 77.

15. In the past, most storytellers of different traditions were illiterate. Even if they consulted written texts (either through reading or through oral transmission), they did not try to memorize a fixed text; see Lord 1960, 79; Bordahl 1996, 226–28; Bender 2003, 34, 101, 132.

16. Fang Buhe 1999, 314–15; see also Liu Yonghong 2013a, 225–30. In several other areas of Gansu, for example, Min county (Minxian), special ritual associations still exist that recite *baojuan* in conjunction with folk rituals: Liu Yonghong 2013a, 182–206.

17. Li Yu et al. 2010, 113–15.

18. See, e.g., Li Shiyu 2007a, 24–25; Sawada Mizuho 1975a, 81–90; Johnson 1995, 59–69.

19. *Zhen xin baojuan*, 1919, 12b.

20. Foley 1990, 5–8.

21. McLaren 1998, 32.

22. Fang Buhe 1999, 313.

23. *Zhen xin baojuan* 1919, 12b.

24. See Berezkin 2014.

25. You Zi'an 1999, 153–55; Wang Jianchuan 2014, 241–42.

26. Cited in Sawada Mizuho 1975a, 80.

27. Teiser 1995, 378; Overmyer 2009, 46–49.

28. Sangren 1987, 126–31; Teiser 1988, 43–48; Naquin 1992.

29. On the history of the Western Mahāyāna, see, e.g., Sawada Mizuho 1975a, 70–74; Li Shiyu and Naquin 1988; Ma Xisha and Han Bingfang 2004, 1:492–518; Li Shiyu 2007a, 81–112. On the history of the Vast Yang, see Sawada Mizuho 1975a, 366–408; Ma Xisha and Han Bingfang 2004, 1:370–413; Song Jun 2002; Liang Jingzhi 2004, 32–33, 178–88; Li Shiyu 2007b, 331–90.

30. Ma Xisha and Han Bingfang 2004, 1:141.

31. See, e.g., Shek 1980, 202–68; Zheng Zhiming 1985; Nadeau 1990; Overmyer 1999, 92–135; Ma Xisha and Han Bingfang 2004, 1:132–88.

32. Sawada Mizuho 1975a, 73–74; Li Shiyu 2007a, 52–54, 2007b, 337–41, 333–34.

33. Its original variant is ascribed to another famous writer of the earlier period, Luo Guanzhong 羅貫中 (ca. 1330–1400).

34. *Ping yao zhuan* 1980, 70.

35. *Jin ping mei* 1980, 430–31.

36. *Ping yao zhuan* 1980, 72, 74. The story of Miaoshan's self-cultivation and transformation into merciful Bodhisattva Guanyin is the subject of *Baojuan of Xiangshan* (Xiangshan baojuan; Che no. 1290) that was composed around the fourteenth to the fifteenth century and became one of the major *baojuan* texts of the "Buddhist period." On this text, see Dudbridge 2004, 47–56; Overmyer 1999, 38–46; Yu 2001, 293–352; Che Xilun 2009, 109–16. For the full English translation of its late recension (mid-nineteenth century), see Idema 2008a, 45–159.

37. *Ping yao zhuan* 1980, 70.

38. Ibid., 71–72.

39. One should compare it with the immoral and sectarian characteristics of the Buddhist nuns who perform *baojuan* in *Sequel to Plum Flowers in the Golden Vase: Xu Jin ping mei* 1990, 73:1005–35.

40. See, e.g., Yu 1981 and Brook 1993.

41. Cited in Che Xilun 2009, 130–31.

42. Sawada Mizuho 1975a, 287–88.
43. It also is recited by the nuns in *Plum Flowers*: *Jin ping mei* 1980, 452–53.
44. Che Xilun 2009, 130–31.
45. Ibid.
46. Johnson 1995, 64–65; Che Xilun 2009, 213–15.
47. Han Bangqing 1994, 124, 134. For the English translation, see Han Bangqing 2005.
48. Classen 1995, 54, 77.
49. Hayes 1997, xiv.
50. Zheng Zhenduo 1996, 478–79.
51. Mair 1989a, 116.
52. The texts of the talks on scriptures have not been preserved. Evidence concerning them comes from the miscellaneous notes (*biji* 筆記) of that period; see, e.g., Průšek 1938; Zeng Yongyi 2003, 691–700.
53. Zheng Zhenduo 1996, 479.
54. Li Shiyu 2007a, 50; Sawada Mizuho 1975a, 28–29.
55. Sawada Mizuho 1975a, 28–29.
56. Sawada Mizuho interprets the word *xiaoshi* in the text's title as "completely explained," a reference to its purpose as a tool for propagating Buddhism for the lay audience (Sawada Mizuho 1975a, 27). *Keyi*, literally "rule of the lesson," here stands for line-by-line commentary on the sūtra that was recited aloud during a religious assembly. Overmyer translates this title as *Ritual Amplification of the Diamond Sūtra* (Overmyer 1999, 34). From here on, I use English translations of Buddhist terms as provided in the Digital Dictionary of Buddhism, unless otherwise noted.
57. There are several different recensions of *Liturgy Based on the Diamond Sūtra* (Che no. 1346–49); all of them vary considerably. One of the earliest dated editions (1528) is *Jingang jing keyi* 1999 (Che no. 1346). There is also the expanded recension of this text with a postface dated 1551, included in *MZZ*, 92:118–224 (Che no. 1348). Another recension is quoted in *Plum Flowers* (*Jin ping mei* 1980, 452–53). For the other published recensions of this text, see *MMZJW*, 1:63–125; *MZZ*, 129:129–44.
58. Overmyer 1999, 36–38.
59. Sawada Mizuho 1975a, 29–30.
60. Mair 1989a, 29, 150.
61. Mair 1986.
62. Schmid 2002, 103–10.
63. Mair 1989a, 29.
64. Che Xilun 2009, 50–64. The hypothesis of the scholars from Gansu who tried to prove that modern *baojuan* from Gansu originated from *bianwen* discovered nearby (e.g., Duan Ping 1992b, 51–91; Fang Buhe 1999, 365–82) does not seem to be well substantiated. Che Xilun provided evidence that *baojuan* entered Gansu at the beginning of the seventeenth century following the spread of sectarian teachings westward (Che Xilun 2009, 268–75).
65. Che Xilun 2009, 57–62.
66. Ibid., 62–64.

67. Ibid., 65–80.

68. *Baojuan of Journey to the West* was discovered in the twentieth century among the scriptures of the local Teaching of Demon Masters (Mogongjiao 魔公教) in Guizhou; see Che Xilun 2009, 77.

69. See, e.g., Dudbridge 1970.

70. Overmyer 1999, 50.

71. Lord 1960, 141–220.

72. Foley 1990, 2–5.

73. McLaren 1998, 38–39.

74. Foley 2002, 122–23.

75. Foley 1995, 28.

76. Ibid., 8, 11; see also Foley 2002, 113–17.

77. Foley 1995, 47–56.

78. Ibid., 81.

79. Ibid., 75.

80. Ibid., 65.

81. Ibid., 138.

82. Ibid., 137.

83. Ibid., 136–207.

84. Hanan 1977, 87.

85. Mair 1989a, 120.

86. Ibid., 121.

87. Bordahl 2011, 129.

88. McLaren 1998, 154. The two latter elements seem to be analogues of the "theme" term used by Lord for oral literature; see Lord 1960, 68.

89. Yoshikawa Yoshikazu 2003, 80–96, 111–13.

90. Johnson 1995, 75–77; Chen Fangying 1983, 106–10.

91. Overmyer 1999, 4–5.

92. Kerr 1994, 7.

93. Sawada Mizuho 1975a, 43–59; Zeng Ziliang 1975, 43–60; Che Xilun 2009, 83–85, 172–206.

94. *Puming baojuan* 1979, 126–88. A reprinted woodblock edition of this *baojuan* in Saint Petersburg is dated 1599. It belongs to the Teaching of Yellow Heaven. The copy of this text in the Zheng Zhenduo collection was damaged and thus not available at that time.

95. Zeng Yongyi 2003, 662–717.

96. *Puming baojuan* 1979, 152–64.

97. Wang Li 1958, 53, 50.

98. Ibid., 304, 350, 322, 468.

99. *Puming baojuan* 1979, 152–64.

100. Ibid., 164.

101. Duan Ping 1992b, 132–34; Xue Yibing 2000, 32.

102. See, e.g., Yu Yongliang 1997, 81–82.

103. I do not discuss musical accompaniment of *baojuan* at length here. For initial research of *baojuan* music in different regions, see Duan Ping 1992b, 169–77; Wang Yanhong 2006, 17–31; Shi Lin 2010, 54–62; Li Ping 2012, 96–154.

104. Che Xilun 2009, 158–59.
105. *Puming baojuan* 1979, 151–52.
106. Che Xilun 1978, 9.
107. *Puming baojuan* 1979, 165–67.
108. Che Xilun 2009, 83–84.
109. Xue Yibing 2000, 32.
110. Che Xilun 2009, 162–67.
111. Huang Yupian 1972, 78–79. *Kunqu* is a form of drama based on southern melodies that became popular in the late sixteenth to seventeenth century and is still performed today. On Huang Yupian, see Overmyer 1976, 29–32.
112. Che Xilun 2009, 157–59.
113. Qi Senhua 1997, 810–11.
114. Xue Yibing 2000, 36.
115. Wang Yiqing et al. 2000, iii.
116. Wang Li 1958, 774–75.
117. Ibid., 715–26.

CHAPTER 2

1. For the English translation, see Teiser 1988, 49–54.
2. Demiéville et al. 1978, 68, 295.
3. Teiser 1988, 48–54.
4. Ibid., 21–22, 94–95.
5. For the overview, see Mair 1983, 224–25; Teiser 1988, 21–24.
6. Karashima 2013, 303–4.
7. For some aspects of his image in texts of Buddhist canon, see Teiser 1988, 124–30, 147–58; Zhu Hengfu 1993, 3–8; Liu Zhen 1997, 289–94.
8. Zhu Hengfu 1993, 3–8.
9. Liu Zhen 1997, 6–8; Cole 1998, 41–80.
10. Ch'en 1968, 93–94.
11. *TSD*, no. 1792, 39:509c16–511b28; Teiser 1988, 91–95.
12. Cole 1998, 2–12.
13. On its transmission in other countries of East Asia, see, e.g., Miya Tsugio 1968; Chen Fangying 1983, 111–21; Mair 1986–87; Sa Jae-dong 1988; Nomura Shin'ichi 2007.
14. Teiser 1988, 35–42.
15. Ibid., 24–25.
16. Guo 2005, 98–99; Tanaka Issei 2008, 299–301; Wang Kui 2010, 89–91.
17. Teiser 1988, 63–66, 103–7.
18. As published in *Dunhuang bianwen* 1997, 1005–76. For the description of manuscripts representing these texts (twelve altogether), see Kawaguchi Hisao 1984, 53–55.
19. The most complete version is the manuscript catalogued as S (Stein) 2614, dated to 921. For its English translation, see Mair 1983, 123–66. The next most complete version is P (Pelliot) 2319, which is also available in an

English translation; see Eoyang 1978. For the English translation of *Yuanqi of Mulian* (P 2193), see Schmid 2002, 201–29.

20. For details, see Mair 1989a, 156–58.
21. Ibid., 158.
22. *Jiangjingwen of the Ullambana Sūtra* from Dunhuang seems to be a line-by-line interpretation of the original *Sūtra*. Very little of the text has survived, however, and we cannot say if the commentary reflected any elaboration of the story. There are numerous studies of the Mulian story in the texts of Dunhuang popular literature and its connection with oral storytelling; see, e.g., Teiser 1988, 87–91, 99–103; Mair 1989a, 13–14, 17–18; Schmid 2002, 110–27.
23. Miya Tsugio 1968; Zhu Hengfu 1993, 29; Liu Zhen 1997, 16.
24. Skt. *devās trayas-triṃśāḥ*, Ch. *Daolitian* 忉利天, the second of the six heavens of the desire realm.
25. Mair 1983, 225.
26. In dramas and *baojuan*, the Fu in Fuxiang 輔相 (originally part of a personal name) usually is interpreted as the family name of Mulian's father. In these versions, Mulian's mother has the family name Liu.
27. Jaworski 1935–36; Kawaguchi Hisao 1984, 33–35; Teiser 1988, 58–62, 91–94.
28. Sawada Mizuho 1968, 81–105, 149–54; Teiser 1988, 170–90; Mair 1989a, 62–63; Teiser 1994, 19–86.
29. Mair 1989a, 73, 99.
30. Ibid., 100–101.
31. Ibid., 103.
32. Fan Jinshi and Mei Lin 1996; Teiser 2006, 180–82.
33. Mair 1989a, 80–84.
34. See Berezkin 2015.
35. For the reprint of the Japanese edition, see Miya Tsugio 1968, 156–69. For its critical text (done with reference to the Korean edition of 1537), see Yoshikawa Yoshikazu 2003, 116–22. As the date of the original Chinese edition in the colophon was indicated by cyclic signs, there has been much discussion about this date; see Liu Zhen 1997, 242–44. Yoshikawa Yoshikazu discovered, however, that the cyclical signs of the day of publication and its number in the month, which were both included in the colophon, according to chronological tables, coincide only in one year, 1251; Yoshikawa Yoshikazu 2005, 18–19. Thus 1251 should be regarded as the date of publication of the original.
36. For the transcription of labels and interpretation of images, see Yoshikawa Yoshikazu 2003, 100–111. See also Teiser 2006, 240–41.
37. Sa Jae-dong 1988, 224.
38. Ibid., 219.
39. Mair 1986–87, 90–91.
40. Meng Yuanlao 1956, 49.
41. Liu Zhen 1997, 247–48.
42. Hegel 1998, 166.

Notes to Chapter 2

43. Apparently there were several recensions of this work, one titled *Penitence at Ritual Place of Mercy of Mulian Repaying the Basic* (Cibei daochang Mulian baoben chanfa 慈悲道場目連報本懺法) was introduced by Chinese scholars; see Liu Zhen 1997, 248–55.

44. There are also two woodblock printed copies of the same work at the National Library of China: one approximately dating back to the Ming dynasty (undated), and one dated to 1679.

45. Meng Yuanlao 1956, 49.

46. Zhu Hengfu 1993, 31–49; Liu Zhen 1997, 33–36.

47. Liu Zhen 1997, 36–48.

48. For the original edition, see Zheng Zhizhen 1954; the modern punctuated edition is used here.

49. Zheng Zhizhen 2005, 2.

50. Ibid., 2, 3.

51. Ibid., 503.

52. Ibid., 322.

53. Zhu Hengfu 1993, 75–88; Liu Zhen 1997, 36–48.

54. E.g., Chen Fangying 1983, 127–44; Zhu Hengfu 1993, 118–96; Liu Zhen 1997, 65–158; Guo 2005, 103–48.

55. Dai Yun 2006, 35–42.

56. Chen Fangying 1983, 145–51; Zhu Hengfu 1993, 104–11; Liu Zhen 1997, 209–40; Dai Yun 2006, 46–52.

57. The Mulian story in storytelling genres other than *baojuan* is not discussed here. Based on existing research, it is evident that storytelling-type pieces on the Mulian story were influenced by Mulian dramas: Chen Fangying 1983, 4–5; Zhu Hengfu 1993, 95–96; Liu Zhen 1997, 258–76; Dai Yun 2006, 258–67.

58. Liu Zhen 1997, 43–64.

59. See, e.g., Xu Hongtu and Wang Qiugui 1994; Xu Hongtu 1994, 1995; Zhang Ziwei 1999.

60. For the overview, see Hou 2002.

61. E.g., Xu Sinian 1984; Ke Ziming 1991; Du Jianhua 1993; Shi Shengchao and Li Jianming 1994; Xu Ming and Huo Fu 2007; *Sichuan Mulian xi* 1990.

62. E.g., *Ritual Opera*; Guo 2005; Nomura Shin'ichi 2007; Tanaka Issei 2008, 292–344.

63. Mao Gengru 1994, 56–58, 104–26, 260–371.

64. Dai Yun 2006, 300–329; this bibliography also takes into account separate acts, published (and/or preserved) separately.

65. See also Peng 1994.

66. Zhu Hengfu 1993, 88–91.

67. Ibid., 53–60; Lin Qingxi 1992, 35–37; Liu Zhen 1997, 41–42, 160–62; Mao Limei 1992.

68. Shi Shengchao and Li Jianming 1994, 100.

69. Guo 2005, 178–220.

70. In many cases, actors and priests cooperate: Xue Ruolin 1992, 8–11; Wang Kui 2010, 135–45.

71. Liu Zhen 1997, 159–208. The existence of Mulian dramas in northern China, which are usually shorter than southern redactions, also must be considered. Liu Zhen 1997, 203–8; Hou 2002, 44–46.
72. Tanaka Issei 2008, 304–41.
73. Dean 1989; Seaman 1989; Ch'iu 1989; Li Fengmao 1995; Xu Hongtu 1995; Ye Mingsheng 1999; Duan Ming 1999; Wang Kui 2010, 239–54.
74. Liu Zhen 1997, 63–64, 169; Wang Kui 2010, 114–28.
75. Tanaka Issei 2008, 304–14.
76. Wang Kui 2010, 103–6.
77. Tanaka Issei 2008, 292–304.
78. Liu Zhen 1997, 251–57; Overmyer 1999, 46–47; Yoshikawa Yoshikazu 2005, 24–35; Che Xilun 2009, 72–76.
79. Li Shiyu 2007a, 15–16; Sawada Mizuho 1975a, 24–25.

CHAPTER 3

1. For a part of this text, see Zheng Zhenduo 1996, 486–95. The whole preserved text was published in Yoshikawa Yoshikazu 2003, 123–34. I rely mainly on this published text with a few corrections that I made after comparison with the original manuscript in the National Library of China.
2. For an introduction to this manuscript, see Berezkin 2013a.
3. Zheng Zhenduo mistranscribed part of the title of this *baojuan* as "Ascend to Heaven" (*sheng tian*). Zheng Zhenduo 1996, 486.
4. For the translation of the first section, see Appendix 3.
5. On Ayushiridara, see Goodrich et al. 1976, 1:15–17.
6. *Yuan shi* 1997, 18/47/986; *Ming shi* 1997, 20/327/8463–8464.
7. Yoshikawa Yoshikazu 2005, 27.
8. Ibid., 31–33.
9. *Yuan shi* 1997, 18/138/3341–3349.
10. Cited in Che Xilun 2000, 384.
11. Zongjing 1999, 61.
12. Che Xilun 2009, 92–93.
13. *Dizang baojuan* 2005, 502; *Li sheng baojuan* 1999, 397.
14. *Li sheng baojuan* 1999, 397.
15. *Puming baojuan* 1979, 84; *Li sheng baojuan* 1999, 480.
16. *Mujianlian zunzhe jiu mu baojuan* 1440, 3a.
17. I am grateful to Liu Zhen of the Institute for Advanced Humanistic Studies (Fudan University) who helped me read it.
18. The three treasures of Buddhism (Skt. *Tri-ratna* or *ratna-traya*, Ch. *San bao*) are Buddha, Dharma (his teaching), and Samgha (monastic community).
19. *Mujianlian zunzhe jiu mu baojuan* 1440, 3b.
20. This is not to be confused with the "tales of conditioned origin," preserved in Dunhuang.
21. Che Xilun 2009, 69.
22. *Mujianlian zunzhe jiu mu baojuan* 1440, 4a–6a.

23. Che Xilun 2009, 69.
24. Skt. *tathatā*, "thusness" or "suchness," usually indicates the absolute reality that transcends the multitude of forms in the phenomenal world.
25. It presumably means the Western Land of Buddha Amitābha.
26. Yoshikawa Yoshikazu 2003, 132–33.
27. Che Xilun 2009, 76.
28. *Jingangjing keyi* 1999, 4–14.
29. Xingyun et al. 1989, 6:5310, 5:4636.
30. Ibid., 5:4636, 7:6975.
31. Ibid., 6:6728.
32. Ibid., 4:3784, 5:4636.
33. Che Xilun 2009, 512–23, 526–27.
34. See Sun Kaidi 1956, 85–93; Mair 1986; Schmid 2002, 144–47.
35. E.g., *Dunhuang bianwen* 1997, 679–703.
36. Yoshikawa Yoshikazu 2003, 132.
37. Teiser 1988, 51–52; Yoshikawa Yoshikazu 2003, 118–22.
38. *Dizang baojuan* 2005, 592; *Li sheng baojuan* 1999, 427, 476; *Mulian baozhuan* 2002, 84.
39. Che Xilun 2009, 70–71, 79–80.
40. Berezkin 2010, 101–2.
41. Preface dated to 1417; see *Zhu fo geju* 1885. On this text, see Sawada Mizuho 1975b, 79–100.
42. *Zhu fo geju* 1885, 40a, 4:8a–9a, 5:175a.
43. Yoshikawa Yoshikazu 2003, 90–91.
44. *Mujianlian zunzhe jiu mu baojuan* 1440, 3a.
45. Yoshikawa Yoshikazu 2003, 67–70.
46. Ibid., 79–80.
47. See Berezkin 2010, 91–92.
48. Zheng Zhenduo 1996, 486.
49. Yoshikawa Yoshikazu 2003, 69–80, 121, 129–30.
50. Ibid., 132.
51. Ibid., 131.
52. See Yu 1981, 29–63, 73–75.
53. Berezkin and Riftin 2013, 469–70; ter Haar 2014, 14–18.
54. Berezkin 2013a, 127–28.
55. Yoshikawa Yoshikazu 2003, 128, 130.
56. On the development of the concept of the Ten Courts in China, see Sawada Mizuho 1968, 22–29, 81–112, 149–79; Teiser 1988, 179–90; Teiser 1994.
57. Teiser 1988, 182–84.
58. Overmyer 1976, 1–2, 203.
59. ter Haar 2014, 32–34, 47.
60. See Overmyer 1976, 45–46; Shek 1982; Ma Xisha and Han Bingfang 2004, 1:339–52.
61. See, e.g., Mollier 2008, 209–12.
62. Li Shiyu 2007a, 15–16.
63. Yoshikawa Yoshikazu 2003, 133.

64. Li Shiyu 2007a, 16; the earliest reliable description of Unborn Mother in *baojuan* literature dates to the first quarter of the sixteenth century; see, e.g., Overmyer 1999, 136–77. Earlier works mentioning it are spurious; see, e.g., Overmyer and Li 1992; Che Xilun 2009, 506–13.
65. See, e.g., Overmyer 1999, 136–42.
66. Huang Yupian 1972, 62.
67. Pu Wenqi 1996, 57.
68. Yoshikawa Yoshikazu 2003, 130, 132–33.
69. Ibid., 133.
70. Ibid., 132.
71. On the cosmology of Luo Qing, see Zheng Zhiming 1985, 89–120; Nadeau 1990, 241–42; Overmyer 1999, 118–21; Ma Xisha and Han Bingfang 2004, 1:168–72.
72. *Zhengxin chuyi wu xiu zheng zizai baojuan* 1994, 92.
73. Overmyer 1999, 136–49, 388, 395.
74. For the picture, see Ren Jiyu 1999, 102.
75. Yoshikawa Yoshikazu 2003, 121.
76. Kohn 2001, 162–66.
77. Che Xilun 2009, 492–94.
78. Ibid., 494–96.
79. *Mujianlian zunzhe jiu mu baojuan* 1440, 6b. In the Buddhist discourse eight difficulties refer to the circumstances in which it is difficult to see the Buddha or hear his teaching. The three disasters mean wars, pestilence, and famine at the end of the world.
80. Yoshikawa Yoshikazu 2003, 132.
81. Mair 1989a, 73, 99, 100–103.
82. Yoshikawa Yoshikazu 2003, 131.
83. Ibid.
84. Soymié 1965, 132.
85. Cole 1998, 197–214.
86. *Fo shuo Dazang zhengjiao Xuepen jing* 1967, 414.
87. Soymié 1965, 132–33.
88. Wang Kui 2010, 261–63.
89. Zheng Zhizhen 2005, 371–79.
90. Li Zhengzhong 2012, 157–62, 363–92.
91. Che Xilun 2009, 356–58.
92. Ibid., 79–80.
93. Overmyer 1999, 308–9.

CHAPTER 4

1. *Dizang baojuan* 2005, 591, 553.
2. Li Shiyu 2007b, 367–68.
3. Xue Yibing 2000, 35.
4. Li Shiyu 1961, 7.
5. Huang Yupian 1972, 92–93.
6. Yu Songqing 1994, 205.

7. On the history of this teaching, see Li Shiyu 2007b, 429–63; Sawada Mizuho 1975a, 343–65; *Puming baojuan* 1979, 74–126; Shek 1982; Ma Xisha and Han Bingfang 2004, 1:308–69; Seiwert and Ma Xisha 2003, 293–318.
8. Li Shiyu 1961, 33; x indicates missing characters.
9. Li Shiyu 2007b, 447–48.
10. Personal name Lü Niu, also known as Nun Lü (Lü Gu), Bodhisattva Lü (Lü Pusa), Imperial Aunt (Huang Gu) (ca. 1392/1396–1489). On the legend that connects nun Lü with the Ming emperor Yingzong (1427–1464), see Li Shiyu and Naquin 1988, 133–36; Ma Xisha and Han Bingfang 2004, 1:492–97.
11. Ma Xisha and Han Bingfang 2004, 1:499–508.
12. See Berezkin 2010, 156.
13. *Dizang baojuan* 2005, 519.
14. Ma Xisha and Han Bingfang 2004, 1:496–97.
15. *Dizang baojuan* 2005, 519–20. The same term was used for the moral injunctions composed by the Shengzu (Kangxi) emperor (1662–1722) and intended for regular recitation for an audience of common people. One of their aims was to keep people away from the sects. There is a similarity in the methods used by the imperial authority and sectarian teachers. On the recitations of the *Sacred Edict* in late imperial China, see Mair 1985.
16. Overmyer 1999, 175.
17. *Dizang baojuan* 2005, 522, 575.
18. Sawada Mizuho 1975a, 71; Che Xilun 2009, 140–41.
19. Ma Xisha and Han Bingfang 2004, 1:516, 502.
20. Ibid., 1:310–25.
21. *Li sheng baojuan* 1999, 426.
22. Sawada Mizuho 1975a, 343–65; Ma Xisha and Han Bingfang 2004, 1:314.
23. *Li sheng baojuan* 1999, 429.
24. Ma Xisha and Han Bingfang 2004, 1:314–15; modern scholars argue that *Puming baojuan* now available was compiled by Puming's descendants. *Puming baojuan* 1979, 74; Ma Xisha and Han Bingfang 2004, 1:328.
25. See Berezkin 2010, 163–64.
26. Yan Yuan 2000, 181.
27. Ma Xisha and Han Bingfang 2004, 1:321.
28. *Dizang baojuan* 2005, 504–10.
29. Ch. *Bore boluomi*, perfection of wisdom, one of the major skills for reaching enlightenment in Mahāyāna Buddhism; *Dizang baojuan* 2005, 592–95.
30. *Puming baojuan* 1979, rpt. 5–20, rpt. 212–32.
31. Berezkin 2010, 123–24.
32. *Puming baojuan* 1979, 173.
33. Wang Li 1958, 756, 762.
34. Che Xilun 2009, 163–65.
35. Ibid., 164.
36. The twelve palaces are zodiacal constellations, known in China through the Buddhist tradition.

37. Duan Baolin et al. 1988, 303–4.
38. *Puming baojuan* 1979, 140; Che Xilun 2009, 185.
39. Berezkin 2010, 127–28.
40. Che Xilun 2009, 169–72.
41. Berezkin 2010, 128–31.
42. See ibid., 131–32.
43. *Dizang baojuan* 2005, 592.
44. Berezkin 2010, 132–33.
45. Lord 1960, 30–35.
46. *Dizang baojuan* 2005, 502–3; *Li sheng baojuan* 1999, 402–15.
47. In *Dizang baojuan*, treasure is called *mohe*, which usually is used for the transcription of Skt. *mahā* (great) instead of the usual *moni*. The author probably confused two different Buddhist terms. Later, this treasure also is called "golden pill" (*jindan*), which indicates the mixture of Buddhist and inner elixir terms common in *Dizang baojuan*.
48. *Dunhuang bianwen* 1997, 1031, 1012; Yoshikawa Yoshikazu 2003, 120, 126.
49. *Li sheng baojuan* 1999, 404–8.
50. *Dunhuang bianwen* 1997, 1011, 1025, 1071; Yoshikawa Yoshikazu 2003, 117–18.
51. *Dizang baojuan* 2005, 513–14.
52. Ibid., 516.
53. Pu Wenqi 1996, 99, 408–9.
54. Ibid., 161.
55. Originally an unemployed official but usually an address for a rich person.
56. *Dizang baojuan* 2005, 580.
57. E.g., *TSD*, no. 262, 9:56c3.
58. Sawada Mizuho 1975a, 66.
59. *Li sheng baojuan* 1999, 415–16.
60. Overmyer 1999, 137–77, 329–30, 249–51; Seiwert and Ma Xisha 2003, 283–84, 373.
61. Sudhana (Ch. Shancai tongzi) is portrayed as a pious young layman who visited many bodhisattvas in search of the true teaching in Buddhist scriptures. In popular belief, he became a disciple and acolyte of Guanyin; see Idema 2008a, 30–41.
62. Pūrna (full name Pūrna-maitrāyaṇiputra, Pali Puṇṇa, Ch. Fulouna) is one of the first ten disciples of Buddha.
63. King of Empty Skandhas should be the title of Buddha, but Reverend Lion is a character unknown to me.
64. *Dizang baojuan* 2005, 535.
65. *Li sheng baojuan* 1999, 408.
66. Zheng Zhizhen 2005, 493.
67. Zhu Hengfu 1993, 94–95.
68. Zhang Zhao 1964, vol. 5, part 9.18a.
69. *Li sheng baojuan* 1999, 400–403.
70. Zhang Ziwei 1999, 269–70; also *Qian Mulian* 1982, 129–38.

71. *Mulian wai zhuan* 1982, 410-13; *Sichuan Mulian xi* 1990, 54, 234-35, 35, 262-63.
72. Zhu Hengfu 1993, 51.
73. Ibid.
74. There are several monographs dedicated to the study of Dizang's cult in China, but they use sources mostly of the fifth to thirteenth century and do not discuss details of the connection between Mulian and Dizang; see, e.g., Sawada Mizuho 1968, 101-25; Wang-Toutain 1998; Zhang Zong 2003; Ng 2007.
75. Wang-Toutain 1998, 79-80.
76. On the Central Asian connections of Dizang, see Wang-Toutain 1998, 70; Ng 2007, 229-40.
77. *TSD*, no. 412, see also Mark 2005, 290.
78. Wang-Toutain 1998, 15.
79. *Dizang pusa benyuan jing* 1983, 778-79, 780-81. For the English translation of these episodes, see Mark 2005, 290-94.
80. This hypothesis was proposed by Liu Zhen 1997, 19-20; see also Ng 2007, 109-10, 201-3.
81. Liu Zhen 1997, 25-27.
82. *San jiao sou shen da quan* 1989, 304.
83. Huang Yupian 1972, 92.
84. See Dudbridge 2004, 5-36; Yu 2001, 291, 296.

CHAPTER 5

1. It was related to the millenarian uprising of Xu Hongru in 1622, which significantly shattered the Ming state; see, e.g., Ma Xisha and Han Bingfang 2004, 1:414-33.
2. ter Haar 2014, 47.
3. Overmyer 1976, 135-37; Li Shiyu 2007a, 8-10.
4. Amitābha is called the Buddha of the future in other sectarian *baojuan* (Overmyer 1999, 136).
5. *Dizang baojuan* 2005, 590.
6. Overmyer 1999, 156.
7. Ibid., 56, 141; Seiwert and Ma Xisha 2003, 274.
8. *Dizang baojuan* 2005, 567; the expression "miraculous sounds" (*miaoyin* 妙音) may refer to the sectarian teaching itself.
9. *Dizang baojuan* 2005, 576, 578, 587.
10. Overmyer 1999, 71, 168-69; Seiwert and Ma Xisha 2003, 279.
11. *Dizang baojuan* 2005, 576.
12. Huang Yupian 1972, 94; Overmyer 1976, 139-40.
13. *Li sheng baojuan* 1999, 420; *Puming baojuan* 1979, rpt. 21.
14. The latter is equated with Puming; *Li sheng baojuan* 1999, 475-76; *Puming baojuan* 1979, rpt. 218-22.
15. Two previous assemblies are associated with the three-petaled and six-petaled lotuses: *Puming baojuan* 1979, 94; the Assembly of Nine-Petaled Golden Lotus is also called Dragon-Flower Assembly (Longhuahui).

Dragon-Flower Assembly, presided over by Maitreya, originally was the Buddhist notion, but it was adopted by sectarian teachings and became one of the major concepts in *baojuan* of the sixteenth and seventeenth centuries. Overmyer 1999, 46, 81, 138, 250, 266.

16. *Li sheng baojuan* 1999, 476.
17. *Puming baojuan* 1979, rpt. 224.
18. *Li sheng baojuan* 1999, 476; *Puming baojuan* 1979, rpt. 224–25.
19. Huang Yupian 1972, 58–59.
20. Skt. *pañca-śila*, Ch. *wujie* 五戒, the minimal set of moral restrictions to be observed by Buddhist lay (householder) practitioners.
21. E.g., *Li sheng baojuan* 1999, 422–23.
22. E.g., Overmyer 1976, 93–95; Seiwert and Ma Xisha 2003, 165–85.
23. Topley 1963, 375; Overmyer 1976, 7–11; Liang Jingzhi 2004, 283.
24. *Dizang baojuan* 2005, 551.
25. Ibid., 586.
26. Jordan and Overmyer 1986, 36–49.
27. *Dizang baojuan* 2005, 551. The name of this monastery comes from the metaphor of thunder sounds for the Buddha's preaching.
28. Ibid.
29. Ibid., 521.
30. This name is usually an abbreviation of the *Mahāyāna Sūtra of the Skillful Means for Repaying the Kindness of the Buddha* (Da fangbian Fo bao en jing; TSD, no. 156, 3:124–66). Here, it also may refer, however, to other popular sūtras, such as the *Sūtra of the Difficulty of Repaying the Kindness of Parents* (Fumu en nan bao jing; TSD, no. 684, 16:778–79); on these texts, see Cole 1998, 204, 42–46, 132–51.
31. *Dizang baojuan* 2005, 504.
32. Ibid., 592.
33. Ibid., 506.
34. Ibid.
35. Berezkin 2010, 192–93.
36. *Li sheng baojuan* 1999, 398.
37. *Dizang baojuan* 2005, 586.
38. Mair 1985, 327.
39. Overmyer 1999, 399, 229.
40. *Li sheng baojuan* 1999, 417. These are important terms in the inner elixir theory; see the next section of this chapter.
41. ter Haar 2014, 131–37.
42. Naquin 1985, 259–76.
43. Literally "square inch ground" (*fangcun di*). This term often is used for the heart but here clearly includes other organs.
44. *Dizang baojuan* 2005, 550.
45. *Li sheng baojuan* 1999, 469, 479.
46. Kohn 2000, 464.
47. Skar 2003, 112–56.
48. Kohn 2000, 464.
49. Overmyer 1999, 48–49; Ma Xisha and Han Bingfang 2004, 1:346–47.

50. Kohn 2000, 611–12.
51. *Puming baojuan* 1979, rpt. 12.
52. Kohn 2000, 612.
53. Palace presumably signifies the paradise of the Unborn Mother.
54. The substances of inner elixir are not named in this passage; I translate them as "them," "it," and so on. Presumably, these are *qi* or *jing* (essence) substances of the body.
55. *Liu men*. This is the general name for the apertures in the human body, including the nose, eyes, ears, etc.
56. This is presumably the so-called Middle Palace, the Seat of Destiny (Zhonggong Mingfu), the place where elixir (*jindan*) is formed. This and similar terms represent fantastic geography (it is sometimes not clear whether they refer to the body or the cosmos, or to both simultaneously), so I capitalize them as geographical names.
57. "Flowers of the heart" (*xinhua*) is the Buddhist metaphor for a tranquil and pious state of mind.
58. I was unable to identify this term. I do not note all the unclear terms in this passage.
59. The navel is considered the place where the elixir of immortality is nurtured in the human body in many inner elixir treatises. It also is identified with the Middle Palace and the Elixir Field.
60. The Elixir Field (Dantian) is the place where the elixir of immortality is prepared. Here, it should stand for the lower Elixir Field below the navel.
61. Crossroad of the Three Paths (Sanchakou) is the acupuncture point between genitals and anus. It is regarded as an important point, as it is the intersection of the Channels of Control and Conception (Renmai, Dumai). Hu Fuchen et al. 1995, 1175.
62. This is the particular way of the circulation of *qi*. There are two different explanations of its movement in different texts. According to one of the explanations, this term denotes the circulation of the original *qi*, nurtured in the Elixir Field, upward through the Three Barriers (San Guan): the Coccyx Barrier (Weilüguan), the Spine Barrier (Jiajiguan), and the Jade Pillow (Occiput) Barrier (Yuzhenguan). Hu Fuchen et al. 1995, 1252. The Coccyx and Jade Pillow barriers are mentioned in the text that follows.
63. Located near the back brain bone.
64. *Duoniugong*.
65. Skt. Lokanātha, Ch. Shizun 世尊, one of the ten epithets of Buddha Śākyamuni.
66. Emei 峨嵋 Mountain in Sichuan province is a sacred site of Chinese Buddhism. Here, it refers to the sacredness of human nature, the potential for enlightenment.
67. In Śāla tree forest, where the trees grew in pairs, the Buddha passed into final nirvana, a sacred place.
68. Skt. *catasro-yonaya*, Ch. *si sheng*, the four ways that living beings are born into in the three realms in Buddhist cosmology: viviparous, oviparous, born from moisture, and metamorphic.
69. *Dizang baojuan* 2005, 504–6.

70. Seiwert and Ma Xisha 2003, 280.
71. Berezkin 2010, 185–86.
72. Overmyer 1999, 49.
73. Schipper 1993, 105.
74. For a detailed analysis of the presentation of inner elixir in these texts, see Berezkin 2010, 182–94.
75. *Li sheng baojuan* 1999, 401.
76. Yan Yuan 2000, 181.
77. Kohn 2000, 101.
78. Teiser 1988, 140, 158.
79. Che Xilun 2009, 144.
80. This is a miraculous mirror that can expel demons.
81. *Dizang baojuan* 2005, 512.
82. For discussion of them, see Overmyer 1999, 223–24, 343–46, 351–55.
83. *Taishan Dongyue baojuan* 1999, 16; Overmyer 1999, 343–46, 351–55.
84. *Dizang baojuan* 2005, 566.
85. *Taishan Dongyue baojuan* 1999, 16.
86. The Western Mahāyāna Teaching is a good example; see also Overmyer 1999, 405; Yu 2001, 449–86.
87. *Dizang baojuan* 2005, 561–65.
88. Ibid., 505.
89. Ibid., 565.
90. Liang Jingzhi 2004, 292–94.
91. *Dizang baojuan* 2005, 550.
92. Wang Yanhong 2006, 15.
93. Li Shiyu 2007b, 354–56.
94. Xue Yibing 2000, 35; Wang Yanhong 2006, 10, 15.
95. Seiwert and Ma Xisha 2003, 312.
96. Ma Xisha and Han Bingfang 2004, 1:395.
97. Ibid., 1:462–65. This tendency, however, is not clearly reflected in *Baojuan of Benefiting Living Beings* discussed here.
98. Liu Yonghong 2013a, 85–91, 197–207; see also chapter 7.
99. Naquin 1985, 289.
100. Li Shiyu 2007b, 353.
101. Wang Yanhong 2006, 10.

CHAPTER 6

1. E.g., Qiu Huiying 2010, 214.
2. Duan Ping 1992a, 1:7, 2:911–80.
3. See Berezkin 2010, 207–8, 232.
4. The earliest edition listed in the catalogue by Che Xilun is dated 1881 (Che Xilun 2000, 166).
5. Tan Chanxue 1986, 13. The first page of this edition with this date was reproduced in the first volume of the collection of *baojuan* from Jiuquan (*Jiuquan baojuan* 2011, 1:3); however, the modern edited recension of this text in the third volume of this series is based on the manuscript dated 1890 by

Wang Yong from the same Jiankang prefecture (appendix 2, XVII, no. 4) and closely follows the edition of 1876.

6. The main sponsor of the 1881 edition.
7. *Mulian baozhuan* 2002, 10.
8. Ibid., 13–14.
9. Ibid., 7.
10. Johnson 1995, 88–103.
11. Ibid., 88.
12. *Mulian baozhuan* 2002, 10.
13. The preface by Yinan Zi in this edition is dated 1899, however. It may be a later addition.
14. Ma Xisha and Han Bingfang 2004, 2:820.
15. On Huang Dehui, see, e.g., Ma Xisha and Han Bingfang 2004, 2:819–24.
16. *Mulian baozhuan* 1999, 945.
17. Ibid.
18. For details, see Berezkin 2010, 215–16.
19. *Mulian baozhuan* 2002, 102; Li Rong 1998, 303.
20. Liu Yonghong 2013a, 81–82.
21. You Zi'an 1999, 65, 148, 152.
22. Li Shiyu 1961, 11–12; Sawada Mizuho 1975a, 75–76; You Zi'an 1999, 153.
23. You Zi'an 1999, 155–56.
24. *Mulian san shi baojuan* 1994, 282–335.
25. *Mulian baozhuan* 2002, 154–85.
26. Counting the flow of time.
27. Poetic name of India, the native country of the historical Buddha.
28. *Mulian san shi baojuan* 1994, 240. For citations from *Baojuan of Three Rebirths*, I consulted the complete English translation in Grant and Idema 2011, 35–145.
29. *Mulian san shi baojuan* 1994, 241.
30. I.e., you will be clear.
31. *Mulian baozhuan* 2002, 17.
32. Sawada Mizuho 1975a, 53–55.
33. Duan Ping 1992b, 11; Che Xilun 2009, 297–98; Lu Yongfeng and Che Xilun 2008, 140–41.
34. *Mulian san shi baojuan* 1994, 392–95.
35. See Berezkin 2011a, 18–22.
36. Li Shiyu 2007a, 29–30.
37. Bender 2003, 26, 87.
38. Li Shiyu 2007a, 23; Sawada Mizuho 1975a, 57.
39. *Mulian san shi baojuan* 1994, 367–69.
40. See Berezkin 2010, 231–32.
41. See ibid., 232–33.
42. Li Shiyu 2007a, 23; Sawada Mizuho 1975a, 57.
43. Furthermore, in the edition of 1898, the one primarily used here, the motif of the aria "Crying during five [night] watches" is rendered as

"Tightening silver knot" (Yin niu xi[si]), a popular tune widely used in the central areas of China at the time of the text composition.

44. *Mulian san shi baojuan* 1994, 256–58.
45. Qi Senhua 1997, 810; Sawada Mizuho 1975b, 67–78.
46. *Heyang baojuan* 2007, 1:282; *Jingjiang baojuan* 2007, 1:421.
47. *Mulian san shi baojuan* 1994, 274–75.
48. Chen Ruheng 1958, 245–50; Sawada Mizuho 1975b, 259–90; Qi Senhua 1997, 74–75.
49. Chen Ruheng 1958, 247–48.
50. Ibid., 246.
51. Wang Li 1958, 674.
52. *Jiuquan baojuan* 2011, 1:336.
53. Johnson 1995, 88.
54. *Shisan jing zhushu* 1999, 10:52.
55. *Mulian san shi baojuan* 1994, 274–75. Liu Jia is an evil person who entices his sister into breaking the fast; the character apparently was borrowed from Mulian drama.
56. See Berezkin 2010, 237–38.
57. E.g., Zheng Zhizhen 2005, 88.
58. *Mulian san shi baojuan* 1994, 273.
59. This formula is used exclusively with the ten-character meter verses. The seven-character meter verses are introduced with another formula, "the verse says."
60. Zheng Zhenduo 1996, 486; Johnson 1995, 84, 89, 101.
61. See Berezkin 2010, 242–43.
62. *Mulian san shi baojuan* 1994, 253.
63. Liu Zhen 1997, 120–22.
64. *Mulian san shi baojuan* 1994, 253; *Mulian baozhuan* 2002, 118.
65. *Mulian san shi baojuan* 1994, 253; *Mulian baozhuan* 2002, 118.
66. Wang Yue 1990a, 34–35; *Sichuan Mulian xi* 1990, 229–31.
67. This is preserved in a number of undated manuscripts (unpublished); the contents are summarized in Zhu Hengfu 1993, 65–66; Ke Ziming 1991, 1–7; Lin Qingxi 1992, 28–29.
68. Zhu Hengfu 1993, 53–60; Lin Qingxi 1992, 29–35; Mao Limei 1992, 22; Liu Zhen 1997, 41–42.
69. Hu Tiancheng 1990, 7–9; *Sichuan Mulian xi* 1990, 229, 262; Liu Zhen 1997, 176.
70. *Mulian baozhuan* 2002, 54–58.
71. These details are similar to those in the Putian drama, *Fu Tiandou* (Ke Ziming 1991, 12).
72. *Precious Account of Mulian* also contains the story of Shenguang's apprenticeship to Bodhidharma, which is a popular piece of Chan school lore; see, e.g., *TSD*, no. 2076, 51:218c12.
73. Lin Qingxi 1992; Mao Limei 1992, 22; Li Huaisun 1992, 74; *Hunan xiqu*, 56:141–238; Zhang Ziwei 1999, 142–80; Wang Yue 1990a, 32–33; Wang Yue 1990b, 52–53; *Sichuan Mulian xi* 1990, 260–61; Mao Gengru 1994, 104–5.

74. E.g., Ke Ziming 1991, 2; Mao Limei 1992, 12; Wang Yue 1990a, 35; Wang Yue 1990b, 54.

75. Based on the late Qing script and records of old actors, this was put together and published as a mimeograph in 1962 (Xu Sinian 1984, 80–82).

76. Jinge and Yinge also act in *Precious Account of Mulian*, but there they are the sons of Fu Chong (Mulian's grandfather) and not Fu Xiang (*Mulian baozhuan* 2002, 47).

77. *Jiu mu ji* 1962, 23, 26–29; see also Xu Hongtu 1994, 47–48, 52–55.

78. On the latter, see Che Xilun 2009, 497–500.

79. See Berezkin 2013b.

80. *Mulian baozhuan* 2002, 195.

81. See Berezkin 2010, 292–93.

82. E.g., Zhu Hengfu 1993, 98–99; Liu Zhen 1997, 36; Ke Ziming 1991, 19.

CHAPTER 7

1. *Mulian san shi baojuan* 1994, 330.
2. Ma Xisha and Han Bingfang 2004, 2:858–63.
3. *Shisan jing zhushu* 1999, 10:51; Ma Xisha and Han Bingfang 2004, 2:861.
4. *Mulian san shi baojuan* 1994, 394.
5. This is another name for the Pure Land.
6. *Mulian san shi baojuan* 1994, 372.
7. Ibid., 362–89.
8. Ibid., 281.
9. Wang Shan's name means "righteous."
10. *Mulian san shi baojuan* 1994, 362–89.
11. Ibid., 393.
12. Scriptures here also may mean *baojuan*. Compare with the "telling scriptures" term for *baojuan* performances in Changshu and Jingjiang.
13. Welch 1967, 112–13.
14. *Mulian san shi baojuan* 1994, 359.
15. Yu Yongliang 1997, 76; Yu Dingjun 2012, 104.
16. *Mulian san shi baojuan* 1994, 393.
17. Ibid., 371.
18. Ibid., 244–46, 362–89.
19. Naquin 1985, 285; Seiwert and Ma Xisha 2003, 465–70; Liang Jingzhi 2004, 102–12.
20. I translate *dian* as "to point" because this word has a similar borrowed meaning in English. Apparently it means "teacher's exhortation" here.
21. *Mulian san shi baojuan* 1994, 281.
22. Ibid., 307.
23. Overmyer 1976, 31.
24. The paradox is that propagators of the true teaching also are represented as "single monks" in the text.
25. *Mulian san shi baojuan* 1994, 286.
26. Zheng Zhizhen 2005, 73, 225.

27. E.g., de Groot 1903, 1:197–241; Wang Jianchuan 1996, 2–21; Lin Meirong 2008, 74–81; ter Haar 2014, 180–83, 210–13.
28. Ma Xisha and Han Bingfang 2004, 2:817–58.
29. Wang Jianchuan 1996, 2–3, 117–18.
30. See Che Xilun 2009, 280–81, 405.
31. *Jingjiang baojuan* 2007, 1:407. There is abundant evidence that the Teaching of Non-Interference was active in southern Jiangsu for a long time; see ter Haar 2014, 107, 129, 200–202.
32. On the complex and still not very clear history of the Great Way of Former Heaven, see de Groot 1903, 1:176–96; Topley 1963; Lin Wanchuan 1985, 3–75; Wang Jianchuan 1996, 75–114; Ma Xisha and Han Bingfang 2004, 2:815–71; Lin Meirong 2008, 74–81; You Zi'an 2012.
33. *Mulian baozhuan* 2002, 96.
34. Ma Xisha and Han Bingfang 2004, 2:816.
35. *Mulian baozhuan* 2002, 62.
36. Ibid., 97; see also Berezkin 2010, 265–66.
37. Topley 1963, 376; Li Shiyu 2007b, 110–12.
38. *Mulian baozhuan* 2002, 98–99; Berezkin 2010, 266–67.
39. E.g., Sawada Mizuho 1975a, 34–38; Overmyer 1999, 4–5; Che Xilun 2009, 2–5.
40. Guo 2005, 114–25.
41. Zheng Zhizhen 2005, 249–50.
42. *Shisan jing zhushu* 1999, vol. 5, part 2, p. 581.
43. *Mulian san shi baojuan* 1994, 392–93.
44. Idema 2002, 84–87; Che Xilun 2009, 545–55.
45. Li Shiyu 2007b, 154–208, 259–72.
46. Ma Xisha and Han Bingfang 2004, 2:830.
47. *Mulian san shi baojuan* 1994, 336–37.
48. Yu Dingjun 2012, 102–3.
49. Che Xilun 2009, 394–95. For the reprint of edition dated 1606, see Ma Xisha 2013, 3:425–578.
50. Che Xilun 2009, 389–97.
51. On the Buddhist ceremonies called "Sevens," see Teiser 1994, 1.
52. Yu Dingjun 2012, 103–8.
53. *Mulian jiu mu diyu baojuan* 2004, 15–37.
54. See Berezkin 2011a, 11–12.
55. Liu Yonghong 2013a, 85–86, 225.
56. Tan Chanxue 1986, 11–12.
57. *Jiuquan baojuan* 2011, 1:5.
58. Mair 1988, 12; Che Xilun 2009, 395.
59. See, e.g., Lagerwey 1987, 173–74; Xu Hongtu 1995, 26–27; Wang Kui 2010, 243–44; Yang Shixian 2011, 104.
60. See, e.g., Stevenson 2001; Dai Xiaoyun 2009.
61. Li Shiyu 2007b, 354.
62. *Mulian san shi baojuan* 1994, 255–56.
63. Pillsbury 1978, 11–20.
64. *Mulian baozhuan* 2002, 175–76.

65. See also Che Xilun 2009, 348–54.
66. Yu Dingjun 2012, 104–9.
67. *Jingjiang baojuan* 2007, 1:417–21.
68. Chau 2006, 129–30.
69. Wu Zhongzheng 2005, 26.
70. See Seaman 1989, 174–75; Duan Ming 1999, 159–60; Wang Kui 2010, 230.
71. Xu Hongtu and Wang Qiugui 1994, 46, 90–92.
72. Dai Bufan 1994, 325–26; see also Xu Hongtu 1995, 17, 64–65.
73. E.g., Xu Hongtu and Wang Qiugui 1994, 15–21; Xu Hongtu 1994, 1995.
74. See, e.g., Huang Wenhu 1992.
75. See Berezkin 2013b.
76. Ibid., 100–103.
77. After the ancient Chinese name for the underworld abode of the dead, Yellow Springs (Huangquan).
78. *Mulian san shi baojuan* 1994, 394; see also Berezkin 2013b, 105–6.
79. Teiser 1988, 219–21.
80. Yu Dingjun 2012, 66–67.
81. Ma Shutian 2002, 97–100.
82. Johnson 1995, 102–3.
83. Ibid., 103.

GLOSSARY OF CHINESE, JAPANESE, AND KOREAN TERMS

Abi 阿鼻
Anrentang 安仁堂
Anyanggong 安養宮
Ayushiridara 愛猷識理 (禮、里) 達腊

Ba Xian 八仙
Bai (surname) 白
bai yuan 拜願
baiwen juan 白文卷
banqiangxi 板腔系
Bao en feng pen jing 報恩奉盆經
Bao en jing 報恩經
Bao shi en 報十恩
Bao zu baojuan 報祖寶卷
baochan 寶懺
baojing 寶經
baojuan 寶卷
Baojuan liutong ba fa 寶卷流通八法
Baomingsi 保明寺
Baoshantang 寶善堂
baozhuan 寶傳
Bei Song San Sui Ping yao zhuan 北宋三遂平妖傳
Beizong 北宗
bi'an 彼岸
Bianliang 汴梁

bianwen 變文
biaoshuo 表說
Boluomen nü 婆羅門女
Bore boluomi 般若波羅蜜
bu ti, que (dan) shuo 不提, 卻 (單) 說
bu ti, zai biao 不提, 再表

Can Tang Wudai shi yanyi zhuan 殘唐五代史演義傳
caojuan 草卷
Chahar 察哈爾
Chanding 禪定
chanfa 懺法
Chang'an 長安
Changshu 常熟
Changzhou 常州
chaodu 超度
Che Xilun 車錫倫
Chen (surname) 陳
Chen Duo 陳鐸
Chen Runshen 陳潤身
Cheng (surname) 程
Chenhe 辰河
chenzi 襯字
Chuan lao song 川老頌

213

chui jiang bao 垂繮報
ci (lyrics) 詞
Cibei lanpen Mulian daochang chanfa 慈悲蘭盆目連道場懺法
cihua 詞話
ciquxi 詞曲系

Da fangbian Fo bao en jing 大方便佛報恩經
Da Muqianlian minjian jiu mu bianwen 大目乾連冥間救母變文
Dai Wen 戴文
Daming 大名
Damo 達摩
dangren 當人
Dangyang Fo 當陽佛
dantian 丹田
daochang 道場
daoqing 道情
daoren 道人
daoxuan 倒懸
Dasheng baojuan 大聖寶卷
Dasheng Wuwei gui kong zhi lu baojuan 大乘無為歸空指路寶卷
Dashengjiao 大乘教
Dashizhi 大勢至
Dazang 大藏
dian 點
diewen 牒文
Ding Yaokang 丁耀亢
Dingzhou 定州
diyu 地獄
diyu bian 地獄變
Dizang 地藏
Dizang baojuan 地藏寶卷
Dizang pusa benyuan jing 地藏菩薩本願經
Dizang wang pusa zhizhang

youming baojuan 地藏王菩薩執掌幽冥寶卷
Dong Dashengjiao 東大乘教
Dongguo 東郭
Donghua Zhu 東華主
Dongjing menghua lu 東京夢華錄
Douniugong 斗牛宮
Duan Baolin 段寶林
duanlian 鍛煉
duilian 對聯
Dumai 督脈
dunwu 頓悟
Duobao Fo 多寶佛
Duowentian 多聞天

Emei 峨嵋

fachuan 法船
fang hedeng 放河燈
fangcun di 方寸地
Fatian 法天
fayuanwen 發願文
fei wuzhi wenhua yichan 非物質文化遺產
fen 分
Feng Menglong 馮夢龍
Fo shuo Da Mulian jing 佛說大目連經
Fo shuo Dazang zhengjiao Xuepen jing 佛說大藏正教血盆經
Fo shuo li sheng liao yi baojuan 佛說利生了意寶卷
Fo shuo Mulian jiu mu jing 佛說目連救母經
Fo shuo Yulanpen jing 佛說盂蘭盆經
Fogen zhongzi 佛根種子
Fomen Xiyou cibei daochang baojuan 佛門西遊慈悲道場寶卷

Glossary

Fotai 佛臺
fotou 佛頭
Fu 傅, surname
Fu Chong 傅崇
Fu Luobo 傅羅卜
Fu Tiandou 傅天斗
Fu Xiang 傅相 (or 輔相)
Fubao 甫寶
Fugui 富貴
Fuhai 甫海
fuji 扶乩
Fukun 甫坤
Fulouna 富樓那
Fumu en nan bao jing 父母恩難報經
Fuming 甫明
Fushan 甫善
Fuxian 富賢

gai wen 蓋聞
Gangkou 港口
Gaochun 高淳
Gaotai 高臺
gelü 格律
gezan 歌讚
gong'an 公案
gongsheng 貢生
gousi 構肆
gua bang 掛榜
Gua jin suo 掛金鎖
Guan ju 關雎
guanfa 官法
guang jie liang yuan 廣結良緣
Guangmu nü 光目女
Guanwu shi 冠五氏
Guanyin baojuan 觀音寶卷
Guanyinhui 觀音會
gufeng 古風

guhun 孤魂
gui jia 歸家
Gui jia yuan 歸家怨
Guiyuan 歸圓
Guizhi 桂枝
gutishi 古體詩
Haishang hua liezhuan 海上花列傳
Han Bangqing 韓邦慶
han shizi 含十字
Han Taihu 韓太湖
hanshi 含識
He Yin 賀因
hefo 和佛
Heng sha 恆沙
hetong 合同
Hexi 河西
Hongda Shanshuju 宏大善書局
hongtang 紅糖
Hongyangjiao 弘陽教
Hou Jing 侯景
hou Mulian 後目連
Houtu niangniang lingying cibei yuanliu baojuan 后土娘娘靈應慈悲源流寶卷
Hu Guanglu 胡光祿
Hu Sizhen 胡思真
hua shuo 話說
Huai'an 懷安
huan benxiang 還本鄉
huan yuan 還源
Huang Chao 黃巢
Huang cun 黃村
Huang Dehui 黃德輝
Huang Gu 皇姑
Huang Jiuzu 黃九祖
Huang shi nü juan 黃氏女卷

Huang Yupian 黃育楩
Huangji Gu Fo 皇極古佛
Huangji jindan jiulian zhengxin guizhen huanxiang baojuan 皇極金丹九蓮正信歸真還鄉寶卷
Huangquan 黃泉
Huangtiandao 黃天道 (or 皇天道)
huanxi bujin 歡喜不盡
Huanyuanjiao 還源教
Huiguangsi 慧光寺
huixiang Jingtu wen 回向淨土文
huixiangwen 回向文
Huiyuan 慧遠
huohou 火候

ji 偈, poetry
Jiading 嘉定
jiahui 家會
Jiajiguan 夾脊關
Jian'an 建安
Jian'ou 建甌
Jiande 建德
jiang shanshu 講善書
jiang yinguo 講因果
jiangjing 講經
jiangjing xiansheng 講經先生
jiangjingwen 講經文
Jiangnan 江南
Jiankang 建康
jiao dian 醮殿
jiaxiang 家鄉
Jiaxing 嘉興
jie jie 解結
jie juan 結卷
Jiexiu 介休
Jigu zhangzhe 給孤長者
Jin 金, state

Jin ping mei cihua 金瓶梅詞話
Jin zi jing 金字經
jindan 金丹
jing 經 (scripture)
jing 精 (essence)
Jingang bore boluomi jing 金剛般若波羅蜜經
jingang buhuai zhi ti 金剛不壞之體
Jinge 金哥
Jingjiang 靖江
jingju 京劇
jingtai 經臺
jingtang 經堂
Jingtu Yulanpen jing 淨土盂蘭盆經
jingzheben 經折本
Jintingguan 金庭舘
jintishi 近體詩
Jinxi 錦溪 (town)
Jinxi 金西 (nun)
Jishantang 積善堂
jituo 偈陀
Jiu mu ji 救母記
Jiuhua 九華
jiupin liantai 九品蓮臺
Jiuye jinlian 九葉金蓮
juxiangzan 舉香讚

Kaifeng 開封
kaijingji 開經偈
kaishan zu 開山祖
kaiti 開題
Karashima Seishi 辛島靜志
keyi 科儀
Kinkōji 金光寺
Ku wu geng 哭五更
kunqu 崑曲
Kunshan 崑山

Glossary

Laishui 淶水
Lanling Xiaoxiaosheng 蘭陵笑笑生
lao'an hua 老岸話
Laoshe chaguan 老舍茶館
lei fenfen 淚紛紛
Leiyinsi 雷音寺
Li Bin 李賓
Li Qing baojuan 李清寶卷
Li sheng bao ji 利生寶偈
Li sheng jing 利生經
Li Shiyu 李世瑜
Liang Wu chan 梁武懺
lianhualao 蓮花落
liantaixi 連臺戲
linfan 臨凡
Ling (jiu) shan 靈鷲山
lingyu 鈴魚
Liu (surname) 劉
Liu Jia 劉假
Liu Ju yanyu 六句言語
liu men 六門
Liu Qingti 劉青提
Liu Siniang 劉四娘
Liu Zhengkun 劉正坤
Longhuahui 龍華會
Longhuajiao 龍華教
longpai 龍牌
Longwang 龍王
Lü Gu 呂姑
Lü Niu 呂牛
Lü Pusa 呂菩薩
luan ru ma 亂如麻
Luo Qing 羅清
luobang 螺蚌
Luojiao 羅教

Manao Jingfang 瑪瑙經坊

Meilian 美連
Meng Ke 孟軻
Meng Po Zhuang 孟婆莊
Meng Yuanlao 孟元老
Meng Zi 孟子
miao 廟
miaojing 妙經
Miaoshan 妙善
miaoyin 妙音
Mile 彌勒
Mile Fo shuo Dizang Shi wang baojuan 彌勒佛說地藏十王寶卷
Min 岷, county
mingqian 冥錢
minjian mimi zongjiao 民間秘密宗教
Minsu quyi 民俗曲藝
Minsu quyi congshu 民俗曲藝叢書
Mogao 莫高
mohe 摩訶
[Mohe]Mujianlian [摩訶]目犍連
Molizhi 摩里支
moni 摩尼 (or 末尼)
Mouzi 牟子
Mujianlian zunzhe jiu mu chuli diyu sheng tian baojuan 目犍連尊者救母出離地獄生天寶卷
Mulian 目連 (or 目蓮)
Mulian baojuan 目連寶卷 (or 目蓮寶卷)
Mulian bianwen 目連變文
Mulian jiu mu 目連救母
Mulian jiu mu diyu baojuan 目連救母地獄寶卷
Mulian jiu mu chuli diyu sheng tian baojuan 目連救母出離地獄生天寶卷
Mulian jiu mu san shi de dao quan ben 目蓮救母三世得道全本

Mulian jiu mu youming baozhuan 目連救母幽冥寶傳
Mulian juan quanji 目連卷全集
Mulian san shi jiu mu baojuan 目蓮三世救母寶卷
Mulian xue 目連學
Mulian yuanqi 目連緣起
Mulian zhuan 目連傳
Mulian zun sheng jing 目連尊勝經
Muqianlian 目乾連
muyu 木魚

Naihe Qiao 奈何橋
Naikaku bunko 內閣文庫
Namo Amituo Fo 南無阿彌陀佛
Nan Gaoluo 南高洛
nanxi 南戲
Nanzong 南宗
nian biao 念表
nian gongke 念功課
nianjuan 念卷

Pantaohui 蟠桃會
Piaogao 飄高
pin 品
ping 平, tone
Ping yao zhuan 平妖傳
pingdiao 平調
pinghua 評話
Po xie xiang bian 破邪詳辯
po xuehu 破血湖
pudu 普度
Puming 普明
Puming rulai wuwei liaoyi baojuan 普明如來無為了意寶卷
Putian 莆田
Puxian 普賢

qi 氣
qian Mulian 前目連
qiju 祁劇
Qinding qupu 欽定曲譜
Qing fo ji 請佛偈
Qinglianjiao 青蓮教
Qingti 青提
Qingyang Shanren 青陽山人
Qingzhen Pusa 青真菩薩
qipai 氣拍
qizi fo 七字佛
qu 去, tone
Quan shan jin ke 勸善金科
Quanxiang pinghua wu zhong 全相平話五種
Quanzhen 全真
qupaixi 曲牌系

Randeng 燃燈
ren 仁
Renjitang 仁濟堂
Renmai 任脈
ru 入, tone
rushi wo wen 如是我聞

San bao 三寶
san cong 三從
San Guan 三關
San jiao yuanliu sheng di fozu sou shen da quan 三教源流聖帝佛祖搜神大全
Sanchakou 三岔口
sanqu 散曲
Sawada Mizuho 澤田瑞穗
Shandan 山丹
Shancai tongzi 善財童子
Shang 上, tone
shang cha 上茶

Glossary

shanshu 善書
shanshuju 善書局
Shaoxing 紹興
Sheng Gugu 聖姑姑
sheng tian 升天
shengjuan 聖卷
Shenguang 神光
shengxiang 聖像
shengyu 聖語 (sacred words)
Shengyu 聖諭 (*Sacred Edict*)
shentai 神臺
shentong 神通
shi 詩, poetry
Shi Daochuan 釋道川
Shi wang baojuan 十王寶卷
Shidi Yanjun 十地閻君
Shier gong nei chu xing lianhuale 十二宮內出性蓮花樂
Shijiamuni 釋迦牟尼
shisan zhe 十三轍
shishi 施食
shizanxi 詩讚系
shizi fo 十字佛
Shizi zunzhe 獅子尊者
Shizun 世尊
Shouxing 壽星
shuang tiao 雙挑
shuhewen 疏合文
Shuilu 水路/陸
Shuiluhua 水陸畫
shuo 說
shuo yinguo 說因果
shuo yinyuan 說因緣
shuojing 說經
si 寺
si ju Wuwei 四句無為
si sheng 四生

Sishiba yuan jian xing ge 四十八願見性歌
song fo 送佛
sujiang 俗講
sumu 蘇木
Sun Chuo 孫綽
suqu 俗曲
Suzhou 蘇州

Ta dao ge 踏道歌
Taishan 泰山
Taishan Dongyue shi wang baojuan 泰山東嶽十王寶卷
Taizhou 泰州
Taizu 太祖
Tan Chanxue 譚蟬雪
tanci 彈詞
tanjing 談經
taoshu 套數
Tiangou 天狗
Tianjin 天津
Tianmu 天母
Tianwang 天王
Tiewei Cheng 鐵圍城
tong die 通牒
Tongli 同里
Tongshanshe 同善社
Tudi baojuan 土地寶卷
tuna cailian zhi shu 吐納采練之術
Tuotuo(shi) 脫脫氏

waidan 外丹
wangfa 王法
Wang Li 王力
Wang Sen 王森
Wang Shan 王善
wang sheng zhou 往生咒

Wang Yin 王印
Wang Yiqing 王奕清
Wang Yong 王鏞
Wang Zuoli 王作礪
Wangmu 王母
Wanquan 萬全
Weilüguan 尾閭關
Weituo 韋陀
Weiwei budong Taishan shengen jieguo baojuan 巍巍不動泰山深根結果寶卷
wen zhong biaoshuo 文中表說
Wenchang dijun 文昌帝君
Wenshu 文殊
Wenxiangjiao 聞香教
Wenyi Shuju 文益書局
Wu 吳 (language)
wu chang 五常
Wu Huang 無皇
wu lun 五倫
wu qi 五七
wu sheng wu mie 無生無滅
Wubu liuce 五部六冊
Wudi 武帝
Wujiang 吳江
Wujinyi pusa 無盡意菩薩
Wusheng laomu 無生老母
Wuwei 武威
Wuweijiao 無爲教
Wuxi 無錫
Wuzhe dahui 無遮大會
Wuzong 武宗

Xi 郗, surname
Xi Dashengjiao 西大乘教
Xi Wangmu 西王母
Xia Yuqi 夏雨麒

xiang 鄉
xiangen Fozi 仙根佛子
Xiangshan baojuan 香山寶卷
xianji 仙籍
xiantai 仙胎
Xiantian da dao 先天大道
xiaoqu 小曲
Xiaoshi Jingang jing keyi 銷釋金剛經科儀
Xiaoshi mingzheng diyu baojuan 銷釋明證地獄寶卷
Xieqiao 斜橋
Xijiang yue diao 西江月調
xilai yi 西來意
Ximen Qing 西門慶
Xinan 西南
Xinbian Mulian jiu mu quan shan xiwen 新編目連救母勸善戲文
xingdou 星斗
xingxiangzan 行香讚
Xinhua 新華 (village)
xinhua 心花 (flowers of the heart)
Xiufu 修福
xiulian 修煉
Xiyin Shuju 惜陰書局
Xizhen Xing 喜真星
Xu Hongru 徐鴻儒
Xu Jin ping mei 續金瓶梅
Xuan 宣, family
Xuanguan 玄關
Xuanguan guguang 玄關古光
Xuanguang 宣光
xuanjuan 宣卷
xuanjuan xiansheng 宣卷先生
Xuanzang 玄奘
Xue Yibing 薛藝兵
Xuehu baojuan 血湖寶卷
Xuehu baoku 血湖寶庫

Glossary

Xuehu chanhuiwen 血湖懺悔文
Xuepen Yulan Shenghui 血盆盂蘭勝會

Yan Yuan 顏元
Yancheng 鹽城
yankou 焰口
Yang 楊
yangshen 陽身
yangsheng 養生
Yanluo 閻羅
yanshenghui 延生會
Yanwang 閻王
Yaoshi gufo 藥師古佛
Yaoshi-Mituo 藥師彌陀
Ye (surname) 葉
yecha 夜叉
yi ren xue Dao jiu zu sheng tian 一人學道九祖升天
yi zi chu jia jiu zu sheng tian 一子出家九祖升天
Yiguandao 一貫道
Yihuatang 翼化堂
Yin 鄞, county
Yin niu xi[si] 銀鈕系 [絲]
Yinan Zi 易南子
Yinge 銀哥
Yingzong 英宗
yinyuan 因緣
Yixingbu 宜興埠
Yonngisa 煙起寺
you ji wei zheng, ting wo daolai 有偈為證, 聽我道來
Youming Jiaozhu 幽冥教主
youyuan 有緣
Yu 虞 (publishers)
Yu Songqing 喻松青
Yuan shi 元史

yuanqi 緣起
Yuantong Zhu 圓通主
yuanwai 員外
Yulan da daochang 盂蘭大道場
Yulanpen jing jiangjingwen 盂蘭盆經講經文
Yulin 榆林
Yunkong wang 蘊空王
Yuzhenguan 玉枕關

zaju 雜劇
zan 讚
zanqie fangxia, you tiqi 暫且放下, 又提起
zao zui ru shan 造罪如山
zao zui zhong ru Taishan 造罪重如泰山
ze 仄 (tone)
zhaigong Shi wang 齋供十王
Zhaijiao 齋教
zhaishi 齋事
zhan cao en 展草恩
Zhang (surname) 張
Zhang Jun 張俊
Zhang Xian 張仙
Zhang Zhao 張照
Zhangjiagang 张家港
Zhangjiakou 張家口
Zhangye 張掖
zhaoben xuanke 照本宣科
Zhaozong 昭宗
Zhedong 浙東
Zhen xin baojuan 鍼心寶卷
Zheng Banqiao 鄭板橋
Zheng Qian 鄭騫
Zheng Xie 鄭燮
Zheng Zhenduo 鄭振鐸
Zheng Zhizhen 鄭之珍

Zhengde 正德
Zhengxin chuyi wu xiu zheng zizai baojuan 正信除疑無修證自在寶卷
Zhenjiang 鎮江
zhenjing 真經
zhenkong 真空
Zhenkong Jiaxiang 真空家鄉
zhenru 真如
Zhili 直隸
zhima 紙馬
Zhiyi Zi 知一子
Zhiyuan 至元
Zhong Kui 鍾馗
Zhonggong Mingfu 中宮命府
Zhong-Lü 鈡呂
zhongsheng 衆生
Zhou Shaoliang 周紹良
zhoutian 周天
Zhu Fahu 竺法護
Zhu fo shizun rulai pusa zunzhe mingcheng gequ 諸佛世尊如來菩薩尊者名稱歌曲
Zhu Hengfu 朱恆夫
zhuanbian 轉變
Zhunti 準提
Zitong baojuan 梓童寶卷
Zongjing 宗鏡
Zongmi 宗密
zui ru qiu shan 罪如丘山

BIBLIOGRAPHY

Abbreviations
BJCJ: Zhang Xishun et al., eds. *Baojuan chuji*
Dizang baojuan: *Dizang wang pusa zhizhang youming baojuan*
Dunhuang bianwen: Huang Zheng and Zhang Yongquan, eds. *Dunhuang bianwen jiaozhu*
Heyang baojuan: *Zhongguo Heyang baojuan ji*
Hunan xiqu: *Hunan xiqu chuantong juben*
Jin ping mei: Lanling Xiaoxiaosheng, *Jin ping mei cihua*
Jingang jing keyi: Zongjing, *Xiaoshi Jingang jing keyi*
Jingjiang baojuan: You Hong et al., eds. *Zhongguo Jingjiang baojuan*
Jiuquan baojuan: He Guoning, ed. *Jiuquan baojuan*
Li sheng baojuan: *Fo shuo li sheng liao yi baojuan*
Ming shi: Zhang Tingyu et al. *Ming shi*
MJBJ: Pu Wenqi, ed. *Minjian baojuan*
MMZJW: Wang Jianchuan and Lin Wanchuan, eds. *Ming Qing minjian zongjiao jingjuan wenxian*
MQ: *Minsu quyi*
MQC: Wang Qiugui, ed. *Minsu quyi congshu*
Mujianlian zunzhe jiu mu baojuan: *Mujianlian zunzhe jiu mu chuli diyu sheng tian baojuan*.
Mulian baozhuan 1999: *Mulian jiu mu youming baozhuan-1*
Mulian baozhuan 2002: *Mulian jiu mu youming baozhuan-2*
Mulian san shi baojuan: *Mulian san shi jiu mu baojuan*
MZZ: *Manji zoku zōkyō*
Ping yao zhuan: Feng Menglong, ed. *Ping yao zhuan*
Popular Culture: Johnson, David, ed. *Popular Culture in Late Imperial China*

Puming baojuan: *Puming rulai wuwei liaoyi baojuan*

Ritual Opera: Johnson, David, ed. *Ritual Opera, Operatic Ritual: "Mu-lien Rescues His Mother" in Chinese Popular Culture*

San jiao sou shen da quan: *San jiao yuanliu Shengdi Fozu sou shen da quan*

Shashang baojuan: *Zhongguo Shashang baojuan ji*

Shisan jing zhushu: Ma Xinmin and Li Xueqin, eds. *Shisan jing zhushu (biaodian ben)*

Sichuan Mulian xi: *Sichuan Mulian xi ziliao lunwen ji*

SWCK: Huang Kuanzhong et al., eds. *Suwenxue congkan*

Taishan Dongyue baojuan: *Taishan Dongyue Shi Wang baojuan*

Tongli xuanjuan: *Zhongguo Tongli xuanjuan ji*

TSD: Takakusu Junjirō and Watanabe Kaigyoku, eds. *Taishō shinshū Daizōkyō*

Yuan shi: Song Lian et al. *Yuan shi*

Zhen xin baojuan: Yin Luanzhang, ed. *Zhen xin baojuan*

Zhu fo gequ: *Zhu fo shizun rulai pusa zunzhe mingcheng gequ*

Primary Sources

Dizang pusa benyuan jing (Sūtra of the original vow of the Bodhisattva of the Earth Sanctuary) 地藏菩薩本願經. 1983. Ch. trans. Jisshananda (Ch. Shichanantuo 實叉難陀, 652–710). In *TSD*, no. 412, 13:777–90.

Dizang wang pusa zhizhang youming baojuan (*Baojuan* of Bodhisattva Dizang governing the underworld) 地藏王菩薩執掌幽冥寶卷. 2005. Beijing, 1710 (originally published in 1679). Reprinted in *MJBJ*, 110:501–95.

Duan Ping 段平, ed. 1992a. *Hexi baojuan xuan* (Selected *baojuan* from Hexi) 河西寶卷選. 2 vols. Taibei: Xinwenfeng (continued in 1994: vols. 3–6).

Feng Menglong 馮夢龍, ed. 1980. *Ping yao zhuan* (Pacification of demon's revolt) 平妖傳. Xianggang: Qingnian Chubanshe.

Fo shuo li sheng liao yi baojuan (Expounded by Buddha *baojuan* on benefiting living beings and understanding of the [true] meaning) 佛說利生了意寶卷. N.p., n.d. Reprinted in *MMZJW*, 5:397–480.

Fo shuo Dazang zhengjiao Xuepen jing 佛說大藏正教血盆經 (Blood bowl sūtra of the true teaching in the great canon pronounced by the Buddha). 1967. In *MZZ* 1, no. 23: 414.

Han Bangqing 韓邦慶. 1994. *Haishang hua liezhuan* 海上花列傳 (Stories of flowers on the sea). Ed. Jueyuan 覺園 and Yugu 愚谷. Shanghai: Shanghai Guji Chubanshe.

He Guoning 何國寧, ed. 2011. *Jiuquan baojuan* (Baojuan from Jiuquan) 酒泉寶卷. 5 vols. Lanzhou: Gansu Renmin Chubanshe.

Huang Kuanzhong 黃寬重 et al., eds. 2002. *Suwenxue congkan* (Collection of texts of popular literature) 俗文學叢刊. 620 vols. Taibei: Xinwenfeng.

Huang Yupian 黃育楩. 1972. *Kōchū Haja shōben* (*Detailed Refutation of Heresies* collated and annotated) 破邪詳辯校注. Ed. and annot. Sawada Mizuho 澤田瑞穗. Tokyo: Dōkyō kankōkai.

Huang Zheng 黃征 and Zhang Yongquan 張涌泉, eds. 1997. *Dunhuang bianwen jiaozhu* (Dunhuang transformation texts collated and annotated) 敦煌變文校注. Beijing: Zhonghua Shuju.

Hunan xiqu chuantong juben (Traditional drama scripts of Hunan [province] drama) 湖南戲曲傳統劇本. 1980–86. 60 vols. Changsha: Hunan sheng Xiqu Yanjiusuo.

Jiu mu ji 1962: *Jiu mu ji* (Records on rescuing of the mother) 救母記. In *Zhejiang sheng xiqu chuantong jumu huibian* (Collection of the traditional drama scripts of Zhejiang province) 浙江省戲曲傳統劇目彙編. Vol. 76. N.p.: Zhejiang xijujia xiehui, Zhejiang sheng wenhuaju xijuchu (mimeograph).

Lanling Xiaoxiaosheng 蘭陵笑笑生 (Lanling scoffer). 1980. *Jin ping mei cihua* (*Plum Flowers in Golden Vase* with lyrics) 金瓶梅詞話. Ed. Liu Bendong 劉本棟. Taibei: Sanmin Shuju.

Li Zhengzhong 李正中. 2012. *Zhongguo baojuan jingcui* (Selected Chinese *baojuan*) 中國寶卷精粹. Taibei: Lantai Chubanshe.

Ma Xinmin 馬辛民 and Li Xueqin 李學勤, eds. 1999. *Shisan jing zhushu (biaodian ben)* (Thirteen Classics with commentaries and subcommentaries [punctuated edition]) 十三經注疏（標點本）. 13 vols. Beijing: Beijing Daxue Chubanshe.

Ma Xisha 馬西沙. 2013. *Zhonghua zhenben baojuan* (Rare Chinese *baojuan*) 中華珍本寶卷. Ser. 1, 10 vols. Beijing: Shehui Kexue Wenxian Chubanshe.

Manji zoku zōkyō (Continued Tripitaka of Manji) 卍字續藏經. 1967. Reprinted as *Xu zangjing* (Continued Tripitaka) 續藏經. 151 vols. Xianggang: Xianggang Yingyin Xu Zangjing hui.

Meng Yuanlao 孟元老. 1956. *Dongjing menghua lu* (The records of bright dreams about eastern capital) 東京夢華錄 (1147). Shanghai: Guji Chubanshe.

Mujianlian zunzhe jiu mu chuli diyu sheng tian baojuan (*Baojuan* of Reverend Maudgalyāyana rescuing his mother [and helping her] to escape from hell and be born in heaven) 目犍連尊者救母出離地獄生天寶卷. Manuscript dated to 1440. 3 vols. State Hermitage Museum, Saint-Petersburg.

Mulian jiu mu youming baozhuan (Precious account of Mulian rescuing his mother in the underworld) 目連救母幽冥寶傳. N.p., 1899. Reprinted in *MMZJW*, 8:945–1001.

Mulian jiu mu youming baozhuan 目連救母幽冥寶傳. N.p., 1893. Reprinted in *SWCK*, 352:5-196.

Mulian jiu mu diyu baojuan (*Baojuan* of Mulian rescuing his mother from hell) 目連救母地獄寶卷. 2004. Manuscript by Yu Dingjun (Changshu).

Mulian san shi jiu mu baojuan (*Baojuan* of Mulian rescuing his mother in three rebirths) 目連三世救母寶卷. 1994. N.p., 1898. Reprinted in *BJCJ*, 27:240-394 (same edition reprinted in *MJBJ*, 111:134-72).

Mulian wai zhuan (Outer biography of Mulian) 目連外傳. 1982. In *Hunan xiqu*, 56:259-413.

Pu Wenqi 濮文起, ed. 2005. *Minjian baojuan* (Folk *baojuan*) 民間寶卷. Vols. 101-20 of *Zhongguo zongjiao lishi wenxian jicheng* (Collection of scriptures of Chinese religions 中國宗教歷史文獻集成). Hefei: Huangshan Shushe.

Puming rulai wuwei liaoyi baojuan (*Baojuan* of Tathāgata Puming Who Understood the Meaning of Non-interference) 普明如來無為了意寶卷. 1979. [Beijing?], 1599. Reprinted in *Baotsziuan' o Pu-mine*. Edited, Russian translation, and commentaries by Elvira S. Stulova. Moscow: Nauka.

Qian Mulian 1982. *Qian Mulian* (Prehistory of Mulian) 前目連. In *Hunan xiqu*, 56:1-141.

San jiao yuanliu Shengdi Fozu sou shen da quan (Overview of the origins of spirits, sage emperors, and buddhas of the three religions) 三教源流聖帝佛祖搜神大全. 1989. N.p., n.d. Reprinted in *Zhongguo minjian xinyang ziliao huibian* (Collection of materials on Chinese popular beliefs) 中國民間信仰資料彙編. Ed. Wang Qiugui 王秋桂 and Li Fengmao 李豐楙. Vol. 3. Taibei: Xuesheng Shuju.

Song Lian 宋濂 (1310-1381) et al. 1997. *Yuan shi* (History of the Yuan [dynasty]) 元史. In *Ershisi shi* (Twenty-four histories) 二十四史. Vol. 18. Beijing: Zhonghua Shuju.

Taishan Dongyue Shi Wang baojuan (*Baojuan* of the ten kings of Mount Tai, the Eastern Peak) 泰山東嶽十王寶卷. 1999. Beijing: Hongwenzhai, 1921. Reprinted in *MMZJW*, 7:1-26.

Takakusu Junjirō 高楠順次郎 and Watanabe Kaigyoku 渡邊海旭, eds. 1983. *Taishō shinshū Daizōkyō* (Newly revised Tripitaka of the Taishō reign) 大正新修大藏經. Reprinted as *Da zangjing kanxinghui* 大藏經刊行會 ed., *Da zangjing* 大藏經. 100 vols. Taibei: Xinwenfeng (originally published: Tokyo: Taishō Issaikyō Kankōkai, 1924-32).

Wang Jianchuan 王見川 and Lin Wanchuan 林萬傳, eds. 1999. *Ming Qing minjian zongjiao jingjuan wenxian* (Scriptures of folk religions of Ming and Qing periods) 明清民間宗教經卷文獻. 12 vols. Taibei: Xinwenfeng.

Wang Qiugui 王秋桂, ed. 1994-. *Minsu quyi congshu* (Studies in Chinese ritual, theater and folklore series) 民俗曲藝叢書. 60 vols. Taibei: Shi Hezheng Minsu Wenhua Jijinhui.

Xu Hongtu 徐宏圖, ed. 1994. *Shaoxing "Jiu mu ji"* (Records on rescuing mother from Shaoxing) 紹興救母記. In *MQC*, ser. 3, vol. 22.

———, ed. 1995. *Zhejiang sheng Dongyang shi Mazhai zhen Kong cun Hanren de Mulian xi* (Mulian drama among Han nationality of Kong village of Mazhai township of Dongyang city of Zhejiang province) 浙江省東陽市馬宅鎮孔村漢人的目連戲. In *MQC*, ser. 3, vol. 23.

Xu Hongtu 徐宏圖 and Wang Qiugui 王秋桂, eds. 1994. *Zhejiang sheng Mulian xi ziliao huibian* (Collection of materials about Mulian drama in Zhejiang province) 浙江省目連戲資料彙編. In *MQC*, ser. 3, vol. 13.

Xu Jin ping mei (Sequel to *Plum Flowers in the Golden Vase*) 續金瓶梅. 1990. Reprinted in *Guben xiaoshuo jicheng* (Collection of old editions of the novels) 古本小說集成, ser. 4, vols. 71–74. Shanghai: Shanghai Guji Chubanshe.

Yan Yuan 顏元 (1635–1704). 2000. *Xizhai si cun bian* (Four essays on existence by Xizhai) 習齋四存編. Ed. Chen Juyuan 陈居渊. Shanghai: Shanghai Guji Chubanshe.

Yin Luanzhang 印鸞章, ed. 1919. *Zhen xin baojuan* (*Baojuan* of rectifying the heart) 鍼心寶卷. Shanghai: Hongda Shanshuju.

You Hong 尤红 et al., eds. 2007. *Zhongguo Jingjiang baojuan* (*Baojuan* from Jingjiang) 中國靖江寶卷. 2 vols. Nanjing: Jiangsu Wenhua Chubanshe.

Zhang Tingyu 張廷玉 (1672–1755) et al. 1997. *Ming shi* (History of the Ming [dynasty]) 明史. In *Ershisi shi* (Twenty-four histories) 二十四史. Vols. 19–20. Beijing: Zhonghua Shuju.

Zhang Xishun 張希舜 et al., eds. 1994. *Baojuan chuji* (The first collection of *baojuan*) 寶卷初集. 40 vols. Taiyuan: Shanxi Renmin Chubanshe.

Zhang Zhao 張照. 1964. *Quan shan jin ke* (Golden rules exhorting goodness) 勸善金科 . In *Guben xiqu kan jiu ji* (Publication of old drama scripts no. 9) 古本戲曲叢刊九集. Ser. 4, part 1, vols. 1–10. Beijing: Guben Xiqu Congkan Biankan Weiyuanhui.

Zhang Ziwei 張子偉, ed. 1999. *Hunan sheng Luxi xian Chenhe gaoqiang Mulian quanzhuan* (Complete story of Mulian, a Chenhe drama with *gaoqiang* melodies from the Luxi county in Hunan province) 湖南省瀘溪縣辰河高腔目連全傳. In *MQC*, ser. 7, vol. 70.

Zheng Zhizhen 鄭之珍. 1954. *Xinbian Mulian jiu mu quan shan xiwen* (Newly compiled drama exhorting goodness of Mulian rescuing his mother) 新編目連救母勸善戲文. N.p.: Gaoshi Shanfang, 1583. Reprinted in *Gu ben xiqu congkan chu ji* (First series of the [reprints] of the old editions of dramas) 古本戲曲叢刊初集. Part 8, vols. 8–10. Shanghai: Shangwu Yinshuguan.

Zhengxin chuyi wu xiu zheng zizai baojuan (*Baojuan* of self-determination [needing] neither cultivation nor verification, which rectifies belief and dispels doubt) 正信除疑無修證自在寶卷. 1994. N.p., 1598. Reprinted in *BJCJ*, 3:1–340 (same edition reprinted in *MJBJ*, 101:372–457).

———. 鄭之珍. 2005. *Xinbian Mulian jiu mu quan shan xiwen*. Hefei: Huangshan Shushe.

Zhongguo Heyang baojuan ji (Collection of *baojuan* [texts] of Heyang in China) 中國河陽寶卷集. 2007. 2 vols. Shanghai: Shanghai Wenhua Chubanshe.

Zhongguo Shashang baojuan ji (Collection of *baojuan* from the Sandbank in China) 中國沙上寶卷集. 2011. 2 vols. Shanghai: Shanghai Wenyi Chubanshe.

Zhongguo Tongli xuanjuan ji (Collection of scroll recitation [texts] from Tongli in China). 2010. 中國同里宣卷集. 2 vols. Nanjing: Fenghuang Chubanshe.

Zhu fo Shizun Rulai pusa zunzhe mingcheng gequ (Tunes with the names of all buddhas, world-honored Rulai, and reverend bodhisattvas) 諸佛世尊如來菩薩尊者名稱歌曲. 1885. In *Dai Nihon kōtei Dai zōkyō* (Revised Tripitaka of Japan) 大日本校訂大藏經, vol. 40a, parts 4–5. Tokyo: Kōkyō Shoin.

Zongjing 宗鏡 (act. ca. 1242). 1999. *Xiaoshi Jingang jing keyi* (Liturgy based on *Diamond Sūtra*) 銷釋金剛經科儀. [Beijing?], 1528. t. in *MMZJW*, 1:1–62.

Dictionaries and Reference Works

Che Xilun 車錫倫. 2000. *Zhongguo baojuan zongmu* (Catalogue of Chinese *baojuan*) 中國寶卷總目. Beijing: Yanshan Shuju.

Demiéville, P., et al., eds. 1978. *Répertoire du Canon Buddhique Sino-Japonais: Fascicule annexe du Hōbōgirin*. Paris: L'Académie du Inscriptions et Belles-Lettres, Institut de France.

Duan Baolin 段寶林 et al., eds. 1988. *Minjian wenxue cidian* (Dictionary of Chinese folk literature) 民間文學辭典. Shijiazhuang: Hebei Jiaoyu Chubanshe.

Goodrich, Carrington L., et al., eds. 1976. *Dictionary of Ming Biography, 1368–1644*. 2 vols. New York: Columbia University Press.

Hu Fuchen 胡孚琛 et al., eds. 1995. *Zhonghua daojiao da cidian* (Large dictionary of Chinese Daoism) 中華道教大辭典. Beijing: Zhongguo Shehui Kexue Chubanshe.

Li Rong 李榮, ed. 1998. *Chengdu fangyan cidian* (Dictionary of Chengdu topolect) 成都方言詞典. *Xiandai Hanyu fangyan da cidian, fen juan* (Big dictionary of Chinese topolects. Separate volumes) 現代漢語方言大詞典, 分卷. Nanjing: Jiangsu Jiaoyu Chubanshe.

Li Shiyu 李世瑜. 1961. *Baojuan zongmu* (Catalogue of *baojuan*) 寶卷綜目. Beijing-Shanghai: Zhonghua Shuju.

Ma Shutian 馬書田. 2002. *Zhongguo minjian zhu shen* (All folk deities of China) 中國民間諸神. Beijing: Tuanjie Chubanshe.

Pu Wenqi 濮文起, ed. 1996. *Zhongguo minjian mimi zongjiao cidian* (Dictionary of Chinese folk secret religions) 中國民間秘密宗教辭典. Chengdu: Sichuan Cishu Chubanshe.

Qi Senhua 齊森華, ed. 1997. *Zhongguo quxue da cidian* (Large dictionary of Chinese drama study) 中國曲學大辭典. Hangzhou: Zhejiang Jiaoyu Chubanshe.

Wang Yiqing 王奕清 et al., eds. 2000. *Kangxi qupu* (Schemes of arias of Kangxi [reign]) 康熙曲譜. Changsha: Yuelu Shuju.

Xingyun 星雲 et al., eds. 1989. *Foguang da cidian* (Large dictionary of the Buddha's light) 佛光大辭典. 7 vols. Gaoxiong: Foguang Chubanshe.

Studies and Translations

Bäuml, F. 1984. "Medieval Texts and the Two Theories of Oral-Formulaic Composition: A Proposal for a Third Theory." *New Literary History* 16, no. 1: 37–42.

Bender, Mark. 2001. "A Description of 'Jiangjing' (Telling Scriptures) Services in Jingjiang, China." *Asian Folklore Studies* 60, no. 1: 101–33.

———. 2003. *Plum and Bamboo: China's Suzhou Chantefable Tradition*. Urbana: University of Illinois Press.

Berezkin, Rostislav. 2010. "The Development of the Mulian Story in *Baojuan* Texts (14th–19th centuries) in Connection with the Evolution of the Genre." PhD diss., University of Pennsylvania.

———. 2011a. "Scripture-telling (*jiangjing*) in the Zhangjiagang Area and the History of Chinese Storytelling." *Asia Major*, 3rd ser., 24, no. 1: 1–42.

———. 2011b. "An Analysis of 'Telling Scriptures' (*jiangjing*) during Temple Festivals in Gangkou (Zhangjiagang), with Special Attention to the Status of the Performers." *CHINOPERL papers* 30:25–76.

———. 2013a. "A Rare Early Manuscript of the Mulian Story in the Baojuan (Precious Scroll) Genre Preserved in Russia and Its Place in the History of the Genre." *CHINOPERL: Journal of Chinese Oral and Performing Literature* 32, no. 2: 109–31.

———. 2013b. "Transformation of Historical Material in Religious Storytelling: The Story of Huang Chao in Baojuan of Mulian Rescuing His Mother in Three Rebirths." *Late Imperial China* 34, no. 2: 83–133.

———. 2014. "Printing and Circulating 'Precious Scrolls' in Early Twentieth-Century Shanghai and its Vicinity: Towards an Assessment of Multifunctionality of the Genre." In *Religious Publishing and Print Culture in*

Modern China, 1800–2012, ed. Philip Clart and Gregory A. Scott, 139–85. Berlin: de Gruyter.

———. 2015. "Pictorial Versions of the Mulian Story in East Asia (Tenth-Seventeenth Centuries)." *Fudan Journal of the Humanities and Social Sciences* 8, no. 1: 95–120.

Berezkin, Rostislav, and Victor H. Mair. 2014. "The Precious Scroll of Bodhisattva Guanshiyin from Jingjiang and the Confucian Morality." *Journal of Chinese Religions* 42, no. 1: 1–27.

Berezkin, Rostislav, and Boris L. Riftin. 2013. "The Earliest Known Edition of the Precious Scroll of the Incense Mountain and the Connections between Precious Scrolls and Buddhist Preaching," *T'oung Pao* 99, no. 4–5: 445–99.

Bordahl, Vibeke. 1996. *The Oral Tradition of Yangzhou Storytelling*. Richmond, Surrey: Curzon Press.

———. 2011. "Storytelling, Stock Phrases and Genre Conventions: The Case of 'Wu Song Fights the Tiger.'" In *The Interplay of the Oral and the Written in Chinese Popular Literature*, ed. Vibeke Bordahl and Margaret B. Wan, 83–156. Copenhagen: NIAS.

Bordahl, Vibeke, and Margaret B. Wan, eds. 2011. *The Interplay of the Oral and the Written in Chinese Popular Literature*. Copenhagen: NIAS.

Brook, Timothy. 1993. *Praying for Power: Buddhism and the Formation of Gentry Society in Late-Ming China*. Cambridge, MA: Harvard University Press.

Chau, Adam Yuet. 2006. *Miraculous Response: Doing Popular Religion in Contemporary China*. Stanford: Stanford University Press.

Che Xilun 車錫倫. 1978. *Yun zhe xinbian* (Newly compiled [book] on rhyme tracks) 韻轍新編. Huhhot, Inner Mongolia: Nei Menggu Renmin Chubanshe.

———. 2009. *Zhongguo baojuan yanjiu* (Study of the Chinese *baojuan*) 中國寶卷研究. Guilin: Guangxi Shifan Daxue Chubanshe.

Chen Fangying 陳芳英. 1983. *Mulian jiu mu gushi zhi yanjin ji qi youguan wenxue zhi yanjiu* (Study of the development of Mulian rescuing his mother story and related literature) 目連救母故事之演進及其有關文學之研究. Taibei: Guoli Taiwan Daxue.

Ch'en, Kenneth K. S. 1968. "Filial Piety in Chinese Buddhism." *Harvard Journal of Asiatic Studies* 28:81–97.

Chen Ruheng 陳汝衡. 1958. *Shuoshu shi hua* (Outline of the history of storytelling) 說書史話. Beijing: Zuojia Chubanshe.

Ch'iu, K'un-liang. 1989. "Mu-lien 'Operas' in Taiwanese Funeral Rituals." In *Ritual Opera*, 105–25.

Bibliography

Classen, Albrecht. 1995. *The German Volksbuch: A Critical History of a Late-Medieval Genre.* Lewiston, NY: Edwin Mellen Press.

Cole, Alan R. 1998. *Mothers and Sons in Chinese Buddhism.* Stanford: Stanford University Press.

Dai Bufan 戴不凡. 1994. "Mulian xi he daoshi" (Mulian drama and Daoists) 目連戲和道士. In Xu Hongtu and Wang Qiugui 1994, 322–28.

Dai Xiaoyun 戴曉雲. 2009. *Fojiao shuilu hua yanjiu* 佛教水陸畫研究 (Study of Buddhist water and land paintings). Beijing: Zhongguo Shehui Kexue Chubanshe.

Dai Yun 戴云. 2006. *"Quan shan jin ke" yanjiu* (Study of the *Golden Rules Exhorting Goodness*) 《勸善金科》研究. Beijing: Beijing Shifan Daxue Chubanshe.

Dean, Kenneth. 1989. "Lei Yu-sheng ('Thunder Is Noisy') and Mu-lien in the Theatrical and Funerary Traditions of Fukien." In *Ritual Opera*, 47–85.

Du Jianhua 杜建華. 1993. *Ba-Shu Mulian xiju wenhua gailun* (Outline of the culture of Mulian drama in Sichuan) 巴蜀目連戲劇文化概論. Beijing: Wenhua Yishu Chubanshe.

Duan Ming 段明. 1999. "Chaodu wang hun de guo qiao jisi yishi" (Memorial rites on rescuing soul of the dead by crossing the bridge) 超度亡魂的過橋儀式. *MQ* 118, no. 3: 145–233.

Duan Ping 段平. 1992b. *Hexi baojuan de diaocha yanjiu* (Survey and research on *baojuan* from Hexi) 河西寶卷的調查研究. Lanzhou: Lanzhou Daxue Chubanshe.

Dudbridge, Glen. 1970. *The Hsi-yu chi: A Study of Antecedents to the Sixteenth-century Chinese novel.* Cambridge: Cambridge University Press.

———. 2004. *The Legend of Miao-shan.* Rev. ed. New York: Oxford University Press.

Eoyang, Eugene. 1978. "The Great Maudgalyayana Rescues His Mother from Hell." In *Traditional Chinese Stories: Themes and Variations*, ed. Y. W. Ma and Joseph S. M. Lau, 443–55. New York: Columbia University Press.

Fan Jinshi and Mei Lin. 1996. "An Interpretation of the Maudgalyāyana Murals in Cave 19 at Yulin." *Orientations* 27 (November): 70–75.

Fang Buhe 方步和, ed. 1999. *Hexi baojuan zhenben jiaozhu yanjiu* (Original texts of *baojuan* from Hexi with annotations and research) 河西寶卷真本校註研究. Lanzhou: Lanzhou Daxue Chubanshe.

Foley, John Miles. 1990. *The Traditional Oral Epic: Odyssey, Beowulf and the Serbo-Croatian Return Song.* Berkeley: University of California Press.

———. 1995. *The Singer of Tales in Performance.* Bloomington: Indiana University Press.

———. 2002. *How to Read an Oral Poem.* Urbana: University of Illinois Press.

Grant, Beata. 1989. "The Spiritual Saga of Woman Huang: from Pollution to Purification." In *Ritual Opera,* 224–311.

Grant, Beata, and Wilt L. Idema, trans. 2011. *Escape from Blood Pond Hell: The Tales of Mulian and Woman Huang.* Seattle: University of Washington Press.

de Groot, Jan Jakob Maria. 1903. "Sectarianism and Religious Persecution in China, a Page in the History of Religions." 2 vols. *Verhandelingen der Koninklijke Akademie van Wetenschappen.* Afdeeling Letterkunde, Nieuwe reeks, deel 4, no. 1–2. Amsterdam: J. Miller.

Guo, Qitao. 2005. *Ritual Opera and Mercantile Lineage: The Confucian Transformation of Popular Culture in Late Imperial Huizhou.* Stanford: Stanford University Press.

ter Haar, Barend J. 2014. *Practicing Scripture: A Lay Buddhist Movement in Late Imperial China.* Honolulu: Hawaii University Press.

Han Bangqing. 2005. *The Sing-Song Girls of Shanghai.* Trans. Eileen Chang. Rev. and ed. Eva Hung. New York: Columbia University Press.

Hanan, Patrick. 1977. "The Nature of Ling Meng-ch'u's Fiction." In *Chinese Narrative: Critical and Theoretical Essays,* ed. Andrew H. Plaks, 85–102. Princeton: Princeton University Press.

Hayes, Kevin J. 1997. *Folklore and Book Culture.* Knoxville: University of Tennessee Press.

Hegel, Robert E. 1998. *Reading Illustrated Fiction in Late Imperial China.* Stanford: Stanford University Press.

Hou, Jie. 2002. "Mulian Drama: A Commentary on Current Research and Source Materials." In *Ethnography in China Today: A Critical Assessment of Methods and Results,* ed. Daniel L. Overmyer, 23–48. Taipei: Yuan-Liou Publishing.

Hu Tiancheng 胡天成. 1990. "Sichuan Mulian xiju ben yanjiu liu ti" (Six issues in the study of the Mulian drama script from Sichuan) 四川目連戲劇本研究六題. In *Sichuan Mulian xi,* 1–17.

Huang Weiyu 黃偉瑜. 1992. "Sichuan Mulian xi chu kao" (Initial study of the Mulian drama in Sichuan) 四川目連戲初考. *MQ* 77:73–88.

Huang Wenhu 黃文虎. 1992. "Gaochun yangqiang Mulian xi chu tan" (Preliminary study of Mulian drama with yang melodies in Gaochun) 高淳陽腔目連戲初探. *MQ* 78:217–38.

Idema, Wilt L. 2002. "The Filial Parrot in Qing Dynasty Dress: A Short Discussion of the *Yingge baojuan* [Precious Scroll of the Parrot]." *Journal of Chinese Religions* 30:77–96.

———, trans. 2008a. *Personal Salvation and Filial Piety: Two Precious*

Scroll Narratives of Guanyin and Her Acolytes. Honolulu: Hawaii University Press.

———, trans. 2008b. *Meng Jiangnü Brings down the Great Wall: Ten Versions of a Chinese Legend*. With an essay by Haiyan Lee. Seattle: University of Washington Press.

———, trans. 2009. *The White Snake and Her Son: A Translation of the Precious Scroll of Thunder Peak with Related Texts*. Indianapolis: Hackett.

———, trans. 2015. *The Immortal Maiden Equal to Heaven and Other Precious Scrolls from Western Gansu*. New York: Cambria Press.

Jaworski, Jan. 1935–36. "L'Avalambana Sūtra de la terre pure." *Monumenta Serica* 1:82–107.

Johnson, David, ed. 1988. *Popular Culture in Late Imperial China*. Berkeley: University of California Press.

———. 1989. *Ritual Opera, Operatic Ritual: "Mu-lien Rescues His Mother" in Chinese Popular Culture. Papers from the International Workshop on the Mu-lien Operas*. Berkeley: University of California Press.

———. 1995. "Mu-lien in *Pao-chüan*: The Performative Context and Religious Meaning of the *You-ming pao-chüan*." In *Ritual and Scripture in Chinese Popular Religion: Five Studies*, ed. David Johnson, 55–103. Berkeley: University of California Press.

Jordan, David K., and Daniel L. Overmyer. 1986. *The Flying Phoenix: Aspects of Chinese Sectarianism in Taiwan*. Princeton: Princeton University Press.

Karashima, Seishi 辛島靜志. 2013. "The Meaning of Yulanpen—'Rice Bowl' on Pravāraṇā Day." *Sōka daigaku kokusai bukkyōgaku kōdō kenkyūjo nenpō* (Annual Report of the International Research Institute for Advanced Buddhology at Soka University) 創價大學國際佛教學高等研究所年報 16:289–305.

Kawaguchi Hisao 川口久雄. 1984. *Tonkō hon "Dai Mokkenren minkan kyū bo henbun"* (Dunhuang manuscripts of *Bianwen of Mahāmaudgalyāyana Rescuing His Mother from the Underworld*) 敦煌本《大目乾連冥間救母變文》. Tonkō shiryō to Nihon bungaku (Dunhuang materials and Japanese literature) 敦煌資料と日本文學, 3. Tokyo: Tokyo Bijutsu Co.

Ke Ziming 柯子銘. 1991. "Guanyu Puxian Mulian xi 'Mulian'" (On the Puxian Mulian drama *Mulian*) 關於莆仙目連戲《目連》. In *Fujian Mulian xi yanjiu wenji* (Collection of research articles on Mulian dramas in Fujian) 福建目連戲研究文集, 1–20. Fuzhou: Fujian sheng Yishu Yanjiusuo.

Kerr, Janet L. 1994. "Precious Scrolls in Chinese Popular Religious Culture." 2 vols. PhD diss., University of Chicago.

Kohn, Livia, ed. 2000. *Daoism Handbook*. Boston: Brill.

———. 2001. "Doumu: The Mother of the Dipper." *Ming Qing yanjiu* 明清研究 8:149–95.

Lagerwey, John. 1987. *Taoist Ritual in Chinese Society and History*. New York: Macmillan.

Li Fengmao 李豐楙. 1995. "Fuhe yu bianqe: Taiwan daojiao badu yi zhong de Mulian xi" (Integration and transformation: Mulian drama in Daoist salvation ritual in Taiwan) 復合與變革：臺灣道教拔度儀中的目連戲. *MQ* 94:83–110.

Li Huaisun 李懷蓀. 1992. "Gulao xiqu de huo huashi: Chenhe gaoqiang Mulian xi tansuo" (Living relic of ancient drama: The study of Mulian drama with *gaoqiang* melodies in Chenhe) 古老戲曲的活化石：辰河高腔目連戲探索. *MQ* 78:61–102.

Li Ping 李萍. 2012. "Wuxi xuanjuan yishi yinyue yanjiu—xuanjuan zhi yishixing chongfang" (Ritual soundscapes of Xuanjuan in Wuxi: A revisit of ritualization in Xuanjuan) 無錫宣卷儀式音樂研究——宣卷之儀式性重訪. PhD diss., Shanghai Yinyue Xueyuan.

Li Shiyu 李世瑜. 2007a. *Baojuan lunji* (Collection of articles on *baojuan*) 寶卷論集. Taibei: Lantai Chubanshe.

———. 2007b. *Xianzai Huabei mimi zongjiao (zeng ding ban)*. (Modern secret religions in Northern China [revised and expanded edition]). 現在華北秘密宗教（增訂版）. Taibei: Lantai Chubanshe.

Li, Thomas Shiyu, and Susan Naquin. 1988. "The Baoming Temple: Religion and the Throne in Ming and Qing China." *Harvard Journal of Asiatic Studies* 48, no. 1 (June): 131–88.

Li Yu 李豫, et al. 2010. *Shanxi Jiexiu baojuan shuochang wenxue diaocha baogao* (A fieldwork report on the Baojuan prosimetric literature in Jiexiu county of Shanxi) 山西介休寶卷說唱文學調查報告. Beijing: Shehui Kexue Wenxian Chubanshe.

Liang Jingzhi 梁景之. 2004. *Qing dai minjian zongjiao yu xiangtu shehui* (Folk religions and rural society during the Qing dynasty) 清代民間宗教與鄉土社會. Beijing: Shehui Kexue Wenxian Chubanshe.

Lin, Kwang-Ching, and Richard Hon-chun Shek, eds. 2004. *Heterodoxy in Late Imperial China*. Honolulu: University of Hawaii Press.

Lin Meirong 林美容. 2008. *Taiwan de zhaitang yu yanzi: Minjian fojiao de shijiao* (Vegetarian halls and mountain temples in Taiwan: From the perspective of folk Buddhism) 臺灣的齋堂與巖仔：民間佛教的視角. Taibei: Taiwan Shufang.

Lin Qingxi 林慶熙. 1992. "Fujian Puxian xi 'Mulian' kao" (Study of the Puxian drama "Mulian" of Fujian) 福建莆仙戲《目連》考. *MQ* 78:25–38.

Lin Wanchuan 林萬傳. 1985. *Xiantian dao yanjiu* (Study of the Way of Former Heaven) 先天道研究. Taibei: Taiwan Qingju Shuju.

Liu Yonghong 劉永紅. 2013a. *Xibei baojuan yanjiu* (Study of *baojuan* in northwestern China) 西北寶卷研究. Beijing: Minzu Chubanshe.

———. 2013b. *Qinghai baojuan yanjiu* (Study of *baojuan* in Qinghai) 青海寶卷研究. Beijing: Zhongguo Shehui Kexue Chubanshe.

Liu Zhen 劉禎. 1997. *Zhongguo minjian "Mulian wenhua"* (Chinese folk "culture of Mulian") 中國民間目連文化. Chengdu: Bashu Shushe.

Lord, Albert Bates. 1960. *The Singer of Tales*. Cambridge, MA: Harvard University Press.

Lu Yongfeng 陸永峰 and Che Xilun 車錫倫. 2008. *Jingjiang baojuan yanjiu* (Study of *baojuan* from Jingjiang) 靖江寶卷研究. Beijing: Shehui Kexue Wenxian Chubanshe.

Ma Jianhua 馬建華. 2007. "Josei no kyūsai—Pu-Sen Mokurengi to 'Chi bon kyō'" (Women's salvation: Mulian drama in Putian and Xianyou and the Sūtra of the Blood Bowl) 女性の救済——莆仙目連戲と《血盆經》. In Nomura Shin'ichi, *Higashi Ajia no saishi denshō to josei kyūsai: Mokuren kyū bo to geinō no shosō*, 353–408.

Ma Xisha 馬西沙 and Han Bingfang 韓秉方. 2004. *Zhongguo minjian zongjiao shi* (History of Chinese folk religions) 中國民間宗教史. 2 vols. Beijing: Zhongguo Shehui Kexue Chubanshe. Original ed., Shanghai: Shanghai Renmin Chubanshe, 1992.

Mair, Victor H. 1983. *Tun-huang Popular Narratives*. Cambridge: Cambridge University Press.

———. 1985. "Language and Ideology in the Written Popularizations of the Sacred Edict." In *Popular Culture*, 325–59.

———. 1986. "Oral and Written Aspects of Chinese Sūtra Lectures (*chiang-ching-wen*)." *Hanxue yanjiu* (Chinese studies) 漢學研究 4, no. 2 (cumulative 8): 311–34.

———. 1986–87. "Notes on the Maudgalyayana Legend in East Asia." *Monumenta Serica. Journal of Oriental Studies* 37:83–93.

———. 1988. *Painting and Performance: Chinese Picture Recitation and Its Indian Genesis*. Honolulu: University of Hawaii Press.

———. 1989a. *T'ang Transformation Texts: A Study of the Buddhist Contribution to the Rise of Vernacular Fiction and Drama in China*. Cambridge, MA: Harvard University Press.

———. 1989b. "What Is a Chinese Dialect/Topolect? Reflections on Some Key Sino-English Linguistic Terms." *Sino-Platonic Papers* 29:2–32.

———. 1997. "The Prosimetric Form in the Chinese Literary Tradition." In *Prosimetrum: Crosscultural Perspectives on Narrative in Prose and Verse*, ed. Joseph Harris and Karl Reichl, 365–86. Suffolk: Boydell and Brewer.

Mao Gengru 茆耕茹. 1994. *Mulian ziliao bianmu gailüe* (Outline of the collection of materials on Mulian [story]) 目連資料編目概略. In *MQC*, ser. 1, vol. 2.

Mao Limei 毛禮鎂. 1992. "Yiyang qiang Mulian xi" (Mulian drama with Yiyang melodies) 弋陽腔目連戲. *MQ* 78:9–24.

Mark, Lindy Li, trans. 2005. "Legends of the Original Vow of the Bodhisattva of the Earth Sanctuary." In *Hawaii Reader of Traditional Chinese Culture*, ed. Victor H. Mair et al., 288–94. Honolulu: University of Hawaii Press.

McLaren, Anne E. 1998. *Chinese Popular Culture and Ming Chantefables*. Leiden: Brill.

Miya Tsugio 宮次男. 1968. "Mokuren kyū bo setsuwa to sono kaiga—Mokuren kyū bo kyō e no shutsugen ni tsunde" (Illustrated scripture on the story of Mokuren rescuing his mother) 目連救母說話とその繪畫—目連救母經繪の出現に因んで. *Bijutsu kenkyū* (Journal of art studies) 美術研究 255 (January): 154–78.

Mollier, Christine. 2008. *Buddhism and Taoism Face to Face: Scripture, Ritual, and Iconographic Exchange in Medieval China*. Honolulu: University of Hawaii Press.

Nadeau, Randall L. 1990. "Popular Sectarianism in the Ming: Lo Ch'ing and His 'Religion of Non-Action.'" PhD diss., University of British Columbia.

———. 1993. "Genre Classification of Chinese Popular Religious Literature: Pao-chüan." *Journal of Chinese Religions* 21:121–28.

———. 1994. "Domestication of Precious Scrolls: The *Ssu-ming Tsao-chün pao-chüan*." *Journal of Chinese Religions* 22:23–50.

Naquin, Susan. 1985. "The Transmission of White Lotus Sectarianism in Late Imperial China." In *Popular Culture*, 255–91.

———. 1992. "The Peking Pilgrimage to Miao-feng-shan: Religious Organization and Sacred Site." In *Pilgrims and Sacred Sites in China*, ed. Susan Naquin and Chün-fang Yu, 333–77. Berkeley: University of California Press.

Ng, Zhiru. 2007. *The Making of a Savior Bodhisattva: Dizang in Medieval China*. Honolulu: University of Hawaii Press.

Nomura Shin'ichi 野村伸一. 2007. *Higashi Ajia no saishi denshō to josei kyūsai: Mokuren kyū bo to geinō no shosō* (Traditions of offerings and women's salvation in East Asia: Mulian rescues his mother and various forms of performing arts) 東アジアの祭祀伝承と女性救済：目連救母と芸能の諸相. Tokyo: Fukyosha.

Overmyer, Daniel L. 1976. *Folk Buddhist Religion: Dissenting Sects in Late Traditional China*. Cambridge, MA: Harvard University Press.

———. 1985. "Values in Chinese Sectarian Literature: Ming and Ch'ing Pao-chüan." In *Popular Culture*, 219–54.

Bibliography

———. 1999. *Precious Volumes: An Introduction to Chinese Scriptures from the Sixteenth and Seventeenth Centuries.* Cambridge, MA: Harvard University Press.

———. 2009. *Local Religion in North China in the Twentieth Century: The Structure and Organization of Community Rituals and Beliefs.* Boston: Brill.

Overmyer, Daniel L., and Thomas S. Y. Li [Li Shiyu]. 1992. "The Oldest Chinese Sectarian Scripture, the *Precious Volume Expounded by Buddha on the Results of [the Teaching] of the Imperial Ultimate Period.*" *Journal of Chinese Religions* 20:17–31.

Peng, Fei. 1994. *Chinese Mulian Plays: Resources for Studies of Ritual and Performance.* Ed. Gary Seaman. Los Angeles: Ethnographics Press, University of Southern California.

Pillsbury, Barbara L. K. 1978. "'Doing the Month': Confinement and Convalescence of Chinese Women after Childbirth." *Social Science and Medicine* 12:11–22.

Průšek, Jaroslav. 1938. "The Narrators of Buddhist Scriptures and Religious Tales in the Song Period." *Archiv Orientální* 10, no. 3: 375–89.

Qiu Huiying 丘慧瑩. 2010. "Jiangsu Changshu Baimao diqu xuanjuan huodong diaocha baogao" (Report on a survey of scroll recitation activities in the Baimao District in Changshu) 江蘇常熟白茆地區宣卷活動調查報告. *MQ* 169:183–247.

Ren Jiyu 任繼愈, ed. 1999. *Zhongguo guojia tushuguan gu ji zhen pin tu lu* (Illustrated catalogue of the valuable old books in the State Library of China) 中國國家圖書館古籍珍品圖錄. Beijing: Beijing Tushuguan Chubanshe.

Roy, David Tod, trans. 1993–2013. *The Plum in the Golden Vase, or, Chin P'ing Mei.* Princeton: Princeton University Press.

Sa Jae-dong 史在東. 1988. "Zhong-Han Mulian gushi zhi liubian guanxi" (Interaction relations between Chinese and Korean versions of Mulian story) 中韓目連故事之流變關係. *Hanxue yanjiu* (Chinese studies) 漢學研究 6, no. 1: 213–41.

Sangren, Steven P. 1987. *History and Magical Power in a Chinese Community.* Stanford: Stanford University Press.

Satō Yoshifumi 佐藤仁史 et al., eds. 2011. *Chūgoku nōson no minkan geinō: Taiko ryūiki shakaishi kōjutsu kirokushū 2* (Folk performing arts in the Chinese village: Collection of oral records of social history in Taihu Lake Basin) 中国農村の民間藝能: 太湖流域社会史口述記錄集 2. Tōkyō: Kyūko Shoin.

Sawada Mizuho 澤田瑞穗. 1968. *Jigoku hen: Chūgoku no meikaisetsu*

(Transformations on hell: Legends about underworld in China). 地獄變: 中國の冥界說. Kyoto: Hōzōkan.

———. 1975a. *Zōho hōkan no kenkyū* (Study of *baojuan*, revised and expanded edition) 增補寶卷の研究. Tokyo: Dōkyō Kankōkai.

———. 1975b. *Bukkyō to Chūgoku bungaku* (Buddhism and Chinese literature) 仏教と中国文学. Tokyo: Kokusho Kankōkai.

Schipper, Kristofer. 1989. "Mu-lien Plays in Taoist Liturgical Context." In *Ritual Opera*, 126–54.

———. 1993. *The Taoist Body*. Trans. Karen C. Duval. Berkeley: University of California Press.

Shek, Richard Hon-shun. 1980. "Religion and Society in Late Ming: Sectarianism and Popular Thought in Sixteenth and Seventeenth Century China." PhD diss., University of California, Berkeley.

———. 1982. "Millenarianism without Rebellion: The Huangtian Dao in North China." *Modern China* 8, no. 3 (July): 305–36.

Shi Lin 史琳. 2010. *Suzhou Shengpu xuanjuan* 蘇州勝浦宣卷. Suzhou: Guwuxian Chubanshe.

Seaman, Gary. 1989. "Mu-lien Dramas in Puli, Taiwan." In *Ritual Opera*, 155–90.

Schmid, David N. 2002. "*Yuanqi*: Medieval Buddhist Narratives from Dunhuang." PhD diss., University of Pennsylvania.

Seiwert, Hubert, and Ma Xisha. 2003. *Popular Religious Movements and Heterodox Sects in Chinese History*. Boston: Brill.

Shi Shengchao 石生朝 and Li Jianming 黎建明. 1994. *Mulian xi: Nanxi yuanliu yu shengqiang xingxiang yanjiu* (Mulian drama: Study of origins of Nanxi and musical forms) 目連戲: 南戲源流與聲腔形象研究. Beijing: Wenhua Yishu Chubanshe.

Sichuan Mulian xi ziliao lunwen ji (Collection of articles on materials of Mulian drama in Sichuan) 四川目連戲資料論文集. 1990. Chongqing: Chongqing shi Chuanju Yanjiusuo.

Skar, Lowell. 2003. "Golden Elixir Alchemy: The Formation of the Southern Lineage and the Transformation of Medieval China." PhD diss., University of Pennsylvania.

Soymié, Michel. 1965. "Chibon kyō no shiryō teki kenkyū" 血盆經の資料的研究 (A textological study of *Sūtra of the Blood Bowl*). In *Dōkyō kenkyū* (Studies on Daoism) 道教研究, ed. Yoshioka Yoshitoyo 吉岡義豐 and Michel Soymie, 1:109–66. Tokyo: Shōrinsha.

Song Jun 宋軍. 2002. *Qing dai Hongyangjiao yanjiu* (The study of the Vast Yang Teaching during the Qing dynasty) 清代弘陽教研究. Beijing: Shehui Kexue Wenxian Chubanshe.

Stevenson, Daniel B. 2001. "Text, Image and Transformation in the History of the *Shuilu fahui*: The Buddhist Rite for Deliverance of Creatures of Water and Land." In *Cultural Intersections in Later Chinese Buddhism*, ed. Marsha Weidner, 30–70. Honolulu: University of Hawaii Press.

Sun Kaidi 孫楷第. 1956. *Sujiang, shuohua yu baihua xiaoshuo* (Lectures for laity, oral narratives, and stories in vernacular) 俗講、說話與白話小說. Beijing: Zuojia Chubanshe.

Tan Chanxue 譚蟬雪. 1986. "Hexi de *baojuan*" (*Baojuan* from Hexi) 河西的寶卷. *Dunhuang yuyan wenxue yanjiu tongxun* (Newsletter of Dunhuang language and literature of studies) 敦煌語言文學研究通訊 1:11–15.

Tanaka Issei 田仲一成. 2008. *Zhongguo jisi xiju yanjiu* (Study of Chinese ritual theater) 中國祭祀戲劇研究. Chinese trans. Bu He 布和. Beijing: Beijing Daxue Chubanshe.

Teiser, Stephen F. 1988. *The Ghost Festival in Medieval China*. Princeton: Princeton University Press.

———. 1994. *The Scripture of the Ten Kings and the Making of Purgatory in Medieval Chinese Buddhism*. Honolulu: University of Hawaii Press.

———. 1995. "Popular Religion." *Journal of Asian Studies* 54, no. 2: 378–95.

———. 2006. *Reinventing the Wheel: Paintings of Rebirth in Medieval Buddhist Temples*. Seattle: University of Washington Press.

Topley, Marjorie. 1963. "The Great Way of Former Heaven: A Group of Chinese Religious Sects." *Bulletin of the School of Oriental and African Studies* 26, no. 2: 362–92.

Wang Jianchuan 王見川. 1996. *Taiwan de Zhaijiao yu luantang* (Religion of fasting and phoenix halls in Taiwan) 臺灣的齋教與鸞堂. Taibei: Nantian Shuju.

———. 2014. "Morality Book Publishing and Popular Religion in Modern China: A Discussion Centered on Morality Book Publishers in Shanghai." In *Religious Publishing and Print Culture in Modern China, 1800–2012*, ed. Philip Clart and Gregory A. Scott, 233–64. Berlin: de Gruyter.

Wang Ku i 王馗. 2010. *Guijie chaodu yu quan shan Mulian* 鬼節超度與勸善目連 (The salvation rituals of the Ghost Festival and Mulian's exhorting goodness). Taibei: Guojia Chubanshe.

Wang Li 王力. 1958. *Hanyu shilü xue* (Study of Chinese poetry meters) 漢語詩律學. Shanghai: Xin Zhishi Chubanshe.

Wang-Toutain, Françoise. 1998. *Le bodhisattva Kṣitigarbha en Chine du Ve au XIIIe siècle*. Paris: Presses de l'École française d'Extrême-Orient.

Wang Yanhong 王延泓. 2006. "Nan Bei Gaoluo baojuan yanjiu" (Study of *baojuan* in Northern and Southern Gaoluo [villages]) 南北高洛寶卷研究. Master's thesis, Yinyue Yanjiusuo, Zhongguo Yishu Yanjiuyuan.

Wang Yue 王躍. 1990a. "Chuanju de sishiba ben Mulian xi" (Mulian drama in Sichuan drama [tradition] in forty-eight volumes) 川劇的四十八本目連戲. In *Sichuan Mulian xi*, 18–51.

———. 1990b. "Chuan ju 'Mulian zhuan' jianghu ben yanchang tiaogang de neirong, tedian ji xueshu jiazhi" (The content, special features, and artistic value of the outline of the scenic script of the "wandering" [troupe] version of the Sichuan drama "Story of Mulian") 川劇《目連傳》江湖本演唱條鋼的內容、特點及學術價值. In *Sichuan Mulian xi*, 52–59.

Welch, Holmes. 1967. *The Practice of Chinese Buddhism, 1900–1950*. Cambridge, MA: Harvard University Press.

Wu Zhongzheng 吳忠正. 2005. "'Xuehu keyi' guanjian" (My views on the ritual of Blood Pond) "血湖科儀" 管見. *Shanghai daojiao* (Daoism in Shanghai) 上海道教 4:23–27.

Xu Ming 徐明 and Huo Fu 霍福. 2007. *Qinghai Mulian xi* (Mulian drama of Qinghai province) 青海目連戲. Xining: Qinghai Renmin Chubanshe.

Xu Sinian 徐斯年. 1984. "Man tan Shaoxing Mulian xi" (Discussion of Mulian drama in Shaoxing) 漫談紹興目連戲. In *Mulian xi xueshu zuotanhui lunwen xuan* (Selected papers of the scholarly conference on Mulian drama) 目連戲學術座談會論文選, 80–99. Changsha: Hunan sheng Xiqu Yanjiusuo.

Xu Yunzhen 許允貞. 2010. "Cong nüxing dao nüshen: Nüxing xiuxing xinnian *baojuan* yanjiu" (From a woman to goddess: The study of the concept of female self-cultivation in *baojuan*) 從女性到女神：女性修行信念寶卷研究. PhD diss., Zhongguo Shehui Kexueyuan.

Xue Ruolin 薛若鄰. 1992. "Hangai duo yuan sixiang, rongbao duo zhong yishu: Lun Mulian xi jianji hai nei wai de yantao qingkuang" (Embracing multiple aspects of ideology, containing multiple sorts of art: Discussion of Mulian drama altogether with the situation of its study in China and abroad) 涵蓋多元思想，容包多種藝術：論目連戲兼及海內外的研討情況. *MQ* 77:5–22.

Xue Yibing 薛藝兵. 2000. "Hebei Yixian, Laishui de 'Houtu baojuan'" (*Baojuan* of the Earth Goddess of Yi and Laishui counties) 河北易縣、淶水的《后土寶卷》. *Yinyue yishu—Shanghai yinyue xueyuan xuebao* (Journal of Shanghai Conservatory of Music) 音樂藝術——上海音樂學院學報 2:31–37.

Yang Shixian 楊士賢. 2011. *Taiwan minnan sangli wenhua yu minjian wenxue* 台灣閩南喪禮文化與民間文學 (Funerary rituals of South-Fujian people in Taiwan and folk literature). Taipei: Boyang Wenhua.

Ye Mingsheng 葉明生. 1999. "Zhangping daotan po shazhai yishi zhi yinyue ji xuju gaishu" (Overview of music and scenic quality of the ritual of destroying sand fortress in Daoist altars of Zhangping) 漳平道壇破砂寨儀式之音樂及戲劇概述. *MQ* 117:1–48.

Yoshikawa Yoshikazu 吉川良和. 2003. "'Kyū bo kyō' to 'Kyū bo hōkan' no Mokuren mono ni kansuru setsuchō geinō teki shiron" (Preliminary discussion of the storytelling art characteristics concerning the story of Mulian in *Sūtra of Rescuing Mother* and *Baojuan of Rescuing Mother*)《救母經》と《救母寶卷》の目連物に関する說唱藝能的試論. Hitotsubashi daigaku "Shakaigaku kenkyū" (*Studies in Social Sciences*, annual bulletin of Hitotsubashi University) 一橋大學《社會學研究》41:61–135.

———. 2005. "'Kyū bo kyō' to 'Sei ten hōkan' no seisho nendai shōken" (Discussion of the time of composition of the *Sūtra of Rescuing Mother* and the *Baojuan of Rebirth in Heaven*)《救母經》と《生天寶卷》の成書年代商榷. Kanagawa daigaku "Jinbun kenkyū" (*Studies in Humanities* of Kanagawa University) 神奈川大學《人文研究》155:9–43.

You Zi'an 游子安. 1999. *Quan hua jin zhen: Qing dai shanshu yanjiu* (Golden rules, exhorting for goodness: Study of morality books of the Qing dynasty) 勸化金箴：清代善書研究. Tianjin: Tianjin Renmin Chubanshe.

———. 2012. "Xianggang Xiantiandao de maiyuan yu fazhan: Jianlun daotong zai Gang, Tai diqu zhi yanxu" (The origins and development of the Way of Former Heaven in Hong Kong: In connection with the succession of this teaching in Hong Kong and Thailand) 香港先天道的脈源與發展——兼論道統在港、泰地區之延續. In *Shanshu yu Zhongguo zongjiao: You Zi'an zixuanji* (Morality books and Chinese religions: Collection of articles by You Zi'an) 善書與中國宗教：游子安自選集, 205–333. Taibei: Boyang Wenhua.

Yu, Chün-fang. 1981. *The Renewal of Buddhism in China: Chu-hung and the Late Ming Synthesis.* New York: Columbia University Press.

———. 2001. *Kuan-yin: The Chinese Transformation of Avalokiteśvara.* New York: Columbia University Press.

Yu Dingjun 余鼎君. 2012. "Jiangsu Changshu de jiangjing xuanjuan" (Telling scriptures and scroll recitation in Changshu of Jiangsu province) 江蘇常熟的講經宣卷. *Mazu yu minjian xinyang: Yanjiu tongxun* (Bulletin on the research of Mazu and folk beliefs) 媽祖與民間信仰研究通訊 2:49–114.

Yu Songqing 喻松青. 1994. *Minjian mimi zongjiao jingjuan yanjiu* (Research on the scriptures of folk secret religions) 民間秘密宗教經卷研究. Taibei: Lianjing Chubanshe.

Yu Yongliang 虞永良.1997. "Heyang baojuan diaocha baogao" (Report on the study of *baojuan* in Heyang) 河陽寶卷調查報告. MQ 110:67–88.

Zeng Yongyi 曾永義. 2003. *Suwenxue gailun* (Overview of Chinese popular literature) 俗文學概論. Taibei: Sanmin Shuju.

Zeng Ziliang 曾子良. 1975. "Baojuan zhi yanjiu" (Study of *baojuan*) 寶卷之研究. Master's thesis, Guoli Zhengzhi Daxue, Taibei.

Zhang Zong 張總. 2003. *Dizang xinyang yanjiu* (Study of beliefs in Dizang) 地藏信仰研究. Beijing: Zongjiao Wenhua Chubanshe.

Zheng Zhenduo 鄭振鐸. 1996. *Zhongguo suwenxue shi* (History of Chinese popular literature) 中國俗文學史. Beijing: Dongfang Chubanshe.

Zheng Zhiming 鄭志明. 1985. *Wusheng laomu xinyang suyuan* (Sources of the Unborn Venerable Mother belief) 無生老母信仰溯源. Taibei: Wenshizhe Chubanshe.

Zhu Hengfu 朱恆夫. 1993. *Mulian xi yanjiu* (Study of Mulian drama) 目連戲研究. Nanjing: Nanjing Daxue Chubanshe.

INDEX

Amitābha, 31, 61, 65, 88, 90, 99, 100, 109, 110
Analects, 134, 144
Anhui, 43, 45, 46, 167
Anrentang, 123
arias, 18, 28–33, 49, 58, 59, 66, 77, 78, 81–83, 130–136, 173
Assembly of Nine-Petaled Golden Lotus, 101
Avalokiteśvara, *see* Guanyin
Avīci, 38, 49, 77, 87, 95, 112, 127, 141, 166

baojuan, introductions of, 54–56, 79, 80, 86, 87, 103, 129, 135
baojuan, periods of; early, 5, 8, 22, 31, 61, 69, 73, 78, 101, 102; late, 8, 14, 15, 19, 27, 28, 62, 92, 118–143, 149, 153, 154, 160, 168–170, 172, 174; middle, 8, 11, 14, 31, 52, 54, 58, 69, 71, 78, 81–83, 116, 127, 128, 130–132, 142, 172; modern, 5, 6, 19, 125, 154, 176
baojuan, sectarian, 4, 6, 16, 47, 52, 60, 64, 65, 67, 89, 90, 94, 100, 107, 108, 110–112, 116, 117, 124, 153, 160, 172
baojuan, visual aids in, 28, 39, 41, 47, 159, 161, 172, 175
Baojuan of Benefiting Living Beings, 8, 27, 33, 52, 72–97, 100–102, 104–108, 111–113, 124, 136, 137, 142, 152, 167, 172
Baojuan of Deeply Rooted Karmic Fruits, Majestic and Unmoved Like Mount Tai, 51
Baojuan of Hell, 156
Baojuan of Journey to the West, 22, 57
Baojuan of Mulian Rescuing His Mother from Hell, 120, 156
Baojuan of Mulian Rescuing His Mother in Three Rebirths, 7, 8, 12, 27, 60, 95, 118–155, 161–163, 167–170, 172–174
Baojuan of Rectifying the Heart, 13, 15
Baojuan of Reverend Maudgalyāyana Rescuing His Mother [and Helping Her] to Escape from Hell and Be Born in Heaven, 6, 8, 22, 27, 33, 36, 40, 47, 48–71, 77–81, 85, 86, 91, 97, 111, 112, 136, 137, 155, 171, 172, 174, 175
Baojuan of the Blood Pond, 120, 133, 151, 163–165
Baojuan of the Great Vehicle of Non-Interference on Returning to Emptiness and Pointing the Way, 156
Baojuan of the Incense Mountain, 96, 192
Baojuan of the Origin and Development of Merciful and Miraculous Earth Goddess, 72
Baojuan of the Ten Kings, 113, 156, 157
baojuan performances, 5, 7, 17, 19, 30, 31, 67, 130, 134, 151, 158, 159, 161, 169; modern, 12, 27, 30, 59, 114, 130, 142, 143, 158, 163, 173–175
Baoming nunnery, 73, 74
Baoshantang publishers, 118, 126, 154
Beijing, 6, 44, 50, 66, 72, 73, 74, 122
Bianliang, 41, 43
bianwen, 20, 21, 22, 26, 27, 37–42, 60, 62, 65, 68, 71, 85, 133, 158, 159, 172; *Bianwen of Mahāmaudgalyāyana*, 37–40, 60, 67, 86, 91
Blood Bowl, 68, 69, 70
Blood Pond, 69, 70, 154, 163–166, 169, 172, 173

243

Blue Lotus Teaching, 155
Bodhidharma, 140, 151
Bodhisattva, 67, 73, 75, 79, 80, 88, 94, 96, 130, 201, 202
Bordahl, Vibeke, 26
Brahman Woman, 95, 96
Buddha, 6, 8, 17, 18, 31, 35, 36, 40, 42, 52–54, 56, 57, 61, 63–69, 75, 80, 86–88, 90, 92, 93, 95, 99, 100, 101, 103–105, 109, 111, 124, 128, 137, 140, 147, 152, 157
Buddhism, 18, 21, 35–37, 50, 51, 54, 56, 57, 61, 62, 74, 79, 90, 94, 96, 103–105, 114, 144, 146
Buddhist monks, 21, 23, 35, 114, 115, 147
Buddhist nuns, 11, 58
Buddhist scriptures, 22, 38, 47, 48, 56, 61, 71, 81, 84, 87–89, 96, 103, 105, 135, 174

Celestial Mother, 65, 66
Chan school, 56, 61, 103, 128
chanfa, see penitence books
Changshu, 5, 8, 9, 12, 17, 30, 116, 119, 120, 130, 131, 133, 146, 151, 155–160, 164, 165, 167, 168
Changzhou, 5, 118, 121, 126
Che Xilun, 22, 31, 82
Chen Duo, 18
Chen Runshen, 15
Chenhe, 93
ci, see lyrics
cihua, 11, 14, 27
City Enclosed in Iron, 127, see also Avīci
classical Chinese, 3, 33, 81, 83, 123
Complete Perfection school, 108
Complete Version of Baojuan of Mulian, 141
Complete Volume of Mulian Rescuing Mother, 119
Confucianism, 37, 144
cosmology, 39, 62, 66, 97, 100, 107, 200
Cundi, see Zhunti

Dai Wen, 88, 91, 114
Dai Yun, 45
Daoists, 4, 13–15, 36, 46, 52, 62, 65, 69, 107, 108, 110, 111, 116, 132, 133, 144, 155, 159, 164–166
daoqing, 132, 133
Dark Barrier, 152
Dashizhi, Bodhisattva, see Mahāsthāmaprāpta
Desnitskiy, Vladimir A., 48
Dharma, 54, 64, 74, 99, 100

Dharmadeva, 41
Dharmaraksha, 35
Ding Yaokang, 11
Dīpamkara, 99
direct speech, 59, 131
Dizang, 77, 80, 86, 87, 95, 113, 114, 153
Dizang Baojuan, 8, 18, 27, 33, 39, 52, 64, 72–117, 124, 136, 137, 142, 152, 153, 156, 157, 167, 169, 172, 175
Dragon-Flower, Teaching of, 150
drama, 4, 27, 29, 31, 32, 69, 82, 83; Mulian drama, 7, 37, 38, 43–47, 59, 60, 91–95, 97, 121, 125, 134, 136, 137, 139–143, 149, 153–155, 166–170, 172, 173, 195, 197, 198, 208
Dunhuang, 20, 21, 37–39, 40, 56, 61, 172

Eastern Mahāyāna Teaching, see Incense Smeller Teaching
Eight Immortals, 109, 110
Emperor Wu of the Liang Dynasty, 114, 139, 14
eunuchs, 16, 51
exorcist practices, 92, 167, 168, 169, 174

Fatian, see Dharmadeva
Feast of Peaches, 100
female deities, 65, 100, 113, 145, 150, 172
Feng Menglong, 17
filial piety, 36, 37, 42, 44, 54, 61, 69, 85, 95, 104, 165
Five Books in Six Volumes, 16, 21, 51, 65, 75, 98
Five dynasties, 20
Five Hundred Archats, 88
Foley, John M., 24–27, 79, 80, 84, 92, 131, 138
folklore, 9, 11, 12, 14, 19, 23, 24, 26, 27, 33, 84, 175
formulas (in language), 23, 24, 26–28, 39, 55, 59, 71, 80, 83–85, 135, 136, 208
fotou (performers), 12, 17, 119, 157, 164, 166
Fu Chong, 139
Fu family, 138, 139, 141
Fu Luobo, 86, 95, 96, 140, see also Luobo
Fu Tiandou, 139, 140
Fu Xiang, 38, 86, 93, 137, 139, 140, 141, 147, 151
Fubao, 74, 102, 103
Fugui, 88, 114, 115
Fuhai, 74

Index

Fujian, 42, 45, 46, 95, 139, 150, 151, 166
Fukun, 74
Fuming, 74
funerary rites, 46, 47, 70, 114, 116, 138, 143, 156, 157, 158, 159, 160, 164, 165, 166, 170
Fushan, 74, 102

Gangkou, 157, 159
Gansu, 5, 6, 9, 12, 13, 116, 121, 122, 125, 142, 153, 157, 158, 170
Gaochun county, 95, 166
gāthās, 55, 56, 79, 81, 84, 105, 106, 127, 129, 130, 132, 135, 156
Ghost Festival, 35, *see also* Ullambana
Golden Elixir, 108, 124, 152
Golden Rules Exhorting Goodness, 44, 45, 92
Great Way of Former Heaven, 124, 140, 151–154
Guangdong, 46, 166
Guanshiyin, 74, 135
Guanwu, Mr. 123
Guanyin, 65, 90, 94, 96, 113, 133, 137, 141, 142, 146, 147, 154, *see also* Guanshiyin
Guiyuan, nun 16, 74, 75, 102
Guizhou, 155

Han Bangqing, 19
Han dynasty, 16, 19, 50, 100
Han Taihu, 16
Hanan, Patrick, 26
Hangzhou, 93, 151
He Yin, 141, 142, 145, 146, 147, 154
Heart Sūtra, 54
Heaven of the Thirty-three Celestials, 38
Hebei, 5, 6, 9, 12, 30, 31, 72, 73, 76, 88, 93
hell, 6, 38, 39, 46, 49, 57, 62, 65, 66, 69, 70, 77, 86–89, 91, 92, 95, 97, 103, 112, 113, 127, 128, 137, 141, 142, 144, 147–149, 152–158, 160–162, 164, 166, 167, 169, 173
Hexi corridor, 5, 12, 13, 30, 121, 129, 134, 158
Hong Kong, 8, 119, 126
Hongda publishers, 13, 119, 121, 126, 154
Hongyangjiao, *see* Vast Yang Teaching
Hu Guanglu, 43
Hu Sizhen, 123
Huang Chao, 27, 92, 140–142, 167, 173
Huang Dehui, 124
Huang Yupian, 31, 73, 96, 101, 105
Huangtiandao, *see* Yellow Heaven

Huanyuanjiao, *see* Returning to the Origin Teaching
Huiyuan, monk, 36
Hunan, 46, 93, 94
hungry ghosts, 35, 37, 38, 49, 114, 142
hymns, 25, 55, 56, 58, 59, 129, 130; Hymn of Old Man Chuan, 55, 56, 57, 64

illustrations in baojuan, 15, 39–42, 49, 51, 52, 54, 61, 65, 68, 71, 77, 119, 162, 172
images in baojuan, 40, 52, 53, 59, 61, 64, 68, 77, 97, 107, 110, 114, 136, 157–160, 162, 175
Incense Smeller Teaching, 98
India, 22, 87, 88, 94
inner elixir, 75, 82, 83, 106–112, 117, 148–150, 152, 153, 172

Jade Emperor, 141
Japan, 40–42
Jiading county, 14
Jiang, imperial concubine, 51
jiangjing, *see* telling scriptures
jiangjingwen, 21, 22, 37, 56
Jiangsu, 4, 5, 15, 46, 88, 95, 114, 116, 119, 121, 122, 129–131, 133, 141–143, 151, 155, 163, 164, 166–168, 170
Jiangxi, 46, 95
Jiankang prefecture, 122
Jiaxing, 88, 113, 114
Jin state, 86
Jingjiang, 5, 8, 9, 12, 17, 30, 69, 119, 120, 130, 133, 151, 155, 157, 163–166, 168
Jintingguan, 122
Jinxi, nun, 74
Jishantang, 123
Johnson, David, 13, 168

Kangxi reign, 75, 106, 133
karma, 21, 39, 139
karmic causation, 17, 85, 89; talks on, 17, 22
Kerr, Janet, 28
keyi, 3, 12, 18, 21, 193
Korea, 40, 41
Kṣitigarbha, *see* Dizang

Lady Bright Eyes, 95
Laishui county, 6, 31, 32, 72, 115, 117
lectures for laity, *see* sujiang
Li Shiyu, 12, 72, 73, 76, 78, 79, 120
Liang dynasty, 114, 139
Lingshan, *see* Numinous Mountain
liturgy, *see* keyi

Liturgy Based on the Diamond Sūtra, 18, 21, 22, 51, 55, 57
Liu Jia, 134, 137
Liu, Ms. 65, 134, 137, 138, 140, 154
Liu Qingti, 38, 65, 86; *see also* Liu, Ms.
Longevity Star, 110
Longhuajiao, *see* Dragon-Flower Teaching
Lord, Albert B., 23
Lotus Pond of the Ninth Grade, 61
Lü, nun 74, 102, 103, 106, 108, 151
Luo Qing, 16, 21, 51, 52, 54, 62, 65, 66, 75, 107, 150, 166
Luobo, 17, 38, 140; *see also* Fu Luobo
lyrics, 29, 32, 132

Mahāsthāmaprāpta, Bodhisattva, 88
Mair, Victor H., 21, 26
Maitreya, 99, 101, 150
Manao Sūtra Store, 154
Mañjuśrī, *see* Wenshu
Mao Gengru, 45
Marīcī, *see* Molizhi
Master of Medicine, Buddha, 90, 100
McLaren, Anne E., 27
medieval period, 35, 36, 39, 62
Meng Yuanlao, 41, 43
Meng Zi, 134
meter (of verses), 28, 30, 31, 49, 81, 82, 84, 129, 132, 133
Miaoshan, Princess 17, 96
Min county, 116, 157
Ming dynasty, 4, 16, 18, 31, 32, 44, 50, 51, 61, 62, 69, 70, 72, 73, 94, 96, 105, 106, 167, 171
miraculous birth, 93, 140, 172, 173
Mogao caves, 39, *see also* Dunhuang
Molizhi, 66
Monastery of the Light of Wisdom, 151, 152
Mongolia, 50
monks, 4, 13, 22, 36, 52, 61, 115, 146–149
morality books, 5, 14, 15, 118, 125, 126, 154, 155, 158
Mountain of Torn Money, 149
Mouzi, 36

Newly Compiled Drama Exhorting Goodness of Mulian Rescuing His Mother, 43, 45, 47, 60, 62, 92, 94, 137, 138, 140, 149, 154, 172
Ningbo, 40
Non-Interference, Teaching of, 16, 61, 67, 150, 151, 156
northern China, 4, 72, 77, 108, 114, 115, 118, 125, 156
Northern lineage (of inner elixir), 108

novels, 4, 11, 17, 19, 27, 115, 167, 168, 172, 173, 175, 191
Numinous Mountain (Lingshan), 87, 145

offerings, 35, 37, 95, 146, 157, 158
oral: literature, 11, 14, 23–25, 47, 84, 123, 143, 172; performance, 67, 68, 85; tradition, 23, 25, 138, 139, 175; versions, 12, 14, 38, 173; -derived texts, 14, 24, 25, 33; -formulaic theory, 23, 24
Overmyer, Daniel L., 22, 28

Pacification of the Demons' Revolt, 17, 19, 115, 175
Palace of Dipper and Cow, 99, 109
pantheon, 65, 88, 113
paradise, 87, 99, 100, 110, 113, 116, 145, 152, 167
Parry, Milman, 23
Parry-Lord Formulaic Theory, 24
Pass of Demons, 127
penitence books, 21, 42, 69, 114, 174
Penitence of Emperor Wu of the Liang [Dynasty], 114
performance arena, 24, 25, 26, 28, 57, 80, 84, 129, 131, 161
performance-oriented texts, 23, 27, 33, 175
philanthropic societies, 15, 125, 126, 154
picture scrolls, 39, 42, 68
pinghua 12, 42
Plum Flowers in the Golden Vase, 11, 17, 58, 191, 193
Prajñā-pāramita, 80
Precious Account of Mulian, 7, 8, 27, 33, 62, 95, 118–143, 151–155, 157, 162, 163, 167–170, 172, 174
professional performers, 12, 13
prosimetric literature, 3, 136
Pṛthivī, 94
Puming, 29, 30, 73, 75, 76, 80, 81, 90, 91, 100, 101, 105, 106
Puming baojuan, 29, 30, 75, 76, 80, 81, 100, 101
Pure Land, 38, 61, 80, 88, 90, 130
Pūrṇa, Reverend, 90
Putian county, 45, 46, 95, 139
Puxian, Bodhisattva, 73, 94
Puyintang, 72, 115

Qing Dynasty, 4, 11, 16, 21, 26, 31, 44, 51, 52, 54, 62, 65, 66, 73–75, 94, 105, 107, 124–126, 150
Qinghai, 5, 125

Index

Qinglianjiao, *see* Blue Lotus Teaching
qu, *see* arias
Queen Mother of the West, 100, 109, 110, 145

rebirth, 6, 17, 18, 35, 38, 46, 49, 57, 61, 65, 68, 71, 76, 86, 88, 92–94, 96, 100, 110, 111, 115, 138–142, 145, 154
refrain, 31, 67, 157
Refutation of Heresies, 32, 73
Register of Arias of Kangxi Reign, 32, 82, 83, 133
Returning to the Origin, Teaching, 156
rhyme, 81, 82, 106, 132, 133
rituals, 18, 21, 22, 26, 28, 42, 46, 47, 54, 56, 57, 61, 62, 69, 80, 114, 116, 130, 149, 155, 159, 160, 164–166, 168, 169, 171, 173–175

Sacred Edict, 74, 106, 147
Sage Nun, 17
Śākyamuni, Buddha 99, 104
Samantabhadra, *see* Puxian
Sangha, 54
Sanskrit, 36, 38, 54, 56, 103
Sawada Mizuho, 21, 22, 89, 90, 92, 93
scroll recitation, 3, 4, 11–14, 17, 19
Sea of Suffering, 87, 99, 100
sectarian groups, 4, 77, 98, 101, 103, 105, 116
sectarian teachings, 3, 60, 62, 64, 69, 83, 87, 98, 105, 106, 115, 144–146, 151–153, 165, 169, 172, 174
Sequel to Plum Flowers in the Golden Vase, 11, 192
Shancai, *see* Sudhana
Shandong, 18
Shanghai, 13–15, 19, 118, 119, 121, 126, 154, 161, 162, 166
shanshu, *see* morality books
Shaoxing, 5, 30, 140, 141, 143
shellfish, 73, 76, 87, 92, 93, 94, 111
Shengzu (Emperor), 75
shuojing, 20
Sichuan, 46, 93–95, 118, 125, 139, 143, 166
Singapore, 46
sing-song girls, 19
Skanda, 53, 54
Song dynasty, 20, 21, 22, 41, 43, 46, 82, 133
South Gaoluo, 6, 72
southern China, 46, 139, 140, 143, 150, 166
Stories of Flowers on the Sea, 19
storytellers, 4, 12–15, 22, 23, 26, 68, 84, 119, 133, 158

Stulova, Elvira S., 29, 30, 31
Sudatta 80
Sudhana, 90, 137, 202
sujiang, 21, 37
Sun Chuo, 36
sūtras, 3, 21–23, 35, 41, 53–56, 79, 80, 85, 104, 105, 111, 129, 138, 146, 172, 174; *Sūtra of Great Mulian*, 40, 41; *Sūtra of Mulian*, 40, 41, 42, 57, 60, 65, 70, 71, 86; *Sūtra of the Original Vow of the Bodhisattva of the Earth Sanctuary*, 94–96; *Sūtra of Ullambana*, 35–38, 103; *Sūtra on Repaying the Kindness [of Parents]*, 103
Suzhou, 5, 8, 9, 12, 30, 118, 119, 154, 166

Tai, Mount 75, 113
Taiwan, 7, 8, 46, 119, 126, 150, 151, 166
Tan Chanxue, 122
tanci, 12, 13
Tang dynasty, 6, 20, 30, 36, 39, 40, 56, 96, 108, 132, 133, 142, 167, 173
tanjing, 20–22
telling scriptures, 12, 17, 30, 69, 155, 156, 157, 164, 165, 168
Ten Courts of Hell, 61, 62, 128, 155, 156
Ten Kings of Hell, 63, 77, 91, 113, 116, 156–158, 160, 169, 173
Three Barriers, 148
Three Teachings, 53, 95, 144
Three Treasures, 56, 79, 147
Tower of the Mirror of Sins, 127
transformation texts, *see* bianwen
Tunes with the Names of all Buddhas, 58
Tuotuo, 50

Ullambana, 35–38, 46, 55, 57, 68, 95, 167
Unborn Venerable Mother, 63–66, 74, 75, 82, 87–90, 97–102, 104, 109–113, 115, 116, 145, 150–153, 170, 172
underworld, 36, 39, 40, 61, 62, 64, 88, 91, 97, 127, 149, 154–156, 165, 167, 169
universal salvation, 37, 89, 116, 167, 169

Vast Yang Teaching, 11, 16, 72, 77, 98, 115–117, 159, 189, 192
vegetarianism, 101, 116, 129, 146, 150, 153, 154
vernacular, 3, 19, 26, 27, 33, 38, 39, 41, 43, 54, 59, 71, 171

verses, 17, 26, 28–30, 56, 57, 59, 61, 63, 67, 78, 81–85, 91, 99, 105–107, 119, 128–132, 136, 145–147, 154, 175; shi genre, 30–32, 132; 132; five-character, 30, 31, 49, 77, 78, 80, 81, 130, 131; four-character, 79, 124, 131; seven-character, 29, 31, 58, 72, 77–81, 93, 127, 128, 130, 131, 152; ten-character, 29, 30, 31, 58, 77, 79, 82, 84, 85, 102, 128, 132

Wang Li, 30
Wang Shan, 146, 147, 154
Wang Yin, 51
Wang Zuoli, 122, 123
Wanquan county, 73, 76
Water-and-Land Service, 159, 160
Way of Pervasive Unity, 144, 151, 154
Weituo, see Skanda
Wenshu, Bodhisattva, 94
Wenxiangjiao, see Incense Smeller Teaching
Western Heaven, 128, 133, 145, 146
Western Mahāyāna Teaching, 16, 73–75, 77, 98, 99, 102, 105, 107, 113–117, 189, 192, 206
woodblocks, 40, 52, 72, 75, 77–79, 118–122
Wusheng laomu, see Unborn Venerable Mother
Wuweijiao, see Non-Interference
Wuxi, 5, 8, 119

Xi, Ms. 114, 140
Xi Dashengjiao, see Western Mahāyāna Teaching
Xi Wangmu, see Queen Mother of the West
Xia Yuqi, 122, 123
Xiantian da dao, see Great Way of Former Heaven
Xuanguang reign, 50

xuanjuan, see scroll recitation
Xuanzang, monk, 22

Yan Yuan, 61, 76, 111, 155
Yancheng, 15
Yangzi valley, 13
Yanwang (Yanluo), 39, 61, 62, 88, 155, 156
Yellow Heaven, Teaching of, 53, 62, 73, 75–77, 90, 98, 100, 102, 105, 107, 108, 111–113, 116, 117, 189
Yiguandao, see Way of Pervasive Unity
Yihuatang, publishers, 15, 126, 154
Yijing, 107
Yili, 138
Yinan Zi (Qingyang Shanren), 123, 124, 152
Yixingbu, 12, 115, 117, 159
Yuan dynasty, 32, 45, 50, 59, 60, 70, 76, 111, 171
yuanqi, 21, 37, 38
Yulin caves, 40

zan, see hymns
Zhaijiao, 150
Zhang Jun, 51
Zhangjiagang, 5, 119, 156, 157
Zhejiang, 4, 5, 40, 46, 121, 122, 141, 166
Zheng Qian, 66
Zheng Xie (Zheng Banqiao), 133
Zheng Zhenduo, 20, 48, 63
Zheng Zhizhen, 43, 45, 92, 93, 94, 137, 172
Zhengde reign, 16
Zhenjiang, 118, 126, 154
zhima, 114, 157
Zhiyi Zi, 123
Zhongyuan Festival, 35, 37, 41, 43, 46, 68, 115, see also Ullambana
Zhu Fahu, see Dharmaraksha
Zhu Hengfu, 93
Zhunti, 65
Zongjing, monk, 18
Zongmi, monk, 36

www.ingramcontent.com/pod-product-compliance
Lightning Source LLC
Chambersburg PA
CBHW030614230426
43661CB00053B/1989